THE GENE CONLEY STORY

One *of a* Kind

KATHRYN R. CONLEY

One Of A Kind by Kathryn Conley

Copyright © 2004 by Kathryn R. Conley
All Right Reserved

ISBN: 0-9754332-5-3

Published by: Advantage Books
             www.advbooks.com

Library of Congress Control Number: 2004113562

First Printing: November 2004

04 05 06 07 08 09 10 8 7 6 5 4 3 2 1

Printed in the United States of America

"In a distant time, when baseball fans are rounding up memories over a few cool ones out in the kitchen, one achievement is certain to be recaptured and replayed.

It won't be Mickey Mantle's four successive homers or Stan Musial's four big blasts, or Bill Mombouquett's near perfect game, or Earl Wilson's no-hitter, or Sandy Koufax's 18 strikeouts, or Floyd Robinson's six for six.

The feat that will keep the 1962 season alive in memory was the historic stroll by Gene Conley, the wayward bus rider.

Behind this redwood of a man came this slender Boston Red Sox teammate, 6' Elijah (Pumpsi) Green. This modern-day Don Quixote and Sancho Panza march off together to tilt at the windmills of conformity.

Like the original Don Quixote, Conley ignored the timid voices that told him "you can't do that here" or "it will never work."

And then he added the most delirious touch of all to this wondrous adventure, the trip to Israel."

Bill Gleason, Boston Globe, April, 1964

Kathryn Conley

Endorsements

Many have tried to become world champion two-sport professional athletes, the most well known may be Bo Jackson, Deion Sanders, Danny Ainge or even Michael Jordan. There is only one who actually achieved this goal and his name is Gene Conley.

One Of A Kind chronicles Gene's amazing career where he was able to win world championships in Major League Baseball and the National Basketball Association.

One reason that you might not recognize the name of Gene Conley is that he won the World Series with the 1957 Milwaukee Braves and three NBA Championships with the Boston Celtics in 58/59, 59/60 and 60/61.

If Gene had achieved this today he would have multi-million dollar contracts with both teams, multi-million dollar commercial endorsement contracts and perhaps be the biggest name in sports.

Gene played in an era with some of the all-time greats in both sports. Here is what some of them had to say about him and this book.

"Gene Conley was one of the greatest athletes of our generation. There was no tougher or more competitive player than Gene. He is the only man, to my knowledge, to be a member of a championship baseball team and basketball team in the same year. That is quite an accomplishment."
Arnold "Red Auerbach, Boston Celtics President. Red shares Phil Jackson's honor as the "winningest" coach in the NBA.

"Gene and I were both Rookies when we broke into the Majors with the Milwaukee Braves in 1954. I could tell right away that he was going to be a great big league pitcher. He was a natural athlete. He could pitch, run and had a good bat. I enjoyed him as a friend and teammate for several years. I was playing in the 1955 All Star game in Milwaukee when he got the win and we both played together in the 1959 All Star game in Los Angeles. I was not surprised that he was able also to play several years with the World Championship Boston Celtics. What a great achievement to be able to perform at the highest level on World Championship teams in both baseball and basketball. We are to this day, great friends".

Hank Aaron: Present all time Home Run Leader. Inducted into Baseball's Hall of Fame, played in 21 All Star Games, 23 years in the Majors, 1 World Championship.

"Gene Conley was a great pitcher, a tough basketball player, a winner, and dedicated athlete who had a unique way of looking at life. I roomed with Gene, he made me laugh and cry. I know he will do the same for you in this book."

Tom Heinsohn: In Basketball's Hall of Fame, he was on 8 World Championship teams with the Celtics, 9 years with them as a player, 6 time all star, 2 World Championship NBA titles as a coach.

"Gene was really something. I don't know of anyone else quite like him. He has a World Series ring and an NBA Championship ring. To have a great success in two sports is rare. To me, Gene was a Giant figure on the mound. He really scared me. You had to respect him. I did and I still do. A great guy."

Willie Mayes: Inducted into Baseball's Hall of Fame, played in 20 All Star Games. Was on one World Series Championship team. Twice, MVP of the National League. Played 22 years in Major League Baseball and was known as the greatest all around baseball player of all times.

"Gene Conley was an extraordinary Major League pitcher as well as a good hitting pitcher with the pennant winning world's championship Milwaukee Braves, Philadelphia Phillies and Boston Red Sox."

Joe Morgan, Red Sox Manager

"Gene was my teammate for two years with the Red Sox. One night in Cleveland, he pitched a shut out and hit a home run and two singles. He had a line drive hit back at him which he caught in the webbing of his glove, but it broke through and hit him in the nose. He ended up catching it anyway. He was a heck of an athlete."

Bill Mombouquette, Boston Red Sox teamate, inducted into the Red Sox Hall of Fame, pitched for 11 years and was in 3 All Star Games.

"In addition to his dominating figure on the mound, in the 1955 All Star Game, Gene Conley struck out, in one inning; Mickey Vernon, Al Rosen and Al Kaline. Gene went on to win on Stan Musial's home run"

Johnny Logan, Short-Stop with the World Championship Milwaukee Braves team of 1957, played in 3 All Star Games. Director of the Milwaukee Historical Association

"Gene was a fine athlete, a great roommate and has an interesting story to tell. We knew playing sports sure beat working for a living"

Robin Roberts: Inducted into Baseball's Hall of Fame, played in 6 All Star Games and one World Series with the Philadelphia Phillies. Was a 6 time 20 game winner and one of the original "Wiz Kids". Along with Lew Burdette, was recognized as one of the best National League RH pitchers of the fifties.

"Gene is one of the great story-tellers. If this book contained only the one's I've heard, I'd still buy it! Gene could not only pitch but was also respected as a hitter. This book may be his biggest hit yet!"

Dick Radatz, Inducted into the Red Sox Hall of Fame, played in 2 All Star Games. Also known as the "Monster" as he was a devastating reliever for 10 years

"Gene was a welcome addition to the Red Sox team his last three years in the Majors. He was a great competitor on the mound and helped himself to victories with the bat. He's been a good friend and I know you will enjoy his book."

Frank Malzone: Inducted into the Red Sox Hall of Fame. Played in 8 All Star Games. Won three Golden Gloves as a third baseman.

"During my first year with the Celtics, and Gene Conley's last year with them, before going to the NY Knicks, we shared a great year winning the NBA's World's Championship. Gene was a hard nose competitor, not dirty, but the competition respected him as did his Celtic teammates. He and I have enjoyed a close friendship over the years. Being a Celtic is being a fraternity of brothers."

Tom "Satch" Sanders: Played 13 years in the NBA, and won 8 World Championships with the Boston Celtics. Present Director of the NBA Legends' Foundation.

"Gene Conley was probably the GREATEST Major League two sport athlete ever! He is the only player to ever earn and win championship rings in pro-baseball and pro-basketball. At 6'8", he had outstanding speed and agility. Because both sports over-lapped, it hindered some of his playing time and potential. Nevertheless, he was still a very valuable asset to BOSTON CELTICS' Championships".

Bill Sharman, Inducted into Basketball's Hall of Fame as a player and as a coach, voted as one of the 50 best NBA players of all time. Eight time All Star, four time World Champion with the Celtics. As a coach, he won championships in 3 professional leagues, the only basketball coach to do so.

"We knew from watching him win the World Series that Gene was a great pitcher. When he came on board with the Celtics, he quickly proved to be a solid rebounder and superb defender in low post. Playing alongside and as a back-up to Bill Russell, Gene played with tremendous motivation and heart, contributing to three more World Championships. A bona fide double legend in two sports, Gene never lost his smile, his team spirit or his positive attitude. Thanks to Katie Conley for insuring his phenomenal accomplishments won't be forgotten."

K. C. Jones, Inducted into Basketball's Hall of Fame, K.C.Jones played 9 seasons with the Celtics, was on eight World Championship teams and coached two World's Championship teams in the NBA. Friend since the fifties.

"Gene was one of our starting pitchers in the mid fifties who helped us win two National League titles with the Milwaukee Braves. At that time, we went against the American League title holder, the NY Yankees, winning a World Series against them in 1957. I also watched him help the Boston Celtics while they were winning World Championships in the NBA. Gene and I have remained friends over the last forty-six years."

Lew Burdette: Starting Pitcher with the World Championship Milwaukee Braves, 3 time All Star and MVP of the 1957 World Series for the Milwaukee Braves. Along with Robin Roberts, was recognized as one of the best National League right-hand pitchers of the fifties.

1961 WORLD CHAMPION BOSTON CELTICS

Front row:, left to right, (inset) Lou Pieri, treasurer, K. C. Jones, Capt. Bob Cousy, Coach Red Auerbach, President Walter A Brown, Bill Sharman and Frank Ramsey, Standing, Trainer Buddy LeRoux, Tom Sanders, Tom Heinsohn, Gene Conley, Bill Russell, Gene Guarilia, Jim Loscutoff, Sam Jones. (Photo Buckley.)

Introduction

Gene Conley has always been a hero to me from afar, pitching for the Braves in 1952. As an eleven year old kid growing up in Wilmington, Delaware, I was crazy about him. As a Phillies fan I was intrigued with this enormous 6'8" baseball pitcher, a true phenomenal athlete, the likes of which baseball had never seen.

It gets better. I was also an avid Philadelphia Warior basketball fan and shortly after that, watching games at old Convention Hall, there was Gene again on the front lines as a Boston Celtic, playing against my beloved Warriors.

In the history of sports, there has never been a duo act like Gene Conley put together. There has been a few multiple sports athletes, most recent, Bo Jackson and Deion Sanders but Gene did it over a longer period of time and with greater success than anyone in history.

In recent years, Gene and his wife, relocated to Orlando and I've gotten to know Gene personally. In other words, one of the heroes of my youth has become a flesh and blood friend and one thing I have learned, Gene Conley is a magnificent story teller. His memory is unwavering and captures all of his special moments in this wonderful new book.

As you read about this remarkable person, I know you will become to enjoy and appreciate Gene Conley as much as I do. Get ready for an enjoyable read and "Goodnight Pumpsi Green, wherever you are".

Pat Williams, Senior Vice President of the Orlando Magic.
November, 2004

TABLE OF CONTENTS

PROFESSIONAL CAREER

Born:
Donald Eugene Conley
11/10/30, Muskogee, OK

Gene was the most successful two sport American Professional athlete in that he is the only man in pro sports history to play in and win world championships in both MLB (Major League Baseball) and the NBA (National Basketball Association). He played longer than any other two sport athlete in Professional Basketball and Baseball. Gene played professional baseball thirteen years with ten plus years in the Major Leagues and three in the minors. He played seven years of Major League Professional Basketball and two years in Minor League Basketball (one year as an Eastern League player/coach). Finishing up at age thirty-eight, he was chosen an "All Star" in each of the previous two seasons he played for the Eastern Basketball League. In all, he played twenty-two years in professional sports.

Only man in American pro sports history to win three NBA world championships (Boston Celtics) and two National League Championships (Milwaukee Braves) and one Major League Baseball World Series Championship (Milwaukee Braves).

Within a year and a half, he was on a World's Series Championship team in MLB in 1957 and a NBA World's Championship team - 1958/1959

Championship rings for three NBA World Championships - 1958/1959, 1959/1960, 1960/1961 and one MLB World Series Championship in 1957

Only man in American professional sports history to win two "Most Valuable Player Awards" in the Minor Leagues in Baseball. (Plaque in Baseball's

Hall of Fame - Minor League section - One while in the Eastern League and the other while playing in the American Association).

In Major League Baseball, Gene pitched in three All Star Games, striking out the side (Al Rosen, Al Kaline and Mickey Vernon) in the 12th inning to win the 1955 All Star Game. In 1959, Gene won the Sporting News, "Comeback Player of the Year Award". (Philadelphia Phillies)

In 1961, nine days after he finished helping the Boston Celtics win its third consecutive World's Championship, Gene pitched nine innings to win the game against the Washington Senators while with the Boston Red Sox. While playing both sports consecutively, he packed thirteen pressure packed seasons of Major League sports (baseball and basketball) into six and a half years and never had a day off during that time, unless injured or, as in the case of baseball, the game was rained out.

Teams in the Majors: BASEBALL: Boston Braves, Milwaukee Braves, Philadelphia Phillies, Boston Red Sox. BASKETBALL: Boston Celtics and the NY Knickerbockers. In 1962, the year he won 15 games for the Red Sox, he made an aborted trip to Jerusalem in the middle of the season, which is probably better remembered than any of his athletic honors. It made National headlines in most major newspapers and TV channels in the country as he went awol for four days.

TRIVIA

Gene held the record for being the tallest man in Major League Baseball for forty years until Randy Johnson of the Arizona Diamondbacks joined the Major Leagues.

Gene is the only professional athlete to play for three Major League teams in one city. (The Boston Braves, Celtics, and the Boston Red Sox)

PRESENT DAY

He is on the boards of the NBA Legends Foundation, The Retired NBA Players Association, was the Director of the NBA Oldtimers Association and served as a board member at Fuller Memorial Hospital, the Lincoln Seventh-day-Adventist Church and the Industrial Board in the town of Foxboro, Massachusetts. He owned and operated the Foxboro Paper Company for 35 years, which provided specialty packaging for Industry.

His hobbies are skiing and golf. (In 1976, he won the Class A Golf Championship at the Foxboro Country Club.) Gene has a wife, Katie, three children; Dr. Gene Conley Jr., Diane Kathryn (Kitty) Conley Quick, R.N./B.S.N. and Susan (Kelly) Conley, R.N. He has seven grandchildren; Katie, Patty Grace, and James Quick, Stacey, and Ryan Malcomson, and Kimberly and Gene (Buddy) Conley III.

1953

1954

1954

1955

1956

1961

1960

1962

1955

1957

1963

1958

1961

1959

1964

1957 WORLD CHAMPION MILWAUKEE BRAVES

In Celebration of The 40th Anniversary
of Their World Championship.

First Row, (bottom): Lew Burdette, Frank Torre, Gene, Warren Spahn
Second Row: Juan Pizarro, Johnny Logan, Bob Buhl, Joe Adcock
Third Row: Manager, Fred Haney
Fourth Row: Billy Bruton, Red Schoendienst, Andy Pafko, Del
Crandall, Henry Aaron
Fifth Row: Eddie Mathews, Wes Covington & Don McMahon

ACKNOWLEDGMENTS

To express our appreciation to our son-law, Dr. Gregory Quick, for dragging me, kicking and screaming, into the twenty-first century in order for me to become computer literate, Dr. Gene Conley for his editing, Pat Williams, Sr. Vice President of the Orlando Magic, "The NBA Oldtimers", our granddaughter, Katie Quick, Al and Bonnie Johnson, Charlie Rosenzewig, NBA Marketing, Todd Caso, the NBA archivist and friend, Jeff Twiss, Vice President of Media Relations with the Boston Celtics, the NBA for their many favors.

Dick Bresciani, Vice-president-Boston Red Sox, MLB, Dan Shaughnessey, columnist with the Boston Globe, Joe Fitzgerald, columnist with the Boston Herald, Jim Murray of the Los Angles Times and Dave Anderson of the New York Times and all the other columnists who helped with promoting the NBA Oldtimers' pension effort but especially, for the fifty-three years spent living with my subject.

Picture that appeared in the Boston Herald just before the Surgery—1989

CHAPTER 1

IN THE BEGINNING

The Boston Herald, Tuesday, June 6, 1989

A LOVE STORY, Joe Fitzgerald

"She was just a kid, 20, who'd come to his town - Richland, Wash., - looking for a job, and he was just a kid, too, also 20, for whom the world was about to open up in a big way, four months after they began to date, with the signing of his first professional baseball contract.

"It was 1951, and Tommy Holmes had just retired as a player with the Braves," Gene Conley recalls. "He'd seen me pitch and wanted me to play for him at Hartford (Eastern League), so I signed with them (Braves' organization) and Tommy took me with him to spring training at Myrtle Beach, S.C."

"One day I caught him by the barracks. "Tommy,' I said, 'I've been writing to this girl back home for quite a while now, and I really want to marry her. We don't head north for a couple of weeks, so this would be a good time, wouldn't it?' He said it would.' I told him, 'but I don't have any money.' So he smiled and said 'OK, how much do you need?' I told him $300.00 ought to do it.'

"Now I call Katie to tell her the good news, and she tells me that she's already saved $600.00. 'Sweetheart,' I said, 'come on down!' Then I took Tommy's $300.00 and bought her a ring. Three days later she arrived in

Charleston, S.C. I took a cab up to meet her. Cost me $35.00 Big spender. Oh, man, I couldn't wait to see her. So I get there, and the first thing she says is, 'Gene, my Mother told me I have to have a church wedding.' I said, 'O.K., honey, let's go find one right now.'

"We went to this big church in Charleston called Citadel Sq. Baptist and I told the pastor the whole story about how I was a ballplayer just starting out, and how this girl had flown down to become my wife, and how we wanted to be married in a church. He said, 'OK, kids, I'll tell you what. We're having a big meeting here tonight, about 500 people. I'll ask them to stay around.' Well, they all did; some doctor even gave Katie away. In fact, his wife started to cry, so I leaned over to Katie and whispered, 'She probably sees what you're getting yourself into!'"

Conley a bear of a man at 6'8", was so gifted that he's still the only athlete to have won world championship rings in two pro sports. He was on the Braves' pitching staff when they beat the Yankees in the 1957 World Series, and he was Bill Russell's backup center on the Celtics team that won NBA crowns in 1959, 1960, and 1961. In addition to pitching for the Braves and Phillies, he also spent three seasons with the Red Sox; indeed, in 1961 he pitched them to a 6-1 victory just 14 days after helping the Celts vanquish St. Louis. All told, as a two-sport pro, Conley crammed 17 seasons into 11 years.

"You know," he says, wistfully, "when you're young, caught up in a big league career - I don't care what sport it is - you really don't appreciate all that's going on around you. I surely didn't. Katie was both mother and father to our kids all the time I was gone. Then one day it's all over. You hang 'em up and come home for good, and suddenly it hits you that your kids are basically grown and you've had nothing to do with it.

"Look at me. I've got a son who's a doctor in California and two daughters who are RN's, and, honestly, I've got to say all the credit for that goes to Katie. We've got three great kids, six beautiful grandchildren, and our phone rings every day with calls from them. It's a tight, loving family. The kids look at her and say to me 'Boy, dad, you lucked out.' What can I say? They're right."

When Conley retired in 1963 he was hardly rolling in dough. I had $11,000.00 to my name," he recalls. "That's all. So Katie and I started a little business of our own - Foxboro Paper Co. (packaging supplies) - and we ran it out of the basement of our little Cape. I'd be out peddling my supplies, and when I'd come home at night I'd find her down in that cold, damp cellar, wearing boots and a stocking cap while typing letters or setting up files. Oh, man, the stories I could tell you about this gal.

"Well, our desks have been side by side for 25 years now, and today the business is going nicely. Sometimes I'll call in from the road, and as I'm listening to her I'll be thinking, 'This is more like talking to a friend than talking to a wife.' And that's the way it should be. She always likes to say she can tell when it's 5 o'clock because I turn into a lover at quitting time.

"I guess we're at what you'd call a beautiful time in our lives. We're both 58, enjoying our kids, and enjoying each other more than we ever have before."

Four months ago that "beautiful time" was abruptly rocked when Conley suffered what he calls a "mild" heart attack. Katie was so caught up in her concern for him that she disregarded an increasing discomfort she was experiencing from a recurring ache in her ear.

"She thought she was going to lose me." Conley remembers. "I could see it in her eyes. She was crying all the time because she felt so bad for me... and now, it's funny, she sees the same look in my eyes, because I feel so bad for her."

Once satisfied that her husband was on the mend, she sought treatment for her own ailment from a specialist who decided upon examination, further tests were needed. When the results came in he summoned the two of them.

"He asked if Katie could bring me with her when she came." Conley said, his voice growing thicker. "As soon as I heard that, my heart started beating like crazy. Why would he want to see me too? I guess we both sensed something wasn't good. Sure enough, he sat us down and started explaining how he'd spotted this tumor at the base of her brain, right by the jugular vein, and how it was going to have to be removed. I was numb. I just sat there looking at her. She didn't say much either, not until we stepped out into the hall where we could be alone. Then I put my arms around her and we both cried."

He paused for a long moment. It was not an easy story to relate.

"I'd better talk fast," he said, almost apologetically. "I don't cry easily, but ... well, I'm more or less like the coach, you know what I mean? If a coach shows weakness, it goes right into his team. A coach is not supposed to cry, so I'm doing my best to be strong, because I want to make my player strong. And yet I want the story told - we both do - because we were thinking, if just one husband or one wife reads this, and stops an extra minute to think about how lucky they are, and maybe decides to hang around the house a little longer before heading out the door, just to say a few things that should have been said before ... well, that would make us feel pretty good. We hope it happens. When you have the kind of love we do. I guess you want to share."

Gene and Katie are in Los Angeles this morning. The surgery will be performed there Friday.

"She's a fighter" he said, before they left on Sunday. "There's just no quit in this girl. Never has been and I'm going to be out there right by her side. Count on that. I'll have my pills with me, in case I get a little bit excited. And she and I are going to fight this thing the same way we've done everything else in our lives; we're going to do it together.

Katie & Gene.
You're the best of the best.
God Bless !
Chuck
Connors

One of our "NBA OLDTIMERS"
Two-sport player, Chuck Conners:
Cubs/Celtics

CHAPTER 2

THE NBA OLDTIMERS VS. THE NBA

In the early eighties, Larry Bird and Magic Johnson were just starting to stake their claim in becoming the catalysts which sent the NBA into outer orbit. During this significant period, Tommy Heinsohn had invited all his former teammates from the fifties and early sixties to be at his induction into Basketball's Hall of Fame in Springfield, Massachusetts. It was a superb gathering. Those Celtic players like Bill Russell, Bob Cousy, Bill Sharman, Sam Jones, K. C. Jones, Frank Ramsey, Jim Loscutoff, John Havelchik and Dave Cowens, just to name a few who had battled their way through the longest run of World Championships ever were present. In their era there were only eight very competitive NBA teams, which necessarily meant an embattled playoff series whose outcome was always in doubt until the final buzzer. It was a time in the NBA when bench depth played a vital role in the outcome of successful championships.

During the festivities that evening, adversarial players, who had already attained Hall of Fame status such as Tom Gola, Dolph Schayes, Bob Petit, Ed McCauley and Paul Arizin, were milling about, slapping shoulders (one didn't hug in those days) and generally having the time of their lives. Overheard, during this mutual admiration society, was conversation concerning the NBA pension and about the new collective bargaining agreement. It seems that their agreement had gone back three years to pick up more NBA players who had previously been excluded from pension benefits.

Until that evening, most had never heard of a NBA pension as the league was still in its infancy, being born as recently as 1948. Whether a former NBA player there that night had been included or not was a matter of conjecture. Rumors began circulating through this jovial throng as players wondered if the NBA had gone back far enough to pick up their particular retirement year. It was beginning to shape up as a very interesting and momentous event. Extending this occasion, our resident millionaire, Frank Ramsey and his wife Jean, invited us all to a brunch the following day at one of Boston's most prestigious hotels. Plans were already being formulated to meet after the brunch, to discus the consequences of this last NBA collective bargaining session.

Those players who were clearly eligible like Dave Cowens and Satch Sanders, added their encouragement to those of us who were questionable. Andy Phillips told horror stories of how Fred Zollner, owner of the Detroit Pistons, had prevented his players from talking union, threatening expulsion from the NBA if ever he heard the idea being floated by any of his players. We saw correspondence from Maurice Podoloff complaining in colorful language, about "that damn Frenchman, Bob Cousy, who was always trying to form a union. Why, he had even requested that there be more than one bar of soap in the visiting locker rooms". These small beginnings in sports' negotiations are almost laughable today. During the eighties, it had been reported at one of "baseball's" bargaining sessions, one of the most pressing issues on the player's agenda was insisting that white wine as well as red be served on their chartered flights.

George Senesky who played and coached championship teams for the Philadelphia 76ers related how after a particularly hard fought battle against Fort

Wayne's team, he had transported his team in a couple of taxis to a certain depot in order to catch a train to their next night's game. The snowstorm and the sub-zero temperatures had delayed it. The depot had closed up for the night. With the cabbies gone and after kicking snow around for an hour, they conjectured, (after all, they **were** college graduates) they would freeze to death in this lonely outpost if radical steps were not soon taken. The door was formidable but the windows proved penetrable and the station furniture provided sufficient firewood until the next train came in.

There were harrowing stories about the LA Lakers mode of transportation. On their way to play the Syracuse Nationals, they encountered a snowstorm so bad that no scheduled commercial planes would venture out. However, their owner had purchased a formerly owned plane for just such an occasion. Unable to make the airport because of zero visibility, the pilot had to open his side window in order to **hear** how far off the ground they were to land in a farmer's corn field. Talk about coming in on a wing and a prayer!

At the close of the fifties, the Celtics who were scheduled for a televised game in Syracuse were unable to use a scheduled flight out of Boston because of another especially violent snowstorm. Of course this didn't phase their "fearless leader", as Cousy affectionately calls Red Auerbach. He merely hired two limousines, during the wee hours of the morning, gathered his little flock and motored there, arriving less than an hour before the National Anthem. After suiting up, Red instructed his obedient crew to lay down on their wooden benches, while he turned off the lights. After about 20 minutes, splashing cold water in their faces, the World Champion Celtics jumped up and ran out onto the floor to once again do battle. Can you imagine running that by the Player's Union today?

Syracuse was always a challenge for opposing teams. George Mikan recalls that before going there, he had remarked to his coach that he would prefer it if his teammates would refrain from smoking when he was around because of his allergies. The media somehow heard about the Lakers' star's problem and when they arrived at the arena for another tough tilt, every fan in the building lit up a cigar! After awhile, no one could see the ball!

It was no mystery why the owners refused vehemently to even discus a NBA players' union. Autonomy was a very comfortable position to be in. At this first casual meeting in 1985, these vintage players cemented their friendships, much like veterans of foreign wars. However, it was obvious from where I was sitting, that although these stories were very colorful and humorous at times, (if somewhat pathetic), no one seemed to want to commit to the leadership in addressing this new pension issue. No one was coordinating strategy. No one seemed to be delegating. These Hall of Fame players were in agreement about the virtue of doing something to correct the existing pension structure. Their status and capabilities were undeniable but for whatever reason, no one was volunteering to take the burden of leadership in setting dates for meetings with the current NBA player's union or the offices of the commissioner. This meeting of the minds was slowly slipping away into nothingness.

At this time we hadn't heard the particulars of this new agreement, whether or not Gene's retirement year was to be included in the NBA pension structure. Already in his fifties, he had begun thinking about his future as a self-employed retiree. The IRA's hadn't been instituted as yet and we had just committed the dumbest move of our entire life.

Our kids and theirs, loved visiting us which was a plus. The problem was that our son, who was a Urologist living in the fertile valleys of California, came with a wife and two kids, and our daughter who had married an emergency room doc and had located in the hills of Wyoming, came with a group of five so their stays were necessarily lengthy. Our youngest daughter had become a single parent and though living in Massachusetts, was still too far away for a day trip. Working during the week and utilizing our grandparenting skills on weekends, every weekend, was a burden of love but our environment needed to be updated. To add to this situation, Mother was now in serious need of nursing care and would need our assistance soon. Planning to integrate all these wonderful people into a three bedroom/bath and a half Cape was a daunting task. It only seemed logical to sell and build a place that would fit all concerned.

Only the project got a little out of control. Our daughter, Kelly, our single parent daughter who was a Registered Nurse, could nurse Mom and also keep an eye out for her baby Stacey. Since she would need to be a "live-in", we would have to expand a little, maybe a remote "wing" to our home.(?)   Even though we stocked and shipped our packaging supplies from a warehouse nearby, we billed and conducted our business from our home office. Up to that time, "The Foxboro Paper Company" had fed and clothed us for twenty years.

Suddenly this new project made it obligatory to have yet another separate "wing" to accommodate not only an office space at home but an entrance for our secretary and maybe even for an additional salesperson. (?) Of course, Mom would have to have her "wing" with separate bath on the first floor and since the "Conley's West" extended their visits, we would need a "wing" for them and the kitchen just had to be augmented with all the latest innovations and dining areas. The five extra bedrooms were certainly reason enough for extra bathrooms. The "wings" of man suddenly developed into this monstrosity that began to grow like Topsy.

Our architect was losing hair at an alarming rate as we tried unsuccessfully to communicate our ideas as opposed to the traditional domiciles he was used to designing. This went on for months until we finally got it. He was being contrary with a purpose. Each visit translated into increased and enhanced billings. His misunderstandings kept his own mortgage paid while our costs were increasing expeditiously. After selling our little Cape three years previous to the completion of the new house, we were feeling quite frugal about sacrificing our life style, renting a small apartment in order to make ten percent on the equity's profits. This, all the while, unwittingly losing about one hundred percent on increased property values in Foxboro.

So armed with a slide ruler and scores of grandiose blueprints which feverishly whetted my penchant for perfection, it was becoming clear that it was a little akin to leaving the fox to guard the hen house. People in our new neighborhood thought some sort of church was being built on their corner. When complete, our dream house had 5,300 square feet which represented hundreds of hours of agonizing sweat and tears and took two years to complete.

Upon completion, sadly, Mom had passed away and Kelly had remarried. Not only that, but at the closing, the builder had given us the wrong set of keys. He couldn't be reached (probably hiding out, rubbing his hands in glee while celebrating his good fortune). The builder claimed there was a room in the office wing that had not been on the blueprints for completion and since his men had finished it off in error, he demanded, another $10,000.00. We wound up about midnight at Motel Six. Insult and dumb thing, number two.

It was beginning to look from this point on, that all would be futility. Just as well, as "Vanity", thy name is Katie. To add insult to injury, this urgent need for more elaborate and larger places became totally useless as our daughter, Kitty and family decided to move back into the Foxboro area as her husband had taken a position in the emergency room at Norwood Hospital, just 20 minutes from our six bedroom, five bathroom, many winged "colossus", which was being further afflicted by a rising tax base. Age and panic had come to live amongst us and we eagerly grasped at the possibility of a NBA pension to help fill in the gap between selling and buying down.

Since nothing had come of our little meeting in Boston, we wrote a letter to the Commissioner to find out if Gene had met the inclusion criteria for the new NBA pension change. The response was from the NBA's actuarial firm with a curt quote stating, "if the player was on the roster as of February 15, 1965, he was qualified to be included in the NBA pension". That was all. This meant that half the Celtic roster of the fifties and early sixties which had accumulated all those NBA championships, had been excluded.

From our perspective, this seemed discriminating. Not only that, the Oldtimers we had talked with, felt it just wasn't right, immoral even. Gene managed to pick up a NBA media guide to find out who else had been left behind by retiring before 1965. Being audacious by nature, he called post-1965 Celtic players to ask them just what their pension was and what they understood the criteria to be. It was their understanding at the time, that they were to receive $125.00/month/year of service or $100.00/month/year of service if taking a widow's benefit and that you had to have had five years to qualify.

So searching the media guide to form our list, we hunkered down for a long hard journey. The Foxboro Public Library became my evening office as the NBA was unable to provide us the addresses of former players. From the list of former NBA players with the required five years, we researched their Alma Maters for the Alumni addresses, contacting them for any information they might have concerning that particular player. Somehow, Gene was able to convince them to give us their addresses. Then began our long torturous odyssey contacting each player. We wanted to find out if it was merely the Conleys who thought of this as a grievance. At first Gene was a little apprehensive about this endeavor, understanding it would be a daunting task which might prove to be another one of our ill conceived efforts. Sending out questionnaires, we were able to get their true feelings as to how they felt concerning this pension exclusion. Also, we wanted to find out if any of our players of that era would be willing to lead out in this.

We knew it was David Stern's job to resist adding another expense to his budget and that it would be a tough sell to the active players in their twenties. The most difficult task, we felt, would be educating and convincing new owners who had recently purchased NBA franchises that it was immoral to discriminate in this way. Shutting out an entire era by leaving out the well known as well as the role players from this entitlement, simply by picking an arbitrary date in view of the NBA's expanding good fortunes seemed unjust. Of course we also knew that they were businessmen and their focus would naturally be on their bottom line, not on the glories of the past. It would take a miracle to obtain justice.

Cataloging all this information took us more than a half year before we were able to complete the addresses of these pre-1965 former NBA players. We really could have used the resources of the internet then. The response to this questionnaire was overwhelming. Everyone we had written, responded and with the exception of just one "negative" on just one of the questions, all the questions were answered in the affirmative. Some even sent small checks to fund the effort. The money wasn't much but most assuredly, this gesture put the fearsome weight of responsibility on our shoulders and realized at once that we had grabbed a tiger by the tail. Our hope had been that even though we would help in this endeavor, we had expected that one or more of the higher profile types would volunteer their leadership in this campaign. After all there were 22 Basketball Hall of Fame players on our list who were a great deal more qualified than we and certainly had more celebrity status. Their basketball name recognition would give them a far greater advantage in this awesome task.

When we look back on this small beginning we realize how fortunate we were to have been gently coerced into fifteen years of Youth leadership at church and also the responsibilities of leading out in social committee activities which gave us the skills and experience to carry out this monumental work. We knew that we needed the assistance of every player we contacted and that a meeting was definitely in order. The question was where, how and when.

Since another Basketball Hall of Fame weekend was coming up the following year, we made arrangements for a room from Joe O'Brien, the president of Basketball's Hall of Fame at that time. As previously mentioned, twenty-two Basketball Hall of Fame Inductees were also NBA Oldtimers so we solicited his cooperation in helping us with anything that he could provide for us. Joe gave us the Library.

Just before this meeting, Bob Cousy who had been televising the Celtic games at the time, called us to let us know that Dave Anderson of the New York Times was interested in talking with us. Dave had been his classmate at Holy Cross. Gene was out of town at some Baseball card show. I was reluctant at first to make that call but Lynn Loscutoff, the wife of former Celtic player, Jim Loscutoff, had called immediately following Bob's call and encouraged me to follow through. Hard work never intimidated me but calling a famous columnist at his home, no less, did. However, since we had taken on this enterprise, I felt duty bound to continue and with nerves of putty, made that momentous call. He was so kind and listened intently as he got the story. He was on his way to the

"Masters" and wouldn't be able to make our meeting but he did want Gene to reach him in Georgia for the rest of the story.

Words cannot express how wonderful our NBA Oldtimers were. They cooperated in every way. First in helping to complete the job of finding the missing, writing letters to the "active" NBA player representatives, the owners and David Stern. They made the effort of contacting any member of the print or electronic media in their respective areas, to alert them to our story. This was the most difficult part. It's not glamorous news, not sexy, nor exciting, not even tragic, though we did have our hard luck vignettes to relate.

Actually, when broaching the issue of pension injustices, you'd be surprised how quickly you can clear a room. Eyes can easily be diverted or glazed over, followed by yawns and excuses for a hasty exit.

It wasn't easy for these 108 proud heroes of yesterday to be suddenly put in this position. We had no leverage but made an appointment with the prestigious law firms of "Foley, Hoag & Eliot" in Boston and from Bob Cousy's contact with "Bowditch & Dewey" of Worcester in spite of it. We found that our cause was not a legal alternative. No, this was a moral issue, not a legal one. It simply was "the right thing to do, an idea, who's time had come" as Earl Lloyd once related to us. Bob Harrison supplied us with our Logo and stationery. Our Oldtimers assisted in every way they could and after we had learned to trust them and they us, we appealed to them for an interest in their prayers.

There were doubters among us, but that didn't stop them. The newspapers in all the major cities in the country carried an article about this group not being recognized with inclusion into the NBA pension. Many thanks to the "Fourth Estate" and the First Amendment to the Constitution and for Columnists like Dave Anderson and Sam Goldaper of the NY Times, Jim Murray of the LA Times,

John Stedman of the Baltimore Evening Sun, Jerry Sullivan and Jerry Izenberg of Newsday, Tom Wheatley of the St. Louis Post-Dispatch and of course our own personal favorites, Will McDonnough and Bob Ryan of the Boston Globe who showed real compassion in their publications. They all wrote eloquently about it being an immoral situation that needed to be addressed by both the players and the owners now that the NBA had become so successful. It was becoming an embarrassment to the League as the word that came down from on high was, "tell the Conleys to call off the dogs". Of course that was like waving a red flag in front of a bull.

With all our momentum, we never really had any direct feedback from the Commissioner's office other than the actuaries' report plus Cousy and Gene's hurried helicopter trip to NY to visit some of the NBA officers. So our next strategy was to invite the electronic media plus the print media to our second meeting at the Hall of Fame the following May. This invitation was also extended to the Commissioner, each owner and player rep. Every former involved player that could, showed up at the Hall of Fame luncheon in readiness for interviews. We knew that Boston's channel 56 was on their way for the 3:00 p.m. meeting as Gene had personally invited them just three days before.

About an hour and a half before that, however, Red Auerbach, unfortunately, granted channel 56 an exclusive interview to announce that K. C. Jones, the Celtics coach then, was going to be replaced. That breaking news of course took precedence over our press conference. Russ Granik, the Vice-Commissioner was at the "Hall's" luncheon that day and had requested that the NBA Oldtimer's board meet with him before lunch was completed. This illustrious board consisted of past players like, George Mikan, Bob Cousy, Paul Arizin, George Senesky, Red Holzman, Ed Macauley, Dolph Schayes and of course, Gene.

This was a real breakthrough for us. Russ, however, stipulated to the board that he would only meet with the other former NBA players on one condition, that no media be present. We had more or less called this press conference for the media so of course this was a disappointment to us and to them but we were pleased that the NBA had made the concession to meet with us on this issue. To accommodate Russ, we hurriedly contacted each Oldtimer, who was still eating, to cut short their lunch in order to meet with Mr. Granik an hour and a half earlier than planned. This prevented the film crews from getting a very significant story and they had to be content with a few hurried up interviews afterwards. There had been one lone AP female reporter who had arrived early, waiting for an advance story but she was a casualty of their agreement and was similarly dismissed. Before Mr. Granik's remarks, Gene asked that all present give their names and the teams they played with.

It was a magnificent showing. Even George Yardley was there from as far away as California. Mr. Granik had to be impressed but there were no definite promises made. Still, the dialogue had commenced. We had already made progress with the Player's Union as Gene had made a few visits to New York to establish their support. Charlie Grantham, the Player's vice president, Earl Lloyd, the first African American to play an NBA game, and Gene went on New York's popular sports radio station, WFAN, with Ann Ligouri, August 23, 1987. Charlie was in complete agreement with what Gene and Earl had advocated. But still, no cigar.

Why or what had equipped us for such a terrifying but magnificent obsession? Maybe it's always best to introduce ourselves and start from the beginning...

CHAPTER 3

MY PERSONAL ACCOUNT

World War II was played out in heroic melodramas where dirt piles became bunkers and black cheesecloth, from the greenhouse near our home, hid us as we seriously defeated and liquidated the "Japs" along with Hitler. Looking back as an adult, it is amusing to think how earnest and sincere our child's play was. But it was unquestionably real to us, the heroes of our odyssey.

The home across from us was owned and built by a gold mining family whose heritage was German. Surrounded by gigantic old growth shrubbery, it was a difficult property to penetrate. The brick mansion was set back and seemed oddly out of place in a middle class neighborhood. We could only imagine the wealth that played out in this world. However, our interest wasn't in finding out about the lifestyle of the rich and famous as we stealthily crept up close enough to peer through the thickness of their camouflage. During the early evenings the black cheesecloth disguised us as we managed to catch just enough, to hypothesize yet another espionage plot being planned by the Axis.

War and its ugly reality really hadn't touched our world, being insulated as we were by geography. Nevertheless, the concept of finding some bit of information that would aid our country, fueled our pride and patriotism which remained a constant as we played out our little war games during those years.

**Katie, Mom, Clymer and Homer
& Patti — 1940**

Father was the neighborhood warden, seeing to it that when there was a mock air drill, every window was black so that the enemy would be completely thrown off his target. Father's war game was at least, useful.

Then, there was the tin foil saved, for whatever reason. Our gas was rationed so we hardly used our car, being a "C" card holder, (not on the essential list). There were paper drives and bond drives. It was a busy and meaningful community we all shared and experienced towards our common goal of victory for our country.

I vividly recall the day our nation declared complete victory. It was the event of the century!

We lived a block from the town line so our existence was basically rural but we were still within the city limits of Spokane, Washington and had bus service only a half block away, so when this momentous occasion was announced via radio, Dad, Mother, Patty and I dressed up, took the bus to where it was happening, the center of the city! As it must have been celebrated all over the nation, everyone crowded city streets. It was Pandemonium! Bells were ringing, horns were blowing, people were shouting and singing and everyone was kissing and hugging everyone else.

The war started when I was 10 and ended when I was in my early teens and being quite naive and sheltered, when soldiers grabbed and kissed me, I was in complete shock! Daddy, after awhile, decided we should return and meditate about our good fortune.

Even though the years of war were over, our brothers had not returned right away. There was great anticipation for us, especially for our Mother. She had bravely kept her courage and did all that was expected of her during the war bond drives, the paper drives, and the leadership of our girl scout troop, plus doing solicitation for all the charities. This, while seeing to it we were all fed with the produce Daddy grew in his victory garden, an acre of vegetables and fruits. She canned and preserved everything. We had enough jars and shelves to house the harvest we gathered for ourselves and then, with the extra bounty, donated the rest to those in the old neighborhood of folks that had very little.

I could almost feel Mother's emotion as day after day, she went about quietly preparing for her sons' return. We were all caught up with her strong feelings. Even Father, who was always sentimental but quietly reserved, began to show signs of anxiety. Finally the word came, Homer and Clymer would be arriving just about the same time.

We dressed in our church clothes. Homer was first and was covered with hugs, kisses and tears. Then, a taxi drove up with Clymer emerging with that dimpled wide grin of his. Homer was first to greet him.

We all held back to see how they would both react, not seeing one another for four years.

The boys were men of their times. American society dictated that they never allow the show of affection as it might be construed as an affront to their sex. They were to remain strong and unmoved. No real man wanted to appear effeminate or soft.

They approached one another, tears glistening, and with myriads of dimples and teeth glowing, they stretched their arms wide in mock pretense as though to embrace but just in time, both reached out in firm but hardy handshakes that were pumped over and over again while using their free hands, to pat one another on the other brother's shoulder. They remained, true to their times and gender, manhood intact. Then, we all cried and laughed at the same time and after Mother greeted each of her sons with her kisses and hugs, she went over quietly, to the front window and took down the tiny, sun faded flag with the two blue stars. Her baby boys were home!

NOW THE WAR WAS OVER!

Kathryn Conley

CHAPTER 4

GENE'S ORIGINS

Gene Conley was born in Muskogee, Oklahoma, November 10, 1930. He was Eva Conley's birthday present, born "breach", and as he is always fond of saying, "I've been doing things backward ever since".

He inherited his Mother's dark Cherokee complexion as well as her Irish and German ancestry. It was the luck of the Irish to have a Father who was equally English and of Irish decent.

Les, Gene's Father, had little time to devote to his two sons as survival was the name of the game in the early thirties, but this didn't deter Gene from finding his own sporting activities. If there was a bicycle contest, he won it, along with various bicycle parts. He began to taste the rewards of becoming a "Professional". Even Yo-Yo contests claimed his interest along with first prizes. His swimming contests produced ribbons only. However, with his first place finishes, he gained a great deal of recognition. So much so, that at the tender age of 13, he was taken to Tulsa along with three other fellows for a district meet. His eyes bugged when he joined the others at pool's edge. There were 12 juniors and seniors from Tulsa competing with Muskogee's Junior High's fearless four. He took a side glance at his competition . "They had beards and looked older than my Dad", Gene laughed later. "The pool in Muskogee was 5 yards. x 20 yards. The Tulsa extravaganza was

Les & Eva, Gene's Parents

30 yards. x 50 yards. "I never drank so much water and saw so many bubbles in my life!" This episode brought realism into his life. You don't always win.

The "depression" had settled heavily on the hills and plains of Oklahoma. Little League was far into the future. So it took a great deal of initiative to round up a baseball team on weekends or after school. Just as soon as daylight beckoned, he was out of the house knocking on doors, pleading and convincing others to join his motley crew to field the two needed teams.

Les managed to take his little family to the class D, Muskogee Reds' minor league games from time to time. Sports, in the Conley clan was held in reverence. They debated and spoke with fervor over the merits of players, the game in season or the problems they produced, similar to those who become stimulated in their conversations over politics or religion. Gene joined the "Knot-hole" gang which afforded him access to games at a nominal cost. On one of these occasions, when his Father joined him, Les predicted that a player on the opposing team would make it to the Big Leagues. His name was Stan Musial, who on this particular night, struck out three times. Gene thought perhaps Les might be hallucinating. A few years later, Stan helped the St. Louis Cardinals win the World Series.

There occurred, one day, an incident that has always saddened him, something that a tremendously talented athletic body was powerless to avert. It was the fourth of July and somehow his brother, Sonny and he had managed to obtain a "torpedo" firecracker. For some reason, after lighting this instrument of destruction and waiting patiently from behind a tree for the grand explosion, nothing happened. Curiosity finally got the better of Sonny who went around the tree to see if the fuse had gone out. Detonation! In that split second, the sight of one of his eyes was gone forever. Even though there isn't a reason to feel guilt,

Gene's remembrance of this trauma brings pain and wonder as to why he hadn't looked rather than Sonny.

An interesting facet of Gene's young mind, was that he liked all kinds of action, not only the physical variety. Living in the Bible Belt, there were plenty of vehicles in which to channel this vent. One summer, during one of his wanderings, he happened to notice that there were a great many churches offering Vacation Bible School and at different times. The first one was already in progress and since the music was lively and the participants' attitudes positive, he found himself inside, registering a smile and a willing spirit. Just the kind of person you'd love to have join your group. However, he lacked "staying power" and he was off, once more to another VBS for more of the same.

In one of the churches, a young Baptist businessman, seeing the potential of using athletic activity to attract and win souls, asked Gene if he'd like to join the YMCA. As Gene often remarks, "I thought I'd died and gone to heaven". One catch, however, which wasn't all that hard to take, he did have to attend Sunday School in order to keep the membership in force.

He immediately began the natural progression of learning how to swim, working up the many levels and then competing in neighboring towns, accumulating his vast collection of ribbons. This is where Basketball was introduced. He and his brother, Sonny, who had by this time been proselytized by Gene, joined the church as well and in so doing, gained free access to the "Y". Gene became a hero at a "Y" summer camp, rescuing from drowning of all people, his camp counselor and was awarded the "Camper of the Year".

Gene became a working man at the ripe old age of 10. He had heard that a Soda Shop next to the theater in town needed a Soda Jerk. He awoke the next morning bright and early, to be first in line for the job, threw on his bib overalls, brushed his hair and was off, minus underwear and shoes. These were reserved for school and church. He rushed down to the shop and after interviewing the enthusiastic youngster, the owner said, "okay kid you get the job but when you report next weekend, you gotta wear a shirt and shoes and, oh yes, have something under those overalls".

His schedule ran from dinner time until 2:00 a.m., when he peddled his bike home over dirt roads for four long miles, past empty lots, abundant with dark forbidding trees and shrubbery. All the horrors ever imagined plagued him as shadows lengthened into figures of formidable creatures as he rode under the stars, whistling in defense. All this was done for a social security card and 10 cents an hour!

After two years of this splendid employment, he was ready for a man's job. His next experience in business was as a nurseryman, trimming trees, pulling weeds, etc. He worked for a guy called Herman for a pay upgrade of 15 cents per hour. "Herman, the German", kept three very large alligators in a pit at the front on his property, He would threaten the boys that if ever they loafed or goofed off, he'd have to throw them all into this pit. Needless to say, Herman got his money's worth for fear is a great motivator.

Mark Twain's, Tom Sawyer/Huckelberry Finn stories come to mind as Gene relates these homilies about his life as a youngster in Oklahoma. "We used to visit Aunt Bel who had raised my Mom and her sisters. Her place was out in the country in "Okay". "We used to 'appropriate' watermelon in the different farmers' fields and one day, just as I spotted the biggest melon in the patch, unbeknownst to me, a farmer had spotted me as well and commenced shooting. I took off and ran at least a quarter of a mile to Aunt Bel's house but as I ran up onto the porch,

I noticed, it wasn't Aunt Bel's at all. I had been so scared that I had gone up on a stranger's porch, but I never dropped the melon."

Life wasn't all games and work. When he and his family moved out to his Grandfather Pop's house, he found himself new friends and one of his best was C.P. who just happened to be African American or "Negro", as the word was used to describe people of color in the thirties, but then, Gene wouldn't have really labeled C.P.

Gene and C. P. had "B-B" guns and no feathered creature was safe on the plains and dusty hills of Oklahoma those summers. They didn't waste their ammunition as their quarry was meat on C. P.'s table and Gene always invited himself to dinner. What a kind woman C. P.'s Mother must have been with barely enough for her, C. P. and T.B., to share with their white visitor. Incidentally, T.B. was skinny so "T. B." was short for T-Bone, at least Gene and C. P. made it up that way. C. P. and Gene built their own track as well, complete with a long jump area and a high jump pit. He loved Football more than any other sport up until high school. He would put on a stocking cap and a sweatshirt, fantasizing these were helmet and shoulder pads. Again, it took a roundup to get as many kids in the neighborhood as possible to play real tackle football. Later, in Jr. High School, the real thing was issued him and Gene became some kind of mean "right-end", weighing in at 110 pounds. The coach had the team divide and position themselves at each end of the field. They were to run towards one another for "head-on-tackling". Gene's opponent was HUGE, as he recalls, and as Gene's shoulder pads, rested big and loose on his skinny frame the sound of the collision cracked so loud that the coach, pleased with the volume, remarked, "See, you guys, that's the way it's done...did you hear that "pop"? It was time for a new sport.

It was Christmas, 1941. Most depression kids in Oklahoma expected oranges and nuts for gifts. However, this Christmas Eve was different. Les worked most of the night while the boys slept, digging post holes for basketball goals. Their sponsor at the "Y" was no longer providing YMCA privileges. (Gene must have missed a few Sundays) This Christmas morning, there were no packages, but after being urged to bring in some wood from the backyard, the boys were stunned with pleasure at what they saw. The surface was dirt but it couldn't have been a grander arena!

When Gene was 13, his sister, Billye Lynn was born and Les knew his opportunities in Muskogee were limited for supporting his growing family. He had heard about a town in the state of Washington, providing employment in a great many fields for a company called the Hanford Engineering Works. Les was anxious to apply.

It was 1943 and Hanford needed, first of all, patrolmen to keep the peace in the free wheeling construction town that the government was developing to produce the components for the world's first Atomic Bomb.

The requirements for becoming an officer were, that you had to be at least 6' tall and weigh 160 pounds. Les met the first criteria but his build was slight. He began gorging on bananas, water and cream, especially on weigh-in day. He barely made it and afterwards, lost most of what had been ingested.

The family joined Les in Richland, Washington a year later. This was Paloose country, rolling hills, sage brush, light dusty soil. A sort of "no-mans" land which was just what the Government was looking for. The land, in the past, had produced the most luscious fruits and vegetables anywhere as long as irrigation supplied the missing ingredient. Unfortunately, the development of the "Bomb", at that time in American history, held precedent.

53

This was to be home and it was exciting as it was a boom town where everything was new, but it still had makeshift housing and schools. However, Uncle Sam was generous and took good care of its employees. Rent was very low, utilities were free and salaries were well above average. The school situation was just barely making it however. Gene was able to develop his athletic skills but his teachers were a little weak on Academics. Since he was always younger than the rest in his grade level (he was five when he entered first grade), his reading skills left a lot to be desired. His athletic skills were exceptional and so it was, when it was time to read, his comment of "I pass" seemed to suffice.

Besides placing first place in Conference wins in both basketball and baseball and coming in second in the state in track's "high jump", Gene was chosen to represent the Yakima Valley Conference in baseball at Seattle. Athletes from all over the Northwest met there for a game to decide which of them would represent the area at the "Hearst All Star Game" in New York. Some of the judges were Joe E. Brown and Monty Stratton, (the Major League Baseball pitcher who later lost his leg in a hunting accident). As luck would have it, Gene was the winning pitcher, even though he had started the game as an outfielder. The starting pitcher had a problem in the third, and Gene was enlisted. He shut out the opposition the rest of the way and won the game with a home run and thus became Washington's choice to represent the state in New York.

The Seattle Post Intelligence sent along a reporter to accompany Gene on the journey. In those days, it was a cross country train affair which took about three days to complete. They wanted the correspondent to chronicle each day's adventure. When Gene boarded the train there were photographers and writers to give him a hero's send off. His Father was there as well. Gene dutifully posed for the last shot and had grabbed his one suitcase with his right hand. He suddenly realized that he had no way to shake his Dad's hand in farewell. Les, in his excitement, kissed his son's cheek. It shocked Gene so that it worried him for most of that first day, as he never, ever, remembered his father kissing him.

The game in New York was between the U.S. All Stars versus the greater New York All Stars. There were many more players than would normally be fielded, so as they worked out for their various positions, Gene was chosen to be the U.S. All Stars' starting pitcher. Their managers were Max Carey, a former manager of the Pittsburgh Pirates and Oscar Vitt, affiliated with the Cleveland Indians. The New York team had Mel Ott who is in the Hall of Fame. The opposing pitcher was Frank Torre who later played first base on two professional teams with Gene; the Hartford Chiefs in the Eastern League and the World Champion Milwaukee Braves. The players voted Gene their captain and he became the winning pitcher. Along with buying a new plaid suit at Sax Fifth Avenue, he had quite an eastern swing.

Graduation was approaching and as a senior, Gene had many contacts from very divergent, but interesting universities, encouraging his enrollment on a basketball scholarship. In those days, it was called "tampering" as he was being transported, wined, dined and promised perks along with scholarships for both he and his brother. Those interested were Adoph Rupp of Kentucky, Hank Iba of Oklahoma A & M, Slats Gill of Oregon State, John Warren of Oregon University, the University of Washington, Washington State and Idaho. Since he was only 16 when he had to make his decision and because his brother had already enrolled there, Washington State became his choice.

On his arrival, before registration, they bunked him in with other athletes, including some football linebackers. In the dead of night, he was awakened suddenly, by a couple of Idaho football players. Being very young and inexperienced, when urged to come out to the car where Idaho's Basketball coach waited, he went willingly.

The linebackers in the two upper bunks seemed not to notice the disturbance. Maybe they were a little naive as well. Gene was put in the back seat between these two mammoth Idaho football players, and was cajoled into traveling with them all the way to Idaho State University in Moscow, Idaho.

They took him to casinos to play the slots along with promises of a percentage of same, if he would just enroll at Idaho. Then, it was back to Idaho's gym with other offers of gifts which included money, a scholarship and the use of a car for himself and one for his brother. Being up all night, tiring of all the high pressure salesmanship, he played along, asking to call his Father with the news as dawn approached.

They let him alone, listening in on the other line as Father and son talked. Gene said, "Les, they've taken me here to Idaho State University and want me to enroll with Idaho." Les, realizing the stress in his son's voice, said, "Gene, where do you really want to go?" "Les, I think I'd really rather go to Washington State." When Gene said that, Les yelled into the phone, "You tell them to get you back to Pullman now, or I'm calling the police," interspersed with some very salty language! They couldn't get him into the car quick enough, back to Washington.

Les, who was becoming close to many in the press, called one of the Tri-City reporters to relate the tale. It was an explosive story that appeared in all the west coast newspapers with columns of condemnation against the many universities that were recruiting illegally. After interviewing the Conleys, the commissioner of the entire west coast conference fined each university involved along with a stern reprimand. Then Gene began his college career.

CHAPTER 5

TRANSITION

Under the glowing headlines in 1948, *"Athlete of the Year - - Big Gene"* a Seattle Post Intelligence reporter expounded on Gene's accomplishments: *"One of the few times it will probably be unnecessary to state why the name of Gene Conley should head the list of athletes who have performed in Richland, Tri-City area, Yakima, or the state of Washington during the 12 month period of 1948. An average of 18 plus for a ten game conference basketball schedule, a 15 plus for 26 games, including two tournaments against tough opposition, selected on the all-state basketball team from those who didn't participate in the state tournament, a batting average of nearly .500 for 16 games in high school baseball season and only one loss in 10 starts..that to the state champs (oh, yes, a 18 strikeout average for 16 games), tied for second in the high jump at the state in Pullman with a scissors leap of 6'3", named on the all-state baseball team, collected the longest hit of the two games in three times at bat in the State-Seattle tilt, and performed on the mound with the Orphans, losing only one game. If that isn't enough, we'll throw in his latest accomplishment, starter on the W.S.U. frosh basketball team and named captain for their first game. Quite a guy, this young boy, who is nearer 6'8" than Bob Kurland is to 7' even, and to top the encore, his fedora size is the same as it was a year ago."*

All this excitement didn't really affect the 16 year old even after the kidnapping scare and the subsequent punishments doled out to the various universities for misconduct in recruiting. He landed in the first fraternity offering him room and board. Acacia frat was made up mostly of returning vets from WWII with an assortment of athletes from all over the Northwest, U.S., and Canada. They took a protective and paternal interest in this youngster, and besides, the Alumni had given him a car and expenses which afforded him beer hosting privileges, something that would plague him most of his athletic career.

The athletic programs set up in colleges of that era were scheduled quite differently than what they are today. If you played on a basketball scholarship, you were on the freshman team automatically. Varsity was only imagined until perhaps your Junior year. Because of Gene's outstanding freshman year, filled with victories, it followed that he would make "Varsity" his sophomore year, which afforded WSU the Division Championship. They went on a tear and Gene became the leading scorer in the Northern Division and was compared to Bill Sharman of USC, who was the top scorer in the Southern Division. Bill, later became his teammate on the world champion Boston Celtics and was eventually voted into Basketball's Hall of Fame. At the NBA's 50th year of existence, Bill was voted one of the 50 greatest NBA stars of its history. Gene racked up 217 points in 15 games, with a 14.5 average. He made an average of 45 percent of his shots in a league where 33 percent was considered par. At WSU, he was known as "Jumping Gene," a few years later, "Jumping Geno" became his moniker when Johnny Most, the Celtics radio announcer, dubbed him thus, because of his frantic antics, out-jumping the opposition under the boards.

In an article from Spokane: *"We're involved in another poll again. This time it has to do with All-American basketball players. From the West Coast we nominated Gene Conley, WSU, Louis Soriano, UW, Bill Sharman, USC, and Don Lofgran, San Francisco. Some others that will be hard to keep off, are White of Long Island U and Paul Arizin, Villanova. The whole deal won't be wound up for some time yet,....but if anything will beat Conley out for a spot on the first ten, it will be because he's a sophomore."*

WSU's team won the Northern Division and was well on their way for bigger and better things when they played a final against Johnny Wooden's UCLA team for the West Coast championship. At a Basketball Hall of Fame ceremony in Springfield, recently, John, then in his eighties, had not seen Gene for forty years. When he caught Gene's eye, before hardly saying hello, he immediately retold the strange circumstances of that dramatic game, his second year as coach there. WSU was leading by one point at the diminutive Westwood Gym, with a minute left to go, when Wooden had to replace two players who had fouled out. He put in a "third-string-milk-bottled-glass-wearing-bench-warmer" and in a seemingly futile attempt, from half court, that "third-string-bottled-glass-wearing-bench-warmer", half-heartedly, threw the ball towards the basket for a game winning UCLA goal as the buzzer sounded for the Coast Championship!

Gene's most supportive and best friend was Bill Gammie from Canada who later became an apple magnate. It was a good thing Bill was so outgoing and encouraging during the spring months of Gene's sophomore year. The more big league scouts started arriving in droves to wine and dine Gene along with another athlete, Ted Tappe, the more discouraging the baseball coach, Buck Bailey became. After the former football player- turned baseball coach met with a scout or two, Gene found himself brought out of a game for no other reason than to cast doubt in the scout's mind. Gene wasn't sophisticated enough to know what the score was, but with Gammie's booming voice shouting obscenities towards Bailey, it helped to salve a hurt and bruised ego of a very young and vulnerable youth. He began to grow as a pitcher in spite of the clash in personalities and wound up leading his team in hitting, with a .417 batting average.

Bailey was boisterous and kicked bats, buckets and whatever was handy. Since Gene had been brought up with decorum and southwestern conventionality, this didn't make for a fun time for him as athletics had always been fun and games. He intimidated Gene quite a bit, but in spite of all of this, WSU was able to play past Stanford at Palo Alto, 2 out of 3 games in winning the birth to the NCAA Nationals in Omaha (Gene winning one of the two).

Every big league scout at Omaha was there and Buck dearly wanted to win it all and felt he had the horses. They won 3 to 1 from Tufts, and Gene, slated for the Alabama game was able to win handily, 9 to 1. It was a forgone conclusion that Gene would be facing the Texas Longhorns for the final. Buck was all excited and had Gene all primed. It was not to be. Before the pitchers warmed up, Bailey came over to Gene and let him know that he was going to really throw them off and use a left-hander. It was a low blow, but he warmed up in the bullpen just in case. When Texas advanced during the next two innings with three runs, Gene was called on and proceeded to pitch 7 scoreless innings, but WSU never scored again.. In the cab returning to the hotel, Ted Tappe and Gene were asked to ride with Buck. Bailey half apologized for his error in judgment and said that next year, they would really kill them all, and both boys nodded in mock agreement, knowing full well neither would ever have to be intimidated by "Big Thunder" again.

In his sophomore year, the scouts had been thicker than thieves. Every club in the majors had submitted a bid. Emmett Watson, a columnist from the Seattle PI wrote, *"One scout followed Conley all over the eastern seaboard, plying him with milk-shakes and honeyed words. Embarrassed by the attention (Gene is a modest kid), he tried to shake the scout with an excuse.*

*'I have to get some hair tonic, offered Gene, hoping to lose his shadow.
'Hair tonic! Hair tonic?!' shrieked the scout, happily. 'Why, my club has a special
fund for hair tonic. Have one on me, son.'*

*The scout, frantic to please, disappeared into a drugstore, and Conley
seized the opportunity to disappear into the crowd."*

He was only 19 now, so he would need the permission of his parents to
sign any contract. At first his Mom and Dad felt it only right that he should finish
his college career but the temptations were just too lucrative and they proceeded
to entertain offers. However, in the fifties there were no agents, no "show me the
money" guys, and a Boston Braves scout, Bill Marshall took advantage of their
naiveté in signing him to a $6,000.00 no bonus contract. The UPI Sports Editor
Ken Benham wrote, *"We suspect a good many persons reading the word,
"no-bonus" wonder how good a deal that could be when the memory is fresh in
mind of the whopping $100,000.00, a high school graduate, Paul Pettit, received
for the same amount of penmanship a few months back.*

*"Don't worry. The scouts have been tagging the tall lad for over a year
now and in that much time Conley and his parents have explored all the avenues.
Next year when Gene is cutting teeth in the minor leagues he can read reports of
Pettit's struggle trying to become a major leaguer sitting on the bench for the
Pittsburgh Pirates and be glad his choice was a wise one."*

As it turned out, that's just exactly how it played out as baseball's Pettit
lasted only a year in baseball. In this era, when you signed a bonus contract,
baseball players like Pettit, and basketball/baseball players like Dave DeBusschere
and Danny Ainge, couldn't be sent down to the "minors" so you became the victim
of this type of treatment and their baseball careers, a mere mention.

Besides, Les thought that the Braves's aging pitching staff of Spahn, Sain and Bickford would mean a quicker and easier entrance into the "Bigs" and with the clause that Gene would make the parent club's spring training each year, he would have plenty of exposure. On the surface, it appeared to be a sub-par agreement but with his southwestern savvy, he did manage to elicit a promise that if the Braves were ever to get into a World Series while Gene was pitching, the entire family would be flown to all the Series games, all expenses paid. This promise was to become prophetic.

CHAPTER 6

THE MEETING

Attending Kinman Business University in Spokane had not been my goal after graduation from Upper Columbia Academy. During my senior year, my Father had suddenly died which meant I would have to delay matriculating into a Journalism program at Walla Walla College. I had spent the summer months at Kinman but employment, so far had eluded me. In the wastelands of Richland, Washington, however, 185 miles away, salaries far in excess of what Spokane could provide, were considered and accepted. My friend, Betty Munn, and I exchanged the city lights for sand and sagebrush and a new adventure.

There was almost enough now for my first semester at Walla Walla College. Betty and I were paid four times what she had been making in Spokane. Paying only $11.00/month for our dorm room, daily maid service and fresh linens certainly helped body and soul. So too, did my policy on dates. Without dinner, it just didn't happen.

Since most of our selection in Richland, (interested in us), were of college age, they came equipped with all the standard "raging hormones without conscience", and each night carried with it, an adventure in inventive escape. Sex education hadn't even been imagined then, nor had sexual harassment. Since my experiences at Academy were limited and protected as far as sex tutelage was

The Way We Were

1951

Pictures exchanged
during Gene's first
spring Training:

Gene and Katie

concerned, the struggle for purity was a learn as you go experience and was fast becoming, hardly worth the dinner compensation. Academy life with all its restrictions, now seemed more desirable.

Because I had taken the vows of chastity, dates were a rapid "turn-over" so Betty and I started signing up for classes in fencing, chorale groups, etc. Towards the end of September, however, I met a nice but complicated, Pat Sheeran who had invited me on a double date. Okay, safety in numbers, I thought. Pat, who later became a district judge, was athletic but also extremely articulate, I needed a dictionary just to converse with him most of the time. It was early evening when he and his friend decided to take us by the baseball field before dinner. Standing tall, dark and smiling was a very personable, handsome young man. I vaguely recognized him from a pick-up basketball game I had watched when I had dropped by the local high school for a fencing lesson. Pat and his friend "Red" joked and laughed with him from the car, while we girls waited for an introduction which never came. Then, as Pat drove away, Gene called out, "nice meeting you girls" which broke up Red and Pat. Since it was immediate attraction, I began questioning the boys as to who he was. They mentioned that he was quite an athlete both in high school and college, but since I had never followed sports this wasn't the kind of information I desired.

Things didn't exactly work out with Pat and date avoidance again became my focus.

That lasted, until one night, my roommate and I were rudely awakened by a knock at our bedroom window. It was "Toad" McMillin, who had invited me to his junior prom a few months before. He and his friend wanted us to join them at a house party. I, with great sanctimonious disdain, told him to get lost. My roommate, however, pleaded with me until I finally broke down and got dressed.

It was a Friday night which meant it was Sabbath for me and should have been for my roommate. Partying wasn't part of our perceived Sabbath keeping habits. She was very convincing, however, saying we would just be meeting friends at a family home setting and besides, we would be back in an hour...... probably.

When we arrived at this young couple's home, several young men were in the middle of a card game and the girls were just standing around, trying to look attractive and gay. My conscience was beginning to tug at my value system. Gambling and cards was a "no no" in Adventist circles and on the Sabbath no less! This foible will cost me many a session of heart rendering pleas for forgiveness. I shall most certainly wear out my slacks at the knees. Then, suddenly, I became aware of someone staring at me. It was that same tall, dark, handsome boy/man, and without shame or flinching, he kept staring straight at me! I tried to avert his eyes but there was no escaping! He had locked on to me like radar. His eyes were hazel but more than that, they were so bright, they glistened. They were so full of warmth that it seemed we had known each other forever. However, I was beginning to feel uncomfortably shy about it.

"Hey Gene, Richie owes you a quarter. Here, catch." Since I hadn't been accustomed to people who drink, I hadn't realized that his glistening stare was alcohol induced and when he reached up to catch the quarter, it alluded his outstretched hand and rolled into the bathroom. Always, an anxious person, eager to be of help, I immediately followed the quarter into the lav to retrieve it. As I straightened up, quarter in hand, I felt a presence and a door slam shut. There we were.

What a ridiculous situation, here was this 6' 8" giant staring down at a very nervous and completely disarmed girl/woman in some stranger's bathroom. I didn't honestly know what to do now. He was still staring and smiling.

"What's your name?"

Then, I became ridiculous. "I'm not going to tell you", I responded, blushing coyly.

Guarding the door, he said, "Then I'm not going to let you out until you tell me".

"Well, if you promise to let me out", it's........Katie"

"Katie what?"

"Katie Disney"

"Well, Katie Disney, I'm Gene Conley, and I'm going to kiss you"

"No you're not!" I was smiling as it was hard to act mad when turning red from my toes up.

"Well, I guess we'll have to stay here all night". More smiling and staring but he wasn't budging as I made a lunge for the door knob. I didn't have a prayer and he knew it but then again, he was so disarming that I was beginning to wonder, why not?.

"Well, if you promise to let me out"...

From that moment on, with all the bells, whistles, horns and accompanied fireworks exploding at the same time, life seemed absurd without him. No one had ever kissed me like that! Isn't that just too precious?

Since Gene had come to the party with a young school teacher and I had come with "Toad", it was awkward but Gene had a talk with him outside and we all left together for home. The car was packed with young people. Tom McMillin,

Toad's older brother, challenged Gene to a foot race. Tom was attending Gonzaga University in Spokane on a track scholarship, so he was confident that he could out run an inebriated Gene Conley. So, with Gene's car full of "smashed" teenagers, we raced off to the desert hills above Richland. There were no roads and Gene was driving recklessly towards his goal, his challenge.

I could imagine seeing my poor Mother reading the papers the next day. "The brand new Pontiac, loaded with drunken teenagers returning from a riotous party, crashed and rolled over several times as all perished, their blood spilling out onto the sandy hills of Richland". My Mother, heartbroken, as she mourned. She wouldn't know that her daughter hadn't had alcohol, but she would know that I was in questionable company, and on the Sabbath no less!

The car came to a screeching halt as Gene and Tom tumbled out. The young teacher was told to drive the car up a ways to furnish the finish line. Then, as Toad yelled, "l, 2, 3, go", they were off! Just as Gene was ahead and just about to touch the trunk, for some reason, the young teacher, drove away just as his outstretched hand came in contact with the sharp license plate which tore out a piece of flesh. He laughed and rubbed his wound into the sand and we were off once again. I was more than apprehensive about this whole affair but Gene's easy ways were certainly attractive.

As couple after couple were taken home, in view of all that had happened that night, I wondered how this was all going to play out. Gene, in the dark, out of the young teacher's gaze, reached back where I was sitting on Toad's lap. Thinking this was a cue to hold hands, I reached down in the dark and was totally shocked when he yelled, "ouch, let go." The pain had started to come back into his injured hand. Embarrassed and caught in the act of being foolish, I apologized.

The young teacher seemed surprised when Gene let her off at her door. His cheery, "goodnight" did nothing to appease her dour countenance, as she huffed off in disgust. Now, it was only Gene, Toad and I, as we pulled up to the dorm. Friendly but obviously in pain, this confusing, interesting stranger asked for a date the next night. This guy has nerve as Toad and I were still holding hands. Not to be put off, Toad too asked for a date for the same night. Well, here's a strange set of circumstances. Here I was, humiliated for mistakenly reaching for this fellow's hand earlier and now he's asking for a date in front of mine?

"Well, I really can't say", I heard myself saying as I opened the door and rushed away, "but whoever gets here first tomorrow night, will be my date!" Right back at you buddy!

Kathryn Conley

CHAPTER 7

BITS AND PIECES

"Toad or the handsome stranger? That is the question. What if both showed up at the same time?"

Saturday had passed quite normally for me, church, reading, resting. In the back of my mind, however, was the previous night's wild ride and my new acquaintance. It was starting to unnerve me somewhat. The sun was setting when I leisurely showered and pin curled my hair. (so fifties). The showers were opposite the opening to the lobby. I stopped short, dumbfounded, as just when I turned to go down the hall, my new black haired friend with the glistening hazel eyes, made his entrance. There was absolutely no place to hide. He had said he would be there first, but this was ridiculous! I was hardly dressed for a rendezvous in my robe and slippers and my hair......my hair?....it was tightly glued to my head. I didn't need makeup as my face turned all shades of red! I went into shock but his smile was so broad and inviting that I found it impossible to resist his greeting and besides, there was no way to avoid the situation.

He acted as if nothing was amiss and said that he was all set. (whatever that meant) He had been able to procure a bottle of vodka and his friend and aunt JoEvelyn would be riding with us, over the river into Umitilla, Oregon. Expecting delight, he was a little dismayed at my reaction.

"But I don't drink".

He recovered with that bright infectious smile and laugh of his and asked if I wanted a cigarette.

"I don't smoke either". By now, I was starting to get the picture. No matter how attractive this character was, we just weren't going to make it.

It threw him for a moment, then, all of a sudden, it just didn't seem to matter. "Okay, but hurry up and get dressed as Bud and Aunt JoEvelyn are waiting in the car."

From that moment on, I was completely charmed. My lifestyle, I realized was quite foreign to him but he settled for being intrigued. Our dates were unusual. One night, when challenged as to who was the better tree climber, Gene surprised me with a repertoire of melodies from school songs to "pop" in one tree, while I burst forth in verse and quotations from my designated tree. Just as we were countering with competing witticisms, we were discovered from another part of the park so we withdrew to fight again, another day. We were so simpatico!

From the time we first met on Gene's birthday, November 10, 1950, until family Christmas festivities interrupted, we had been together continuously except for the 8 hour work days. Since I worked for twelve nuclear engineers in the same "area-west" (another word for nuclear hot spot), we even managed lunch at times. Most nights we were in by 2:30 a.m. each morning and four hours later, I had showered, dressed, and ready to return to work. No matter how we promised one another to end our date at 10:00 p.m., it always seemed to wind up at 2:30 a.m. It was a real endurance test!

Shenile was one of Gene's old flames. Since Shenile's parents were out of town and she had access to her parents' liquor stash, everyone who was anyone in Richland, was invited to the big New Year's Eve party at Shenile's big house.

Arriving, I was apprehensive and full of serious guilt. Being raised Adventist, put me in a disadvantaged position and quite out of my element. My comfort level was fast fading as Shenile, though gracious, was most anxious to fill my cup with the vilest of liquids. At first I resisted, but after a great deal of peer pressure and being deemed a "Miss goody too-shoes", I caved. "Just a small amount please". "Of course", Shenile oozed as she gleefully filled my "small" glass with what was then termed, a "zombie". Hardly a first time drinker's friend.

I sipped slowly and at first didn't notice anything different or altered but in a very short span of time, I was sitting down in a chair that I clearly saw across the room. From the floor I was beginning to feel horrible! Gene gently picked me up and even though he was laughing, he diplomatically managed to half carry me out into the snow where I kneeled in supplication, praying for forgiveness, promising sobriety from that point until eternity. Just make the nausea go away. However, the biblical quotation that fit the results of "reaping whatsoever thou soweth", produced prodigious amounts of my supper, lunch and breakfast. I wanted my Mommy!

Gene drove around as the motion of the car seemed to soothe my troubled stomach. He rubbed my back over and over as I tried to return to normalcy. I repaid him by chucking up the remains of the day all over the interior of his brand new Pontiac Chieftan. He and his Father had carefully picked it out with part of the $6,000.00 he had received for signing with the Boston Braves in October. Now I knew I'd never see him again! This was just too much to bear, being separated from both God and Gene.

Consciousness was slowly ebbing over my poor numbing mind and body the following morning, not only feeling physically lousy but morally despicable.

Shenile's revenge had done it's dirty deed so being a positive loser, my thoughts again began focusing on my original goal of college by Fall.

As I was so disposed, Gene was being announced from the lobby. Again, he surprised me by acting as though nothing pitiable had happened the night before. In his same kind, gentle way that I was beginning to know, he was insisting that we go out and get some fresh air, even though I felt like death warmed over. He assured me that fresh air and a little something to eat would set me right.

Eat??!! That would be last on my list of things to do that day but I was so glad to see him, I dutifully followed instructions and we were off across the river to Oregon again. After a bite to eat, I was starting to feel as if I would live. There was a spot beside the river that looked quite flat, a perfect place to show him my full range of talents. I proceeded with all the gymnastics I had ever learned and he seemed duly impressed. We were still truly children but starting to become devoted to one another.

That night, a little over six weeks after meeting, Gene properly proposed marriage. I couldn't answer. I wanted to say yes but I also knew, as an Adventist, that wasn't possible. From childhood, I had been instructed that, "being unequally yoked" was not an option.

In the book, "Why I Joined", Gene wrote, *"Katie deeply impressed me, and it seemed mutual. We knew from the start that we could never live apart from each other, so I asked her to marry me soon after we began dating. I expected her to be ecstatic. After all, I had just signed a Major League contract with the Boston Braves baseball club! Instead, she burst into tears. She told me of her Lord, of her faith, and that her church frowned on marriages outside the Adventist circle. For a few minutes I was filled with anguish until I convinced her that I did believe in God, and had believed since a very young child. She agreed to marry me".*

Aunt Mattie had been right.

In September, I had auditioned for the Tri-City Choral Group and after making the cut we were told that we would be doing a joint concert with the Tri-City Symphony just before Christmas. They had asked for experienced Ballet people for the "Nutcracker" as well, so I eagerly volunteered. We had practiced from September for the Yuletide extravaganza. I was anxious to have Gene see the performance and meet my family. Since my Father had died, my Mother had opened her own Nursing Home. It would really be an effort for her to travel the 150 miles to be there but she said that she, Aunt Mattie and my sister, Patti, would be accompanying her as they were anxious to meet Gene.

The excitement was starting to build in my mind about the performance. The prospect of having Gene see me in a new light was entering my vain little heart. Somewhere out there in the dark, I could just imagine him appreciating each movement that was orchestrated for his benefit. It had been a success! After the performance, I rushed out, without waiting to change my costume as I was so anxious for the family to meet Gene but he wasn't where he said he would be. We waited for some time. I was humiliated!   That was when Aunt Mattie said it......."this is the one she'll marry as he can't be instructed as to what to do, nor when to do it."

Yes, Auntie, you were right!

Kathryn Conley

CHAPTER 8

SEPARATION

It never once occurred to me nor my prejudices that Gene's family wouldn't approve of our match. My own Mother's profound silence following my announcement was an unspoken dissent which I understood, given the differences in our faiths. I knew a certain social stigma would affect my family's value system and status among our friends. Not to mention that this would probably change or eliminate altogether my goals of communicating the gospel of truth to the world.

It was only a week into the new year when Gene told his family of our plans and as Gene explained to me, it took a great deal of effort by his Father to calm his wife's reaction, especially in light of his own misgivings. Gene could see that his joyous plans of marrying Katie Disney wasn't on his parent's agenda.

Somehow, this new situation didn't seem to shake our confidence in our commitment. We still continued to make plans as Gene said he had made up his mind a week into our relationship and when I finally agreed on marriage, there was no longer a question.

After the dust settled, Les proposed a compromise. Gene's $6,000.00 contract had already been diminished by half. He and Les had picked out that large, shiny, but not exactly cool, gray four door sedan so there would only be $3,000.00 left to live on. Hardly a king's ransom. It seemed logical to wait, at least through spring training, as it could also divert Gene's concentration from his first training experience with the parent club and might harm his chances of impressing the Braves. Not only that, we were just too young! All very logical reasons to wait.

The crushing results of this meeting of the minds came to its fruition just three days later. Gene was to leave right away, a month and a half before spring training started, to visit Pat Sherran, a friend stationed in Texas. He had recently been drafted during the Korean Conflict. This would still put him in Bradenton for spring training a few weeks early. His Dad had made all the arrangements. The hope was clear and obvious that this might cool the relationship by putting time and distance between us. At least to me, it seemed so.

As I blinked in disbelief, (in shock, actually), I only half listened to Gene as he outlined his plans for us following the completion of spring training. My thoughts began to race with breathless speed. In my mind, I concluded that, okay, God must have closed this door and will now be opening a window someplace else. Isn't that the way it goes? Slowly, the empty ache of desertion replaced my previous visions of pure joy.

Somehow the next two days went pretty much as the past six weeks had gone, with hugs, kisses and promises, but at this final parting, upon entering my dorm, I felt quite alone, numb and forsaken.

I hadn't shown disappointment or objected in any way to this arrangement, but I was storing away a great deal of unresolved and pent up emotion. I began having feelings of despair and for some reason, my own imminent death. Dismissing thoughts of our life together, I desperately struggled to adjust my plans and focus once again on college and now since I had saved enough for a semester, this was possible. Even with this new resolve, I found that I was unable to shake this feeling of doom. I started experiencing lack of concentration, shortness of breath, rapid heart rate, and a general feeling, at any moment, of fading from existence. My Father's demise just two years before, brought back memories which only colored my soul a deeper hue.

One day as my office manager, who also had been a Major in the war, drove me home from work, I began unloading on him. I told him of my thoughts about dying. In vain, he tried to encourage me with stories of men under his command that were sure they were going to die in battle but hadn't. When these war stories didn't seem to dislodge my despair, he decided that I should go home for two weeks and rest.

Going home usually meant a joyous sense of relief and pleasure but even the thought of returning to a loving and warm family did nothing to discourage my dark thoughts. Mother became worried after a few days and asked a psychiatrist she knew to visit us to check out my weird imaginings . I was truly suffering all right. My symptoms were classic signs of anxiety. She told Mother that only time and a good diet would help me as I was suffering from love unrequited. The winter with all its dreariness fueled my mood.

Somehow, I did get through those two weeks and finally felt strong enough to return to work and to whatever fate dictated. I arrived that night to a surreal scene as I got off the bus in Richland. It was indeed fortunate that Mother had cared for me so carefully as that setting could have pushed a mentally bothered soul over the edge. The surface of the landscape was covered with an icy thin frosting, reflecting the shimmering bright light of a full moon. It was a solitary, lonesome scene as there seemed no one was about. It was a cold and dreary night as I half carried, half dragged my heavy suitcase, breaking the crust of the icy surface.

From that time on, I started to envision life without Gene. There would be some way I was going to get through this. My goals were going to be different now. Nevertheless, with all of my plans of forming a life without Gene, my resolve and determination melted when the postman brought the backlog of Gene's letters that had piled up while I had been away. After that, his letters came every day and sometimes two a day. They didn't vary much but none the less, I treasured each one as they were life blood to me. Yet, lingering in the back of my mind, there was also this nagging reminder that it might not ever come to pass. After all, shouldn't I be about my Father's business doing good works?

I had been educated to be of service to mankind, not satisfy my own ego. The idealism of youth in all its purity, before cynicism colors conscience, causes many to sacrifice themselves in order to benefit mankind. Perhaps I placed too great a value on what I could do for God. So, rationalizing, I began to scoff at my own spirituality as after all, "He" could certainly do what was necessary without me I'm sure.

February passed and then March and even though the letters hadn't stopped, without Gene's actual presence, I began to semi-date. Still, when I accepted an evening out with someone, it was always with someone "safe", as all I talked about was Gene. I shortly found myself alone again. As April returned, so did the warmth of nature. My outlook was beginning to recover from the separation and since I hadn't heard from Gene when spring training had come to a close, I accepted a sort of group date with several journalists who were having a convention in the tri-cities. It was fun and games, but winding up at an after hours "joint", also known as a nightclub, certainly didn't make me feel comfortable. The company was stimulating and far more sophisticated than I had ever been exposed to, but my conversation still couldn't get off the dime as Gene still pervaded my every thought. Even though I really didn't want to continue the evening, in a strange and perverse way, I did, as I was having my private revenge. Not being contacted immediately after spring training was over, had shaken my confidence level.

When I returned that evening, actually morning, I had a message to call Gene. I was rather shocked but naturally, pleased. It was about 4:00 a.m. when I finally reached him. He was torn between being angry about my absence and anxious about telling me his thrilling news of his plans for me to meet him in Charleston, South Carolina to be married!

No mention of his sending me the air fare.

He insisted, since Tommy Holmes, his minor league manager, had loaned him $300.00 and a leave of two days, I was to catch the next plane out. When you worked for the Atomic Energy Commission, it usually took three days to terminate employment. One full day for physicals, another with the F.B.I. and then another to do whatever.

My office manager wanted me to go through all the motions necessary for polite termination but he also knew that there was nothing that was going to hold me back from leaving immediately if not sooner. He managed the impossible. He made calls, he had me signing all sorts of documents, he took me for a quickie physical and on top of all that, he even managed to have an impromptu office party, complete with gifts. I packed just a few things and then the Major drove me out to the airport for the first leg of my long journey.

I had no idea what a professional ballplayer's life would be like. All Gene told me was that he had signed a major league contract to play ball and that he would be paid for it. I didn't understand what major league meant or for that matter, what a minor league was. There were also different classes of minor leagues and this strange term called, "farming out" a ballplayer from a "parent club". There were eight of these in the National League and eight in the American league. It was 1951 and all the major professional teams were in the east. Washington and Oregon people enjoyed sports like hunting, fishing, mountain climbing, hiking, swimming, skiing, etc. It was unusual to find people actually savvy about the professional eastern sporting life. Life, in the fast lane would soon develop into a passion I didn't know I would be capable of enjoying.

In those days, before jets, it took prop planes a full 24 hours to cross from the northwest to the southeast as there were several connections with as many as five to six hour layovers.

When I had received my marching orders to leave immediately, after that all night escapade and the long day's termination from work, I grabbed a "hopper" home to Spokane. My college savings paid for the journey while my sister and Mother helped with the washing, ironing and packing that needed to be done for a wedding, a trip and a lifetime. At midnight, we drove to the Spokane airport just in time to embark. Mother handed me a little white wedding bible she had just purchased and in the rush, the white orchid she so carefully chose, was left in my sister's hand as I ran to make the flight. My Mother's only instructions as she embraced me was that I was to be married in a church and this was to be done just as soon as I arrived!

The only seat in the Stratocruiser was in the belly of the huge aircraft which was also the lounge. Since I had been the last on board, this was where I was put until a seat could be found in the main cabin after takeoff. My six hours to Minneapolis upstairs was spent fending off a sleeping drunk who used my shoulder as his pillow. This wasn't going well at all. There was this one hour layover in Minneapolis and then with another hour and a half to Chicago, there

82

would be another layover of six hours before I would leave for Atlanta. I had been told that if you are ever in Chicago, the place to go would be the Palmer House and to be sure and eat at the Empire Room. Why not?

After being without sleep for two nights and two days, I was almost burned out but with all the excitement of being in a strange and wonderfully exciting city, the adrenaline was starting to kick in. The hotel was as advertised but I really didn't have the chutzpah to make my way into the Empire Room as it looked daunting with those twelve foot doors, attended by two uniformed doormen and everything decorated in green and gold. I definitely wasn't in Kansas anymore! As I was comfortably ensconced in a cushy wing-backed chair in the lobby, an airforce colonel, unbeknownst to me, was circling. He opened up the conversation quite innocently enough and before I knew it, he had invited me to have lunch with him in that Empire Room! Being naturally shy, it was almost more than I could bare but my curiosity won out as I agreed to do lunch with him. Four waiters attended to our every need. I was terribly intimidated and naive. They took my purse and laid it down beside a dozen or so pieces of flatware and crystal. Then my coat disappeared and when they asked for my gloves and handed me a rose, I nearly fell off my green velvet empire sized chair! By then, I was about ready to run to the nearest exit when a white gloved and tux clad waiter, ceremoniously handed me a scrapbook disguised as a menu with all these excessive prices. All I could manage was a faint order from the appetizer list. The colonel tried to convince me to try an entree but I just couldn't let anyone spend that much money on me, especially a stranger.

The stranger, seeing me yawn now and again, suggested that I rest in his room until my plane departed. All he needed was a top hat, cape, and a handlebar mustache to fondle as he pressured this naive and silly wench into his lair. It didn't take a brain surgeon to know the score however. So firmly but awkwardly, my excuses made and not allowing even a ride to the airport to be accepted, I departed Chicago, a little wiser than when I arrived, in that windy city on the Michigan shores.

I was so weary for the next leg of my odyssey that when a young soldier who sat next to me, started telling me of his sad tale of going home to Atlanta to bury his Father, it was five hours later in Atlanta before I realized I had slept all the way. On my arrival, I was surprised to see an engineer I had dated in Richland, who helped pass yet another layover. Small world!

Surely the plane would explode at any moment as this was the last leg of my journey. If it landed, Gene would be there and it was for sure there would be no turning back, I would become an "unequally yoked" person.

As the captain flashed the no smoking and seat belt sign, I looked down on Charleston, South Carolina with all her sparkling lights, and with mixed feelings of anxiety and fear, I wondered if Gene had received the telegram and if he had made all the arrangements.

In the rush to "leave on the next available flight" from Richland, I had forgotten my glasses. I was near-sighted and being dark, my chances of picking Gene out from the crowd as I disembarked, was nil even if he had made it but I smiled as if he were and as if everyone there was welcoming me.

Out of the darkness I heard my name shouted loud and clear in the most melodious and deep sounding voice I had ever heard before or since! I ran with open arms to where the sound was coming from. Gene had jumped the fence and had picked me up in a bear hug that nearly strangled the breath from my lungs. His embrace lasted, it seemed, for hours but to be honest, when you have about a 14" difference in height, the thrill of it all, was tempered by pain. Yet, since the plane hadn't crashed and Gene was physically there, pain was hardly noticed as my heart was over flowing with gratitude.

Kathryn Conley

CHAPTER 9

CHARLESTON TO MYRTLE BEACH TO HARTFORD

"We have gathered together to join this man and this woman in holy matrimony..... forsaking all others.... in sickness and in health.... for richer or poorer..........". What began as a two month courtship in Richland, Washington, a three month separation, culminating in Charleston, S. C. with two weddings in as many days, seems to me, qualifies us for some sort of record. Great fun seeing the different shades of shock wash over folk's faces when told in casual conversation that we owe our compatibility to our two marriages! That's always an attention getter. The silence is deafening.

My Mother's desire that our wedding be upon my arrival and in a church was partially adhered to. Since there wasn't a church available at that hour, Gene had made arrangements for us to be married at a judge's home. Though informal, it was very legal.

Gene assumed that making arrangements at a local Seventh-day Adventist church, in deference to my faith, would be no problem. However, in those days, it was not possible for an ordained minister of the Adventist church to marry anyone other than two members of the church. However, Mother's request was that we be married only in "a" church so wanting to please me by honoring my

Mother's wishes, Gene scouted out the largest church he could find, one in the central square of Charleston, the Citadel Square Baptist Church.

It was Sunday evening and as was customary, Baptists in 1951 nearly always filled their churches on Sunday evenings. As I remember, it seated around 450 folks. The hymns were familiar so I should have felt right at home in the warmth of Southern hospitality but we were being formally married that night.

Prior to leaving for the church we decided to have a salad. Not sure whether it was a wedge of lettuce, the excitement, the dread of coming events or the dull knife, but the wedge, thousand island dressing, including flatware, catapulted and wound up an accessory to the front of my new white suit. Oh joy!

The minister had closing prayer and before anyone had a chance to move, he announced that there was a young couple from the west coast who were to be married that night and wouldn't they all like to just keep their seats and stay for the ceremony. Fainting seemed like a logical option as no one moved. This wonderful doctor and his wife came forward to assist us as best man and matron of honor. The tension was starting to ebb at this kind gesture. Someone seemed to be repeating the correct words which was odd as there hadn't been a rehearsal. It was truly an out of body experience, rather like viewing a movie. Jewelry, in my Adventists' circle, wasn't worn, as a kind and loving heart was considered ornamentation enough. However, I had told Gene that I would wear a simple thin silver wedding band and when he pulled out this flashy diamond studded heavy platinum band, I didn't know whether to be incensed or impressed.

The ceremony accomplished, accompanied by tearful good-byes and wishes of joy and happiness, we found ourselves alone and outside the church door, wondering what to do next. There was no script to follow and being about as unaffected as ever, Gene said, "want to go to a drive-in movie?" Yeah, great idea!

Some honeymoon, we were off for minor league training camp the following morning, arriving by greyhound in Myrtle Beach, South Carolina. This was my baptism by fire for just as soon as we arrived, I was left alone in a very upscale hotel on the ocean's edge. Here I was, Katie Disney, newly married to an almost stranger, left without funds or knowledge of the proprieties of hotel life, three-thousand miles from home, suddenly immersed in Southern Culture. I was to sign checks as opposed to paying cash for meals. (Gene was now without reserves) Amusing myself for about 8 to 10 hours in a strange land, without money was sort of like another salad disaster waiting to happen.

This wasn't the worst of it. Embarrassed but needy, we had to wire our parents for money as we had liquidated the balance of even my meager funds. To add a little salt into the wound, the next day, Gene would be taking a bus with the team for exhibition games on their way up North to home base. This was baseball's way of funding their spring training expenses each year and there was a "no wives need apply" policy. Gene did take me to the airport with instructions to stay at the Bond Hotel in Hartford, CT. as motels would demand money up front. (Gasp, gulp and horrors)

Arriving on a sunny Northern spring day, with trees slightly sprouting tiny pale green promises of summer, made me feel more at home as Hartford reminded me of Spokane. However, the "Bond" frightened me to death as I had never actually registered at a hotel by myself before and as "Mrs. Kathryn Conley" yet. Sounded so strange. Actually, being totally unaccustomed and flustered as to the "Mrs." part, I merely registered as Kathryn Conley.

Then began my days of signing for my accommodations plus meals and whether imagined or not, it seemed every bellhop, waiter and clerk followed my every move with suspicion. There was precious little left from monies sent by our parents and knowing I didn't have the money to cover the checks I was writing, fear and shame pervaded my soul.

How could I possibly last for 7 days! Not only did the male employees seem to be looking with suspicion but could it be that they were leering? The thought suddenly crossed my mind that most of the bellhops had access to the rooms. Since I was unaccompanied and seemingly available, the maitre d' and the concierge started grinning a knowing and lecherous smile each time I made my entrance through the lobby. Now straight out fear accompanied my guilt and to say I was uneasy, is to put it mildly.

Then a miracle occurred. Mary Lenthe, one of the player's wives who had already established herself in Hartford, heard that I was there alone and called me, inviting me to a movie. I was overwhelmed with gratitude as she had not only filled my need for companionship but had generously offered to pay for the ticket. Afterwards, she took me by her place. I really didn't know people lived this way. It was "a" room, with kitchen privileges and it was shared with an older couple in their two bedroom, third floor "walk-up" apartment! The price was right for sure but the set of rules were very rigid and certainly confining. I had a lot to absorb about professional baseball.

It was very late when I returned to the hotel and as usual, the stares, whether imagined or not, were particularly annoying. Exhaustion and paranoia were taking over as for some inexplicable reason, feelings of fear had replaced my former guilt of not being able to cover the debts that were accumulating. The thought had invaded my mind that because I had been so long unescorted, those of the male persuasion might be closing in on their unsuspecting prey. They

90

seemed to be especially attentive with all knowing, indecent looks as I walked towards the elevators. My apprehension was fueling my anxiety and supposing they all must be thinking that I might be setting up business as a lady of the night, I was filled with terror.

Being cognizant of the fact that bellhops had key access, my mind continued to play out all sorts of scenarios. As I reached my floor, I was starting to tremble. Panic was taking over reason. My plan of escape was that after opening the door, if upon seeing someone or even sensing someone in that room, I'd be positioned in such a way as to be able to make a quick exit, screaming down the hallway. As I slowly turned the key, my hand shaking, I began to take up my position while at the same time, pushing open the door to peer in. JUST AS I HAD THOUGHT!

There was someone in the room! I couldn't see who, just his feet at the end of the bed!!! What colossal nerve!!! When I turned to run and scream, this personage bounced up from behind the wall and shouted, "Katie, it's me!"

It was impossible, as Gene was on the road, pitching the opener that evening in Albany, NY

"Gene! How, did you get here?"

"Frank Torre loaned me his car. The game was rained out so I drove down to be with you a couple of hours but I'll have to be back before the skipper wakes up." (Tommy Holmes was their player/manager)

"How did you get into the room?"

"I asked the clerk for the key".

"But Gene, I never told them I was married, what must they all think?" (no wonder they were all smirking)

Gene did make it back in time but unfortunately, lost the opener, 3 to 2 and kept telling Torre, "Really Frank, I can't understand it. I just didn't have my stuff today".

CHAPTER 10

THAT FIRST YEAR

At last, we'd be able to pay our debt to society! The ballclub was due any minute which would mean that our hotel bill and my anxieties would be history.

Amid jokes and laughter, the initial flush of meeting the players, I had observed that something new had been added. Gene's flashing smile and eyes caught the curious look in my eyes. The extra piece of luggage in question was pushed aside to heighten the mystery. Gene obviously was enjoying the moment. Since he owned only one suitcase, it wasn't difficult to spot the addition. Afterwards in the room, Gene could hardly contain himself as the contents spilled out.

The players had been issued their first pay-checks of the season on the road. In Gene's case, this was not an intelligent administrative decision. Giving money to a happy generous boy with time at his disposal with no clue as to how to support himself and his new dependent, naturally led to errors in judgment. After spending seven lonely, frightful and tortuous days in a strange city, worrying about our mounting debt, the sight of all those completely useless gifts of sun glasses, caps, T-shirts, and a cheap camera, left me less than thrilled. Never able to feign an emotion that was not true, whether wise or not, finding out how precious little had been salvaged for our expenses, let alone our past deficit, we..., I launched into a very disagreeable conversation.

At its onset, it didn't look like this was going to be a very good year. Gene won the home outing against the Wilkes-Barre Barons at Buckley Stadium by a score of 2-1 at Hartford. Then began a succession of wins which included nine shutout victories, not only validating his own confidence but winning over Bill Lee, the sports columnist for the Hartford Courant. Gene's initial outing on the road had ended with that 3-2 loss and Lee had written with vivid and virulent comments about Gene's inability to perform at "A" level ball. It had left Gene livid. (That had been the game played the day after he had driven most of the night to surprise me at the Bond Hotel in Hartford, CT and then driven back the rest of the night, to rejoin the team in Albany, NY). To challenge Gene at the beginning was probably the best thing that could have happened to him for he always performed at his peak when insulted.

Gene nearly put himself out of commission in one of those games. After enthusiastically batting in yet another run, he had simultaneously hit himself in the leg with his bat. It was with a sigh of relief several minutes later that he was able to resume his duties.

Gene was a media magnet. Comments about his height were twisted into all sorts of hyperbole, like, "the lanky right-hander who, if he fell down full length would overflow into another league" or "the towering right-hander is half-way to the plate before releasing the ball...", "he throws the ball with the speed of a jet and when landing in catcher Stan Glenn's glove, the sound can be heard in the top row of the right field bleachers", "He can't vote until next year but is so tall he can almost see the batter's tonsils on a clear night, by just leaning over, or, "what a lamplighter he would have made if he had been born 50 years earlier." Average baseball players then were usually 5'9" to 6' and to have this attention brought to his height, made Gene feel a bit like a circus side show. Each year he generously posed for pictures with the shortest guy on the roster. George Selkirk, one of his managers said once, "that he was the only pitcher he ever knew who could slump in such a way that it looked as though he might be able to hide under the rubber."

This increased his anxiety over his height then and has never abated. Avoiding long lines in public has always been observed as it invariably attracts stares and such comments as "how's the weather up there?" Or, "my G.., how tall are you anyway?" Gene usually says, "eighty inches, but you should see my big brother!" Almost always, they'll reply with, "Oh my G.., how tall is he?" Bill Russell, the Hall of Famer with the Boston Celtics, after being asked about the weather, used to say, "it's just fine up here, how's it around my posterior?" Being called, "Shorty", is the most original of course. (NOT) I'm sure that people don't really realize these unsolicited comments are insulting. Anywhere off the basketball court, most giants of that game feel self-conscious.

Getting back to our hotel situation. Unable to pay our first week's rent, we were invited to leave the main part of the hotel and were demoted to their "Annex", a down-scale room in the back of the hotel, awaiting Gene's second check. A little like being sent up the river. After a couple of games, Gene once again was on "the road". As most MLB and NBA fans know or maybe not, the players of today are transported to the airport by limousine or private bus and are whisked aboard their chartered plane which has been stocked with all sorts of fruits, veggies and assorted gourmet foods and drinks. In 1951, it meant squeezing into three aging black rented cars, (probably from the local funeral home) that carried them for hours from one vintage ballpark to the next with stop overs for cokes and hot dogs. Actually, the Class "A" Eastern League was a pretty fast lane in the fifties with extremely strong talent. Their younger players were pretty much set to make it to the "Bigs" or it meant a good place to park their aging big leaguers on their way down but could easily be brought up by the parent club at a moment's notice if injuries dictated. Since the majors had only eight teams per league they had a deep storehouse of choices, not so today of course.

While the players were gone, wives were expected to ferret out places for the summer which was a formidable task as most of us were without cars and little cash. However, interested fans would sometimes post their summer rentals on the player's bulletin board and so it was that I was taken out by a couple who had property. I had already experienced culture shock in Hartford, being stared at and assailed with crass comments like, "who does she think she is, wearing pastels and white shoes before Memorial Day." In Spokane, there wasn't a dress code. The different accents of the region were a given but this day, I learned certain phrases that I had never expected nor encountered.

Upon seeing their place, which they had hoped we would lease, it was love at first sight. It was perfect! Their little white country cottage was on a delightful and beautiful lake. They really didn't have to sell the region to me but, just to seal the deal, they added smiling with confidence, "and of course, it is "restricted", Restricted? What in the world did that mean? Coming from the Northwest, I hadn't a clue about what was so great about this feature so when I pressed them for an explanation, they said, "oh you know". Well, I didn't so finally they said, "you know, Jews and Negroes". I could feel the color and heat travel up my neck and face. I had been so stunned that I just couldn't respond. My best girlfriend in grade school and Junior High was Corrine Jones who just happened to be of African American extraction and lived not far from us. Gene played with black players. I had honestly never encountered bigotry before and didn't know how to handle it. There was a bulletin posted on the player's board the next day for housing in a six bedroom home in West Hartford, and without a thought, jumped at it. The only problem was, the rent was out of sight, half of our salary each month, but this didn't prevent us from being totally, and extravagantly foolish. This was just the beginning of a succession of absurd housing choices.

By the time he had won his 15th game of the season, John Quinn, General Manager of the Boston Braves and Lou Perini, the Owner, paid a visit to view their Boston Brave's prospects. Gene won a shut out victory that night, striking out 10. Quoting from Bill Lee's column, "With Malice Toward None", *"A half hour or so after the game Conley came out of the clubhouse and I joined his charming wife."*

'Gene', "Lou Perini said," 'Mrs. Conley thought you were taking longer than usual.' "I told her you were getting a rubdown and that there was a lot of you to rub down.'

"The Conleys giggled and walked off arm in arm. They looked like a couple of college coeds on their way to a campus drugstore for a chocolate milk shake."

Actually, we were of college age and would have been in our Junior year. Outside of a drug store and a "White Tower Hamburg Haven", one of our favorite places to eat was the "Southern Plantation". It was a very upscale fried chicken dinner restaurant (at least to us) near the ballpark where the players hung out. Very few of them were married and they always joked with Gene about his "child bride" so every time we walked in, someone would put a nickel in the juke box to play Nat King Cole's hit, "Too Young" which became our theme song I suppose.

"Conley Night" was an extravaganza promoted by the front office to attract a full house as by this time, every time Gene pitched, the park was filled to capacity. That night I was sitting in the wives box, beaming from ear to ear as the microphone was brought out for the ceremonies between the seventh and eighth innings. Nothing like being interrupted during a pitching duel.

Anxious to see what the ballclub gave him, I sat relaxed and quite proud but as anyone who reads the scriptures; "pride goeth before a fall". This night was no exception as the loud speaker blasted out with, "we'd like to include Gene's wife, Katie, in our presentation tonight and as we have just found out, Katie is expecting next February".

As usual my face turned several shades of red and then came the coup de grace. "Katie won't you please join us here at home plate?"

It was like a scene out of Dicken's book, "A Christmas Carol" when Jacob Marley, carrying his ball and chains appeared to warn Scrooge. These same five tons of iron accompanied me as I slowly rose to walk out onto the field while a kindly usher opened the little box gate in front of me. The bright lights blinded my vision. Oddly enough, the infield seemed to be covered in some sort of adhesive film as I was struggling to make due haste, only to find my feet strangely attached, preventing any rapid movement.

Home plate seemed farther and farther away as in slow motion, I attempted to reach my goal. It was a nightmare! How can athletes do this night after night with a thousand pairs of eyes following every move made? Having the knowledge of my pregnancy announced on the loud speaker like it was, caused a wave of elbow poking while thousands cheered and whistled. I felt humiliated!

It was surreal. So much ado about this night. It had been so hyped and now at its zenith, expecting something grand, we were actually amused as all the front office was able to muster was a very ugly plastic suitcase in a sickly green with a nondescript shade of cream trim and oh yes, from a local jeweler, who had gotten a lot of mileage from advertising his gift, a man's ring. You could almost feel the fan's disappointment so the management added an announcement that they were going to pass the plate for contributions.

I was beginning to learn about professional sports. It must seem a glamorous life from the civilian prospective but being used is also demeaning. I guess this was mild compared to what players in a lower minor league club endured in Muskogee, Oklahoma where young Gene attended pro games. A local merchant would stand behind the netting in back of the catcher and when a player hit a home run, he would turn to the crowd, with grinning pride and holding up a dollar bill for all to see, poked it through a hole so that the player could pick it up on his way to the dugout. The merchants of today, still play that game but the players have improved their stake.

But then, I digress.

With the conclusion of the home plate ceremonies, Gene proceeded to pitch two remaining perfect innings, a 1-0 shutout against the Wilkes-Barre Barons, to win his 20th game for the season. At the conclusion of the last out, Stanley Glen ran out to meet Gene half way between the catcher's box and the mound, jumped up onto Gene's towering frame, wrapped his legs around Gene's waist, hugged him and exclaimed excitedly, "I loves you like a brother, you did it just like 'ole Satch' used to do" Glen had caught Satchel Paige in the old Negro League and had caught most of Gene's games that year in the Eastern League. That year, Gene pitched 33 games and completed 24 of them, striking out 173 and walking only 53, ending his rookie year with an era of 2.16. These stats won him the "Eastern Leagues' most Valuable Player Award" and when the Sporting News (Baseball's Bible of the fifties and sixties) chose Stan Musial, "Major League Player of the Year", they chose Gene, their "Minor League Player of the Year".

All's well that ends well and "Conley Night" had ended well, plus adding to our great honor was the fan's gift, a "purse" of $652.73. It doesn't sound like a fortune today but when you're making $350.00/month, $652.73 was outstanding. No sooner had he mentioned this bundle when worry replaced our joy.

Everyone in the stands knew of the collection. Why do you suppose that fellow is lurking in the shadows? Those guys over there look kind of scruffy and seem a little shiftless. Are we being followed? All the way home, we tortured ourselves with distressful scenarios. We managed to get our booty into our dark and eerie mansion, hurriedly flipping lights on and off as we checked out each room. It was a typical hot and humid eastern-seaboard type evening. It had been for some time, actually, so we had made it a practice of sleeping on the second-floor screened-in balcony. We began to plot our mode of operation, whispering our grand plan if, per chance, someone had indeed followed us home.

We had a very heavy and large alarm clock by our bedside and as Gene fondled it, he said, "now Katie, if anyone should come up here and opens that door, I'll put a fastball right between his eyes." "Oh Gene, I'm so scared, do you really think anyone would attempt it?" "There are all kinds of stupid and weird people in this world. Besides, they just might think it's more money than we have."

Humidity and fear hung heavily that evening as we slept intermittently. Then, about 2:45 a.m. in the morning, Gene sat up in bed, "Katie do you hear that?" His Indian heritage always gave the first alarm. It was uncanny how he was able to hear things I never heard and while never wearing a watch, able to tell me within a minute or two, what time it was. Sure enough, there was scratching at the back door below our balcony. Someone was breaking in! Gene grabbed his defensive weapon and we held our breath for whatever would happen next.

Just then, another sound, a door opening.

"Henry, you dumb fool! Get over here! You're drunk again and in the wrong house!"

Even though these old Victorian homes in this area were huge, they were built only a small driveway away from each other and apparently, Henry, our next door neighbor was drunk and had mistaken our back door for his, trying unsuccessfully to enter our back door which was only about 20' from his.

After that absurd scare, we slept like babies. A perfect ending to a perfect season!

Kathryn Conley

CHAPTER 11

JOURNEY HOME

"TRIBE GLAD THAT CONLEY QUIT BASKETBALL"

The tribe, more commonly known as the Boston Braves placed that announcement in all the Boston papers. That much attention to a Minor League Player had resulted from "The "Rookie Rocket", a promotional affair orchestrated by Billy Sullivan, the Braves publicity director at the time and the future N.E. Patriots owner and founder. The press was treated to a whirlwind excursion, flying from Puerto Rico to every corner of the country, having dinners for the Braves' most promising rookies in their natural habitat. Rookies like Gene, Hank Aaron, Eddie Mathews, and Ernie Johnson, to name just a few. Since Gene had made "Minor League Player of the Year" that year, the news that he would be giving up basketball in favor of baseball, must of made him worthy news in Boston.

When it became known that Gene was seriously considering playing for the Wilkes-Barre Barons Basketball team, the command went forth that Gene meet with the Braves' officials high atop the "golden stairs", a term commonly used in describing the corporate offices by Braves' players from Babe Ruth's time on. In those days, when the front office decreed an audience with their players and told to "jump", you were expected to say "how high?"

During their last road trip to Wilkes-Barre, PA, Eddie White, the Barron's Basketball manager/coach, had invited Gene to suit up for a scrimmage with his team at King's College gym. Afterwards, they offered him a contract for $5,000.00. This was a princely sum for just a few months' work. Also, we only had $250.00 at the end of the season for our journey home and with the pregnancy and Gene's unemployment, we were seriously considering this option (actually, up until then, our only option).

I was personally excited about going to Boston. To me, it represented famous universities, the arts, music, great architecture and all the historic places I had read so much about. Traveling, to me was akin to heaven. Once, I even convinced Gene after he had pitched a night game in Hartford, to travel down to New York city. When we arrived there, it was about 4:30 in the morning. The drive along the East River, was clear as the moon graced its waters. The city was so peaceful. The streets of New York were damp and shinning as its workers were just accomplishing their task of clearing away the refuse of yesterday, presenting a clean slate for yet another industrious and active day. It brought to mind the words from an old Broadway musical, "Manhattan babies don't sleep tight until the dawn". All my fantasies about New York came to fruition that night and with the lights still on and only a few workers wandering about to break the quiet, I hadn't realized through my excitement that Gene and I hadn't slept the entire night!

After John Quinn, the Braves general manager, had heard of the Wilkes-Barre offer and decreed that Gene come immediately after their last game of the season, we leisurely made our way up to Beantown from Hartford as Gene loved confrontation and looked forward to this command performance. I was learning that although my new husband was a quiet giant, he was never afraid if he thought himself to be in the right. However, he would soon be educated concerning nasty little things like binding baseball contracts which when signed, made you an indentured slave, the only post-civil war kind. Waiting in the car, I observed the citizens of Boston and their busy streets bustling with energy. It was love at first sight. My heart felt at home in Boston. Boston, even in 1951, had a pace and ambiance that inspired imagination and possibilities. Gene wasn't long and came down the steps gingerly, smiling from ear to ear. He had been given a $1,000.00 check in return for his promise never to play basketball again. (at least, not that year) Well, it seems that funding wasn't going to be our problem and we'd be able to make it home after all. Of course, not until after seeing Plymouth Rock.

Grasping a map of the United States, (which still hangs in our study), we were off! First stop was supposed to be Niagara Falls. However, in upstate New York, the day being exceptionally warm for September and spotting this inviting private little lake, Gene knocked on the door of a cottage located alongside its dock and simply asked to use it for a couple of hours. Talk about chutzpa!

After our afternoon swim, Albany, NY which was in the Eastern League, seemed the logical spot to spend our evening. We took just enough clothes into the hotel, for the next day and left our luggage in the car. After a pleasant evening and a delightful breakfast, we rushed to our car anxious to continue our westward trek. We jumped in and were shocked to find that everything we owned was gone! Gone, was the set of "genuine white leather suitcases with their genuine brass locks", Mother and Daddy had saved for my graduation just before Daddy died.

I was devastated but Gene, being at first sympathetic, soon became quite piqued at my not being able to get through this loss. I was fixated on that luggage and my repeated recitation of how my parents had sacrificed for that "genuine white leather luggage with the genuine brass locks" was beginning to wear down Gene's patience. My sorrow and whining turned to dismay as I learned pretty quick that he had a strong and decidedly quick and determined temper. I guess the honeymoon was over! So there we were with only a pair of pajamas between us, clothes for two days and now approaching my fourth month of pregnancy, I was beginning to feel a little uncomfortable in that pair of jeans I had taken into that Albany hotel. We were amazed at Niagara Falls but only stayed for the day as Gene was getting anxious to get through Cleveland and Chicago in order to connect to famous "route 66".

Early on, we both found out that I was somewhat of a pain in the neck about clean motels and it was obvious Gene could care less. He finally, in exasperation said, "we are stopping at the next place we come to as it is l0:00 o'clock and I'm just too tired to go on!" I grew silent in embarrassment and didn't put up an argument. We came, we saw, we rented, and yes, it was the most hideous place in the world! It was way up in the mountains of Pennsylvania. The units were of rough hewed boards, weathered over many years. When the owner offered to get a blanket that seemed to be missing on the bed, we noticed a couple of little bugs racing over the pillow cases onto the sheets. It was then that Gene's resolve melted into laughter and said, "Okay, lets get out of here before he gets back".

We sang and talked incessantly, as we dipped down into Texas on our way to Muskogee, Oklahoma. The temperature was hot and humid and since car air conditioning hadn't been invented yet, or at least not to our knowledge, we searched for a block of ice to set on the floor in a vain attempt at keeping cool. Muskogee was kind of a disappointment to Gene as his grandfather and other assorted relatives must have been someplace else, as they weren't available that day. Since he hadn't been there since he was in Junior High School, he decided to move on. Nevertheless, Gene did talk with some of Les's former co workers and just before departing, I could tell he enjoyed that Oklahoma way of conversing.

The Grand Canyon was next on our agenda and we marveled at its beauty and vastness. The Inn there was all that you've read about and more. When zipping down this lonely stretch of highway on our way to the Carlsbad Caverns, we came to a halt as this huge tarantula as big as a turtle, sauntered across. This spider could have been another wonder of this world! Listening to the game that would determine which team in the National League would represent the league in the Series in 1951, we ran out of gas in the middle of nowhere and missed that shot heard round the sports world when Bobby Thompson hit his famous home run to put the Giants into the World Series that year.

We were tiring as we headed into our third week in transit and our expedition was being made burdensome by continually hand washing our clothes out each night. After viewing the great Salt Lake, we decided that in Boise, Idaho, we would outfit me in maternity wear as I was about to meet Gene's parents for the first time. We had just enough money left to complete our junket and purchase two outfits. It was beginning to dawn on me that I was dreading our meeting with Gene's parents and being in "my condition", (as if it were a disease), started me shaking in apprehension.

Outside of me, these were the people that Gene cared for the most but I also knew that it wasn't going to be a happy occasion for them and I dreaded this meeting. Nevertheless, Gene, being the optimist he was and is, felt that once they were told about the baby, they would be so thrilled, the dark thoughts that had been entertained, would be given up.

We found a little run down log cabin to rent, beside a busy highway while Gene looked for work. Eva, Gene's Mother, loaned us two plates, two sets of flatware, a knife, 2 glasses, a pot, a frying pan, two sheets, two pillows with cases and for our wedding gift, an iron and ironing board. We purchased a washboard as the luxury of a washing machine didn't exist, let alone a dryer. Television access wasn't available. Rather like living in a third world country. The place had a kitchenette, a mattress on the floor and an ugly small bathroom. The spiders were upset by our arrival and took every opportunity to make themselves known.

Gene belonged to the iron workers union so found employment, leaving me in this little dungeon without an agenda, with the exception of cleaning and declaring war on the prolific spider population. Thank goodness the owner soon requested his cabin back so after learning of a small trailer for rent, we jumped at it. It was clean and neat but it had a major drawback, no bathroom! In the middle of winter, we had to trudge our weary bones a block and a half to this unheated bathhouse. It was a bit like being banished to Siberia! To add to this melodrama, at Christmas time when peace and good will to men should have prevailed, Gene was laid off. It wasn't because of his work ethic but because they had to cut back and Gene was expendable as he did have a job in the Major Leagues in a couple of months. Talk about bleak!

Prenatal care was in the future so unless there was something obviously wrong, women didn't usually see a doctor until delivery. At least I hadn't since my pregnancy was confirmed in Hartford. When I developed an infection, my Mother insisted that we come to live with her in Spokane, 180 miles from Richland. We had two more full months to go before we knew the sex of our child, and if I would survive the pregnancy. Hearing that Gene had been talked into taking a $5,000.00 life insurance policy on me, caused me a little apprehension. Though it took two days of constant labor pains, we were blessed with our 9 lb. 3 oz. son. His name, if it were to be a boy, was to be Randy Stuart Conley. However, just after the delivery, while I was still in la la land, Gene requested that his first name be Gene and his middle name, in honor of his Father, Raymond. Made sense to me. Before I became sober he was gone and a new spring training had begun for him.

CHAPTER 12

OUR CUP OF COFFEE

The papers glowed with superlatives about Gene in 1952 and the Braves announced that he was to be their fourth starter. Gene's apparent success had followed him from the Eastern League right into the "Bigs". He allowed very few hits and was pitching six innings regularly in spring training. After playing exhibition games on their way up to Boston, the Braves were penciled in for the "City Series". This was a game played each year between the two Boston teams, primarily to showcase their new talent, which translates into tickets sales. Their profits then, came mostly from attendance before the corporate sponsors in concert with television, made it the extravaganza it is today. His six inning stint in that series established him as a legitimate starter by allowing only two hits and with his outstanding pitching against Major League hitters such as future Hall of Famer, Ted Williams, the front office was convinced; he had arrived!

Speaking of Ted, there were many times during the decades following Gene's career, that he would encounter life-long Red Sox fans at charity golf tournaments or banquets queuing up in small cliques to sing the praises of Teddy Ballgame. Gene would attempt to join in. When finding themselves suddenly confronted with Gene's size, they would ask the usual, "how tall are you anyway?"

"Five feet, twenty inches", would be and is his customary reply. Then, the recurrent inevitable question, "have you ever played basketball?" Answering in the

1952 - Gene's Cup of Coffee - Boston Braves

affirmative and in modesty, would reply, "Yeah, I played about 7 years in the NBA".

This remark most often evokes a little interest but then when that doesn't seem to impress, and knowing they didn't have a clue as to his history, there have been times, especially if abject snobbery is noted, he will add, "Yeah and 10 years in the Major Leagues."

Some will be dismayed and genuinely astonished and either to test his credibility or their sincere desire to know more, will question him further. However, there are always those especially nonplused types who are only aware of the cre'me de la cre'me stars and wanting to dismiss this interloper, and anxious to get on with their praise of Ted, have 'oft served themselves an extra helping of arrogance and in patronizing tones, add, "Yeah but did you ever play with Ted Williams?" (as if this were the litmus test for greatness.)

"No, but I've pitched against him."

In mock dismay, they will almost always interrupt their singular veneration of their most adored hero, while balancing their drinks and in the manners of the elite and privileged born and bred, still incredulous but quite secure in the obvious outcome, continue their inquisition. With leering pleasure, and in haste, parry their final coup de grace by putting an end to this Oklahoma hayseed once and for all, with the usual, but with variations of course, "Oh yes, how'd you do?" " heh, heh", content now to show this alien, their obvious superiority. Gene always, grinning back in charming modesty, replies with a "gotcha" expression, "I struck him out in an All Star Game back in '59".

Of course, this hardly makes friends nor influences people in some New England circles as some have been known to become quite hostile as if "they" had been the ones insulted. It's trivia to be sure but still a honor for Gene to be able to use it on such occasions. There was also that "City Series" when Gene faced Ted but he doesn't remember whether or not Ted ever got a hit off him but I'm sure Ted would remember as when Gene introduced himself to him 30 years later, at a local charity golf tournament, Ted said, "I know who you are Gene, you struck me out on that dinky curve ball of yours in the '59 All Star Game in Los Angeles". What a memory!

Meanwhile, back at the ranch, I was learning to become a Mother, just out of my teens, I proved myself a complete failure. My Mother was a working nurse, not able to be at my beck and call. Baseball had first dibs on Gene and spring training in Florida kept us 3,000 miles apart once again and robbed me of a comforting spouse. My sister was dating most of the time which wasn't bringing aid and comfort to anyone so the process of bringing up baby was my project. Gene Jr. was a royal pain and crying was his project, day and night. Serious infections prevented my sojourn to Beantown. All the while, "The Big Rookie" was having a ball, or at least I imagined it so as I languished. Even being at the low end of the pecking order, he was fast establishing himself as a regular starter but he was also having fun at his teammates expense. On their way up north, they played scores of exhibition games and while waiting for buses, Gene would take bets that he could jump up high enough to touch the 12' to 14' marquees in front of the hotels they frequented which seemed impossible. However, he was always an early riser and had already staked it out, and like his Celtic friend, Frank Ramsey used to say in his Southern drawl, "I may be dumb but I ain't stupid!" He wound up collecting enough to compensate the measly stipend the club would laughingly call, "meal money".

We wrote and received letters daily from each other and finally after six weeks of torture, I flew with this l6 lb. "Baby Huey", 24 bottles of formula and as many cotton diapers, to be reunited with a Big League Baseball Player, who I had imagined had set up a darling little furnished apartment for our new and glamorous life. I had outlined our needs in my correspondence, a crib, a buggy and a place with a clean kitchen to boil bottles and mix formula. Formula in a can hadn't even been dreamed of nor had disposable diapers and when the subject of "buggy" comes into the conversation today, (which it rarely does) young matrons wonder what is this crazy old lady talking about. It was a warm and fuzzy experience, having Gene's comforting arms around us at the airport. We were so full of talk that I hadn't noticed that we were going quite a distance out of town, away from the bustling excitement of the City. We drove for miles out to Saugus or Lynn, or wherever, to a dull yellow run down Motel. Okay, that was all right, just so long as the baby had a crib, a buggy, and the room had a little kitchenette. None of the above applied. One of the drawers of the dresser and a pillow was our son's first bed in the "Bigs", our arms his buggy and waking up the motel manager to use his kitchenette rather than having one at my disposal, was my introduction to life as a Big Leaguer's spouse. Not only that, Gene was scheduled to go on the road the next day. Yipes!

In all honesty though, Gene had purchased a car, not the one we had longed for while waiting for Little Gene's arrival into our life but a new one. (The gray Pontiac sedan had been sold to spring me and Jr. from hospital.) So that was a plus and since having the experience of listening to the sounds of our son's melodic screaming most of his waking hours, Gene knew I needed help, especially in finding a place to live. Even the thought of having my flirtatious younger sister assist me sounded right, so we made haste in arranging to have her fly out. Gene was gone so I was left alone (except for my "little stranger" riding shot gun) to find an airport called "Logan". Through winding streets I warded off drivers who thought it their sworn duty to cut me off in order to observe the time honored

Boston tradition of raising a certain digit while all the time shouting obscenities from lungs of leather. I practically kissed my sister's feet when she at last arrived.

I thought I was having it tough. Gene's first assignment of the season in regulation Big League Baseball was also his baptism by fire. His first pitching assignment was the dreaded Brooklyn Dodgers. Nothing like starting from the top. No easy transition here. It didn't help that just before taking the field, over hearing someone ask, "who's pitching today?"

And hearing the insulting and acid reply from one of the older veteran pitchers, "They say our "PHENOM " will get the assignment"

That rattled his chains.

Sarcasm is the stock and trade of any sports' professional and since Gene's existence so far in baseball had been blessed and never tested, you might just have called the game right there and called it a day. Gene was and is, self-deprecating, his manner, modest , jovial and giving. He has always been able to appear "cool" and the challenge wasn't his problem but the idea of not being liked, especially by his teammates sent his insides into full blown anxiety. He was still new at the professional game, vulnerable and unsophisticated, not even aware that because of his being crowned the fourth starter, meant that the other starter's careers were waning and the crown was not easily relinquished.

Then too, his first start of the season proved intimidating against the World Champion Brooklyn Dodgers, and before he could lick his wounds, his next assignment was against the New York Giants which didn't add luster to his budding career. After his problems with the Dodgers and Giants, he was looking as if he was in a winning groove pitching against the Cincinnati Reds, when the

Braves committed three errors that produced five runs. We started packing our bags.

He was optioned to the Milwaukee Brewers, the Braves, AAA team. Okay, this was all right as the Canterbury Hotel in Boston was one of those run down dowdy "has been" places, fully equipped with dust and musk, even though it did provide the necessary prerequisite kitchenette. Leaving the environs of this dark hole of Calcutta in Boston, was almost joy had it not been for the fact that the parent team did not provide travel expenses and once more, we were without funds. Baseball paid on the first of each month and we had only experienced two. It was the middle of June. There were four of us now; Gene, myself, my sister and Junior. It would take three days to reach Milwaukee as there were bottles to be sterilized, diapers to wash, etc. The day before reaching our destination, we had just enough money left for one hot dog split three ways. Never had a lowly "dog" been so relished!

Since it was against Gene's principles to get an advance, he asked "cabbies" to direct us to a hotel that had kitchen facilities. (in the fifties, you didn't have to show a credit card for admittance and could run up quite a tab) Our new abode proved just as shabby as Boston's worst. The rooms were absolutely cavernous! The owner was only too happy to have company as it didn't look as though he was able to communicate to his son who was grotesque in appearance and sadly retarded. My sister cruelly called him "Egor" under her breath and since it so described him, it became impossible to refrain from joining in as Egor was also a "clinger" who lingered, rattling on and on, oblivious to our need of a good night's sleep. On the road we had slept three in a single bed so we were anxious to enjoy the luxury of having separate beds, not to mention rooms. Patti was only 16 and was put in a room right above us. In the middle of the night, we heard a frantic knock at our door, "Katie, please let me in!" It seems that the Hotel had rented out to wrestlers who were practicing their trade on the floor above Patti's. The sounds were so thunderous, it scared her to death and again, we found ourselves three in a bed.

CHAPTER 13

THE BREWERS, FIRST EDITION FAST FORWARD

Thank goodness the traveling secretary heard of our sojourn at Hotel Hades and directed us to another residential hotel. We were well into June before Gene received his first assignment. His debut started with a 2 hit victory. Again, his strike outs were many and his walks few and the great fans of Milwaukee responded accordingly. It felt good to be in the right place at the right time. He dazzled them with footwork. His talent of jumping uncommonly high to spear towering line drives that were hit through the middle never failed to garner a lot of excitement. His ability to win games with his bat made the season of 1952 a year to remember for us. The night he went five for five in Indianapolis was especially great fun! The writers were generous in their appraisal, plus Gene's size and sense of humor didn't hurt either.

The night the Brewers won the pennant was the night Gene won his 10th. Especially flattering were the remarks of managers and players alike to the writers that he was the best they had seen in the league. We could handle that. This particular triple A league had players like; Roger Maris, Moose Skowron, Frank Howard, Vic Powers, Bob Cerv, Wally Post, Sam Jethroe, Gene Mauch, Billy Klaus, Billy Bruton and many more future Big Leaguers. Gene welcomed his demotion to the Brewers as this meant he would be in a steady rotation which usually translates into success.

In the meantime, hotel life was not conducive to family life, especially since my sister Patti and baby Gene were living with us in our hotel living room, we moved again and found a house rental not far from the park. The only thing remembered about this place was the dated gas stove. Its pilot light had been reported to have a nasty little problem. Lighting it was "tricky", an understatement if ever there was one. When my poor brave sister approached it with lighted match one day, we knew immediately which opponent would come out second best. This sad experience left Patti shaken and quite without brows or lashes. "Old Smokey" had once again claimed the title.

Another episode remembered was the day we decided to cool off on the shores of Lake Michigan during an especially long run of hot and humid afternoons. Armed with all the baby paraphernalia known to exist at that time, we had just settled our encampment, enjoying the cooling breezes from the lake, when a tall Gestapo looking state trooper approached our little gathering and began writing us a citation for indecent exposure. Our crime.....wearing shorts. Horrors!!!! They weren't even short shorts but apparently at that location, a woman had to have slacks on. I had heard that Wisconsin was a conservative state, but this was truly a shocking experience.

Gene's two and a half months' ended with 12 wins (one in playoffs) and 4 losses.

"CONLEY'S CAGE PLAN SQUELCHED BY QUINN", the headlines flashed across the back page of the then, Boston Herald American.

When Gene came to Boston the fall of 1952, he came to play. He carted our little family and all of our worldly possessions (which, by the way could fit into a car trunk and still have room for a TV), not knowing for sure whether the Celtics would sign him or not. This took real faith or naiveté, whichever. John Quinn, General Manager of the Boston Braves was quoted as saying that "he would order Conley not to play with the Celtics". Red Auerbach had obtained negotiating rights for him after the draft meeting in April. In those days, the player could not be drafted until his graduation year from college. It was generally thought that his graduating year was 1953, because of his age but Red had made the discovery that Gene's class would have been 1952 so after obtaining affidavits to prove it, he entered the Celtic rights to him. Once again Red caught the opposition napping. The article mentioned that as a sophomore, "Conley led the northern division of the Pacific Coast Conference in scoring with 220 points in 16 games."

The article went on to quote Quinn as saying that, "Conley is under a major league contract and therefore cannot take part in any outside activities without our O.K." In other words, once signed, the player was merely a slave.

From the Sporting News, November 12, 1952, it was reported, *"A sizable gathering of basketball experts, followers and writers attended the workout at Harvard in order to get a peep at Conley. Among them was Charlie Sands of the Braves' publicity office, who apparently is the staff basketball expert of the Braves."*

"Said Sands to Conley: 'Mr. Quinn would like to see you this afternoon.' But Conley didn't go to see the Braves' general manager. Instead the Mountain, as it were, had to go in pursuit of Mahomet. Quinn went to see the young pitcher

in the lobby of the hotel where Conley and the Celtics were waiting for a bus to take them to an exhibition in Maine."

"Quinn granted his permission." However, he was also quoted as saying, *"if Conley should be shunted to some minor league basketball club, he will need the Braves' permission all over again."* He signed a contract with the Braves and the Celtics within a two day period that year.

Larry Claflin wrote, *"Conley is the best big man available, Hank Iba, great Oklahoma A & M coach told Auerbach a few months ago."* Perini, owner of the Braves was quoted by Jack Barry of the Boston Globe as saying that, *"Conley is one of the most promising major league prospects in baseball."* So the tug of war commenced.

Before all this uproar started, we had taken two weeks to decide on whether or not to subject ourselves to a punishing winter of grinding basketball. However, the prospect of looking for a dead end job during the next five months didn't look promising either. The Celtics had been in training a good month before he joined them and what with making up for lost time, his feet became blistered as he ran, full throttle, not only up and down the basketball floor but up and down the Boston Garden's steps. Jock Semple, the famous running coach of the Boston Marathon and the Celtic trainer at the time, would massage his tortured muscles and split open his blisters as they formed each session and then, sew them back up with thick black string until the oozing wounds healed. At night, usually, his temperature rose and all he could manage was soup. Still, he was determined. He was used sparingly as this was his rookie year and five minutes of play wasn't unusual. However, the media, anxious to see an athlete take on such an unusual task, reported each little positive thing he attempted. It was clear that his jumping abilities were phenomenal from the beginning. Johnny Most, the Celtic TV and radio "voice" for so many years, dubbed him, "Jumpin Gino". His only desire that year was to help the club and his value was clearing the boards as the Celtics were loaded with shooters.

As promised, though, he reported almost on time for baseball's spring training that year, in spite of the fact that the Celtics had come in second in the league and had made the playoffs. Walter Brown had included Gene in their winnings and followed up his appreciation by sending his share, $250.00 per player! His coach, Red Auerbach concluded that "I know that basketball this winter has made Gene more aggressive. He was an easygoing guy at the start of the season. But he has been in closer contact with his opponents, and as a result has learned to retaliate. He has learned that he has to be aggressive or pushed off the court. The same, I think, can be applied to baseball." The Media also reported that because of Gene's conditioning on the floor, he should be able to step right into baseball. No one knows better than Gene that each major league sport uses a different set of muscles and the contrast of sneakers as opposed to "spikes" on the divergent surfaces takes a little getting used to. Also, even though spring training started almost on time for Gene, he missed the extra few weeks the pitchers and catchers had before the official spring training opening.

That year, 1953, Milwaukee became the Braves new home. The city had built a brand new stadium there to house their major league team and Gene was anxious to get started there as his triple A "half year" had been so successful. Having won 12 games in a two month period would logically translate into a 20 win season, barring injuries, if used regularly for the full year. However, Charlie Grimm, deep in very good pitching, felt that Gene would benefit with another minor league year's experience. Gene didn't see it that way and when I picked him up at the ball park that hot and humid afternoon in Bradenton, Florida, I was seeing smoke coming out of every orifice. I cannot remember whether he thought his basketball defiance had caused his delay into the "Bigs" but looking back on how baseball ruled in this era, I certainly could suspicion such an act.

It was a blow to the ego I'm sure but there simply wasn't anything that could be done as this was before the reserve clause had been challenged so if you didn't play the game right with your parent club, you couldn't play the game at all. It made a very indelible impression on me as I had no idea that you were basically bound by your club. I was learning. After finding that Senator Kefaufer was doing some sort of investigation of the Major League Baseball's reserve clause, I wrote him a very fervent letter explaining Baseball's hold on the player. Of course I never received or asked for a response but I watched TV as "Baseball" brought in their big guns; Mickey Mantle and Casey Stengel. They regaled the senators with the virtues of Major League Baseball. That wasn't their articulated description but then again, it was difficult to tell just what they were testifying to but it was clear they were perfectly satisfied with their situation. Naturally. I watched as Baseball manipulated these high profile personalities while Congress fawned over them and consequently, voted to let their "Reserve Clause" stand, as is.

With only 16 teams in the Majors, most players labored in the Minors for years and some, decades, unless someone in their position suffered an injury or retired. There were rare occasions when a player would be let go because of a behavioral problem as it meant the end of a career. If you take the time to read the ages of players that made it to the Majors in the forties and fifties, before Baseball's expansion years and "free agency", the average age of players were usually in their late twenties or early thirties, the short prime years of a professional player's career.

If this was the Braves intention to punish Gene for defying their wishes about playing Basketball, it was to no avail as Gene went on a tear, winning game after game for their triple A team in Toledo, OH.

I'll never forget the time, after winning 10 games by the first part of June, he was slated to pitch before the home town fans but lost. There had been such a tremendous build up in the papers and on radio about that game. Added to that, was the fact that the stadium attendance had broken some sort of record for that date. After I picked up my dejected husband, I could tell there wasn't going to be too much conversation so I drove to a grassy knoll, under a tree, while Gene replayed the game. His regret was not that he lost, it was just that he had disappointed the fans! I couldn't relate to this sort of thinking. Gene's innocence was astounding. I've only seen Gene cry three or four times during our 53 years of marriage and this was one of those times.

Our son was now a toddler and becoming almost human. He was my constant Buddy and we had a great relationship. I was the only game in town. Daddy had been gone a lot during the Basketball season and now as we approached the middle of that 1953 season, he really hadn't developed a close relationship with him. Gene loved his little son with a passion but I was his constant. One night, on a whim, after Gene had won about 18 games, I decided to take Little Gene with me to old Swayne Field. Taking care of him, I rarely got to the games as we weren't into baby sitters. I dressed him in his usual jeans and white tee which was also my usual attire and dropped in on my sister baseball players' wives. Not being a regular, I really didn't know their mode of dress, although I should have. I had liked dressing up for the games in Hartford but after Little Gene arrived, I hadn't bothered, especially after I had had the experience of taking him to a basketball game in Boston at age 6 months. At that time, his shrill little scream had been neutralized as in unison, thousands, rose to their feet with a great thundering roar resounding so loudly that the timbers of old Boston Garden seemed to tremble. It wasn't difficult to conclude that babies need not apply at professional games. Anyway, as I approached the gathering of Toledo's well dressed and pleasant women, I knew straight off, I wasn't on the same planet as one remarked, a little on the sarcastic side, "Oh, cute, Mother and son outfits."

Nothing could rattle my chains though as Gene went on to win 23 games that year and as most pitcher's wives' usually do, will add, "he should have won 30". It was touch and go for Toledo as they struggled to stay on top in their pennant race. It was termed the closest in triple A history. Milwaukee, the Toledo parent team, was struggling for the same prize in the Majors and it was rumored that he would be called up.

The American Association unanimously voted Gene, "The Most Valuable Player in the League and the Sporting News voted him "The Most Valuable Player in the Minors" for the **second** time, the only time a minor league player has ever done so. If anyone is brave and has energy enough to mount the many stairs of Baseball's Hall of Fame in Cooperstown, you will find a floor or section, honoring its heroes of minor league history. There, you will be able to find a small green plaque displayed on an obscure wall, listing the MVP recipients of minor league's MVP's there. Noted on that list, you will find Gene's name listed twice. He broke all time records, winning 23 and losing only 9. He pitched more innings, 261, and struck out the most batsmen, 211, started the most games, 40, faced the most batters, 944, hurled the most shut-outs, 4 and worked two 1-hitters, one 2-hitter, three 3 hitters and one 4 hitter, going on a 7 straight victory streak.

One writer compared it to the time, in Seattle when All Star high school players competed to be in the annual Hearst's National All Star Game in New

York. Speaking of Gene winning 1953's AAA League's MVP title, compared it to 1949's MVP award when he was a 16 year old senior in high school.

"He vaulted to fame in that '49 game at Sick's Stadium, leading the State squad to victory with a 360 foot home run performance that saw him strike out 9 batters in five and a third innings. He was voted the game's outstanding player and went on to represent the Northwest in the Hearst sandlot game in New York."

Gene had done his time in high school, college and the Minors. This time he would not be denied a place on a Major League roster.

Gene Jr. and Katie in the New Milwaukee Apartment — 1954 Our First Home

CHAPTER 14

ABORTING THE NBA
THE MAJORS BECKONED

"Toledo's hopes in the first round play-offs received a terrific jolt last night when it was revealed that Gene Conley, the ace of the Sox mound staff, will be out for the rest of the season with an undisclosed back ailment". So it was that the Kansas City Blues went on to win the best of a seven game series for the American Association's Championship title. It was a wonder Gene could even move his back after pitching so much during the season. Baseball has now judiciously changed their ideas about having starters go the full nine innings in the Major Leagues. In today's game, after a starter finishes his 6 innings, a "closer" is used the rest of the way. By today's standard, Gene pitched about two years worth that '53 season. He spent a week in the hospital, a brand new experience for Gene. He hated that week as they invaded his space. There were x-rays, prodding and poking, as he agonized about not being able to help his team. The docs fitted him with an elaborate and complicated back brace, instructing him to wear it at all times during the next 6 weeks and to report back after that for physical therapy.

As we left, all the while smiling genially to the hospital staff, Gene commented under his breath, while bolting out the front door, "let's get out of here!" When you are a 6' 8" bundle of frustration, working your way into an average size car, fitted with Dr. Frankenstein's monstrous creation of leather, steel, and screws strapped rigidly onto your back, you tend to lose said object. I can't

127

remember if this abnormal unyielding collection of junk was put into the back seat or if it still resides in front of one of Toledo's finest hospitals as a monument of man's inhumanity to man.

We had a winter ahead filled with blank space. Once again, Gene was drawn back to thoughts of the NBA and the Celtics. After a couple of weeks, his back was feeling fine and he was ready to go. Honors meant very little to him. Success just meant he would be able to pitch in the Majors and his ability to make money during the winter, while doing what comes naturally, just meant another way to compete. However, the new Milwaukee Braves weren't about to let this happen. John Quinn called Gene when it was announced that this was his intention. He was once again reminded that he wasn't allowed to. There was no offer of compensation not to play, just a flat "no". So off to Boston we went.

It wasn't until Gene had made the team that Mr. Quinn interrupted his basketball season with an offer of $5,000.00 not to play basketball. Well, since the Braves were that interested, the thought that just maybe he could be injured playing round ball, added affirmation to that offer. Not only that, we had just found out that I was with child once again. Actually, what sealed the deal was that the Celtics had only raised his contract to $5,000.00, and with living expenses being what they were in Boston, staying in Toledo for "our winter of discontent", suddenly sounded appropriate. We might be dumb but we're not stupid!

On the other hand, Walter Brown and Red Auerbach weren't exactly ecstatic over Gene's decision as they had already included him in their plans. Gene felt a little guilty and slightly embarrassed but after returning to Toledo, where an offer to become a weekend disc jockey tweaked his curiosity; the guilt and remorse lessened. Also, a car dealer was anxious to have him on their staff as a Repair Manager. I found this to be totally absurd as changing light bulbs had always been a production for him. However, pushing a button when a car was to be repaired and listing said car's problems didn't take a rocket scientist so he signed up. His weekend job with WFOX was a hoot. How corny did he get? Well, try out this line, "Enough of this chatter, let's spin another platter". If it hadn't been for his sports talk between "platters", it wouldn't have lasted the winter or even another weekend.

By Christmas, we were already thinking spring training and anxiously counting the days until February. Because of our eagerness, the day after January 1, 1954, we were already packed. So off we went in a cloud of dust in our darling little black convertible with the red leather upholstery, stuffed with Toddler paraphernalia, a few of our things and I believe a little black and white TV (our worldly possessions). Snow suddenly disappeared as we reached the middle of Kentucky and by the time we had arrived in Tennessee, the warm sunshine was starting to tranquilize every nerve and fibre of our being as we looked forward to being a part of the big league season.

It was one of those rare and unexpected spring days that belied the fact that we weren't quite into spring yet. The sun was beginning its rise into the heavens above us, the absence of even a small cloud seemed to be an omen of extraordinary and wondrous events to come. The sky seemed so blue and then came the challenge of who could come up with the most oft used cliché's by pitchers in response to the most hackneyed questions posed by the media. For instance:

After a pitcher has had a bad outing, "I noticed that the batters were starting to get to you in the fifth, what happened there?"

"Well, Ed, my curve was beginning to give me some problems so I .... On and on this went until we crossed over into Alabama. Our spirits were soaring as we tired of the "media challenge" and started singing songs. Gene's were mostly fraternity ditties, boy scout songs and Southern church hymns. Mine were mostly Sinatra, Torme, Cole and Como, mixed in with scout and church melodies. We had been following a large white "semi" truck and as I laid Little Gene down for a much needed diaper change, seeing that we had clearance up ahead, Gene began to pass.

Just at that moment for some inexplicable reason, the driver's cab started to make a left hand turn into a wheat field.

As I sat there in shock, a bizarre scene unfolded before me. I heard the sustained sound of Gene pressing on the horn, the sounds of tires laying tread as brakes were applied, and in slow motion knew that we were going to crash. Gene usually drove about 60 to 65 miles an hour. These were the days before seat belts. Luckily, Little Gene was in a prone position when we struck the truck's cab and I had been hunched over his little body. The only thing that I recalled was feeling a tremendous impact against the side of my face. I had no idea where Gene was, or Little Gene.

After this initial impact, I must have blacked out for a second or two as from nowhere I became aware of Gene's presence at the driver's door from the outside, shouting, "how's the baby", where's the baby?"

Gene looked horrible! His mouth and head were bleeding. My jaw hurt and we found Little Gene on the car's flooring. Gene had been shot out of his seat like a cannon ball, rolling over and over for about 30 feet. A tooth was missing from his front bottom teeth, another two were hanging. The baby seemed all right. Terribly shaken and crying of course. He cried a lot that afternoon and night. My jaw seemed wired shut as I could not open it, nor did I want to try as the pain was so intense; and, of course, I was three months pregnant.

The state troopers appeared on the scene almost immediately as the truck driver must have called on his radio for assistance. We could have had a brilliant case against the milling company as besides my pregnancy and the possibility of Gene's career being affected, the fact that the driver's choice of traveling companion was a half empty-pint of whiskey, could have reaped a small fortune. We weren't angry with the driver. We were just overcome with relief that we were still alive.

The driver had a little home back up the hill on the left and I guess there was this little dirt path that led up to it and since he was passing by on his way to the flour mill, without looking back, decided to take this opportunity to visit. Fortunately at that same moment as he began his turn, hearing Gene's loud horn, he reacted in time to barely lesson the impact. It was just the beginning of a split second-right hand turn, but it was just enough to prevent our demise, I'm sure. So in a way, he saved our lives.

The troopers shook their heads in disbelief as the car was totaled. The front motor and seat were pushed up into the back seat. I didn't want to look. We were taken to a local doctor's office where Gene was stitched on the top of his head and forehead. I was filled with questions about the horrific bump I had sustained and about the baby I was carrying.

"What about a blood clot? Don't you have something for that? What about my baby?"

The doc's only reply, "well, yep you could have a blood clot and yep, you could lose the baby. Time will tell." That was it. That was modern medicine in the mid fifties along with, oh, yes, aspirin. The troopers were then kind enough to take us to the dentist where Gene, who had two teeth hanging from his mouth by tiny shreds of tissue, had them extracted. From there, we were transported to a very moldy motel to wait out whatever "time would tell".

We had tried unsuccessfully to down some noodles but I couldn't move my jaw and Gene's newly extracted teeth prevented him from enjoying the "Southern Cookin'." We had just decided to give it up and call it a night when two insurance guys and the flour mill lawyer came "calling". They wanted us to sign a release form. To put it bluntly, if I was going to have a miscarriage, or a blood clot, I didn't think it wise to have them in this little backwoods area of Alabama. Ignoring their liability, we signed the "release" and accepted a brand new convertible in order to get back to civilization and spring training, just as soon as the ink would dry.

Bradenton, Florida was a welcome sight, even though we were a tad on the early side, just to be near a real hospital was encouraging. Florida in the fifties was an amazing place for someone from the great Northwest. Flat sandy terrain replaced the dark rich soil and mountainous ranges of our homeland. Lazy rivers flowed gently quite unlike the wild white capped ones we were used to, but it had a relaxed sunny disposition.

Since most of the Braves players stayed on Anna Maria Island which was surrounded by the bluest of water and sugary sandy beaches, we felt compelled to join the crowd. We found a cottage, actually a shack, but it was right on the water and each night we could hear the surf pounding away on the beach as we drifted off to sleep. The other players used to joke about Gene's feet sticking out the back porch when he went to bed at night. It was tiny, just two rooms but it had a screened in back porch. It was heaven!

This spring training was a great experience for Gene and with his continued success, "Life" Magazine called on him for a feature as did "Look". His height was the usual attraction but his winning the "Minor League Player of the Year" for the second time, a "first" in Minor League history, almost assured him a pitching berth on the Braves pitching staff, which was no small feat in those days.

We couldn't believe the enthusiasm the Milwaukee fans had. They absolutely loved the Braves players and their families to the extent that they offered us free dry cleaning, along with laundry, delivered meats, eggs, dairy products, a car to use during the summer, and the Miller Brewing company, each week, sent over a case of beer. This held no attraction for me, being a life long abstainer (except for that one New Year's Eve fiasco) and out of respect for my principles, Gene refrained from imbibing at home. Our neighbors were only too happy to oblige a friend by taking the case off our hands.

The ballpark was always packed, standing room only. It was a glorious feeling to be in the Majors. Every commercial enterprise tried to get a piece of the action. An upscale clothing store hired most of the Braves' wives to model their latest fashions and were photographed for full page ads in the Milwaukee Journal. So now I can truthfully say, that yes, I once had been a model. Not only that, we were asked to do commercials over radio and television. When we ate out, we were given currency just to be seen dining there. This activity was short lived though as eating in public proved too uncomfortable, appearing anyplace in public was impossible. It was physically and emotionally draining to have hovering baseball fans, singly or in groups, offering praises or second guessing managerial moves or expressing their expertise on how the pennant race was going. All this as each bite was observed, ending with a request for an autograph or a pictorial remembrance of the occasion. We often left meals uneaten.

Charlie Grimm, the jovial manager that year, had a great ballclub. People like, Hank Aaron, Eddie Mathews, Warren Spahn, Lew Burdette, Bobby Buhl, Joe Adcock, Johnny Logan, Billy Bruton, Del Crandall, Andy Pafko, Ernie Johnson, Jim Wilson, Dave Jolly, Jim Pentleton, Charlie White, Ray Crone, Joey Jay, just to name a few. Three became Hall of Fame players. Gene, being a rookie, was not put in rotation but used primarily in spots the start of the year.

His first game was a draw, his second, a loss, marred by several unearned runs and finally on his third try, a WIN!!!! Del Crandall handed Gene the winning ball, his third saved and treasured baseball. He started his collection in 1951 with the one used to win his 20th game, his first professional year in Hartford, CT, the second one was the one saved for his 23rd victory in Toledo. Manager Grimm announced afterwards that Gene now could be used in a five man rotation from this point on. This announcement couldn't have pleased any one of those starting pitchers as to have an impressive year, a starter needs to know that he will be pitching every **fourth** day. I had heard rumors that Lorene Spahn one year, charged the front office to rectify a similar situation. I always admired Lorene as she really knew the game and was no shrinking violet.

Then came a succession of shut outs and wins, gaining Gene not only honors for being the player of the day or week or whatever but actual shekels from various companies. This made it even more significant as we had just moved into a brand new four unit apartment building and it needed to be furnished.

By his fifth victory, he was being touted "to rank with the great pitchers of all time" so said Birdie Tibbets. The atmosphere for the Conleys was getting more rarefied with each appearance and since the past three years had been so glorious with its honors, we took it for granted that it would always be thus. The World's Champion Dodgers and their manager, Walter Allston, especially praised

Gene as for some strange reason, they continued to be frustrated by his success against them in particular, just as Gene was curiously unsuccessful against the lowly Phillies. Against the Dodgers, he had a 1.33 earned run average.

By the time he had won his 7th game, Walter Allston, manager of the Brooklyn Dodgers and the National League's All Star Manager selected Gene for his All Star team. Warren Spahn, had been selected as usual and his remarks at the time were, "I'm just as happy that Conley was named, too. It's a great tribute to Gene to be on an all-star team in his first season as a regular starter in the big leagues. He certainly deserves the honor."

Unfortunately, when he came in to try his hand against the American League's All Stars, Gene gave up two hits and a walk which put him in the clubhouse a little early on. Carl Erskine wasn't able to erase the damage that Gene had started, thus, Gene had his first All Star defeat. To the reporters gathered at his locker afterwards, he admitted to being nervous but smiled and said, "I really goofed things up, didn't I?" "I feel terrible". Many decades later, we were joking around about his All Star Games and his one defeat and he said, in all seriousness, "really Katie, you know what the problem was?" "no", I said. "Well, it was because the outfielders weren't in the right places"...heh...heh...heh...

The end of July brought Gene his ninth win and a brand new baby daughter, Kitty. Gene stayed with me until she was born, then flew out to join the Braves against the Dodgers. As luck would have it, my sister, Patti, was free to fly out to help me as we certainly didn't know anyone in Milwaukee that could. By the way, he won that "birth day" game and went the distance but it wasn't a pretty site, especially with the temperature in the high 90's and the humidity in the 70's. It was a hitter's victory.

By August 16th, Gene had his 12th victory and had gained a new nickname, "High Pockets". At the Boston Gardens, it was "Jumpin' Gino". Hank Aaron tagged him, "Stretch" and still does. Robin Roberts has always called him "Slim" and he also has been referred to as "The Towering Gene Conley" or "Genial Gene Conley" by the media. "A rose by any other name would smell as sweet"... The media always had a field day with Gene, and with that "Okie" accent, one compared his wit and mannerisms to the great Oklahoma humorist, Will Rogers.

Soon after his defeat at the 1954 All Star Game, we received an article from a Washington State writer, referring to Gene's modesty; *"There was this first time he (Gene) was called on as a relief pitcher, when he was a freshman at Richland high and Walla Walla had loaded the bases. Conley walked to the mound, warmed up, delivered his first pitch, and watched it sail out of the park. That night Gene's dad had a serious talk with his gangling son, to the general effect that 'apparently you're not cut out to be an athlete, boy, so you'd better just play for fun'.*

Which perhaps, explains what happened when Conley returned from playing in the annual high school all-star game in Seattle. He walked into the house after an overnight train ride from Seattle, put a big paper sack away in a corner, asked his mother for some sandwiches, and went off to his summertime ditch-digging job.

It wasn't until an excited neighbor who had been listening to the radio came rushing into the house that the Conleys discovered son Gene had been the winning pitcher and hit a home run in the game the night before. And when they looked in the paper bag Gene had stashed away in the corner, they discovered it contained the "Joe E. Brown Trophy" awarded to the game's most valuable player."

The 1954 season came to an abrupt end the latter part of August when Gene injured his back in the middle of a game.

He tried to come back after a two week rest but it wasn't to be. He wound up with 14 wins and 9 loses, and a second place standing for National League Pitchers with a 2.84 era.

First Year as a Milwaukee Brave
Wrigley Field, 1954

CHAPTER 15

A YEAR TO REMEMBER

Gene's back injury wasn't serious but Charlie Grimm or someone from the front office decided to send him to a specialist in Iowa for treatments. Whether this was doing him ill or good didn't matter because we now possessed something more important. Time. Time to just be normal. Not having to deal with being a professional athlete's family. In Iowa, it was state fair time and I had never, nor have I ever since, seen a fair quite like it. Even with a very young baby, we thoroughly enjoyed immersing ourselves in the sights, sounds, and smells of the grandest state fair of them all. The outstanding "down home" exhibits, the remarkable animals and food inspired us into thinking this could be our calling. Like many city dwellers, we began to wonder if farming or ranching might be a pleasant way to make a living.

Visiting our parents in Washington state and Oregon, provided us the opportunity to show off our new six week old baby. It was nothing for us to take off cross country, and the babies were just part and parcel of the whole experience. This unexpected time off gave us the opportunity to get re-acquainted-unlike the short home stands when the schedule amounted to: "the greeting", "the game that ended after 10:00 p.m.", "appropriate showering, dressing, and discussion period", "Gene's trip home again around midnight", "dinner about 1:30 a.m.", "bed around 2:00 or 2:30 p.m.", "sleep late", "eat late light lunch/breakfast" and then, finally, "off to the ballpark for another game" and another round of same until the team left once again for a two to three week road trip usually by train. It's no wonder our first two children are night people.

Somewhere between Iowa and South Dakota on that trip, after the children had nodded off, Gene asked me, "Katie, why do you go to church on Saturdays?"

I was surprised that he hadn't understood what I was really about. I would often try and explain my beliefs and value system. He basically turned me off when I broached the subject of religion but with this "gift of time", I suppose it must have inspired his curiosity.

"Well, Gene, yeah, it is weird isn't it? You've read parts of the bible, right? Think Genesis, honey. As you must know, it states right at the beginning, that God created this world in six days."

"Yeah, what has that got to do with anything?"

"Okay, on the seventh day, God rested from all that he did and he blessed and hallowed that day and that's why, as you may have noticed, (jokingly) why I don't go to ball games on Friday nights and Saturdays".

"Okay, but why two days?"

"That's a fair question. You see, after each day of creation, Moses, the most accepted author of the first five books in the bible, described a 'day' as being an 'evening and a morning'. Later, God's prophets, kings and judges also referred to a 'day' in this same manner. Rather than count a day from midnight to midnight as most of the world does now, some of the followers of God, Jews and several million Seventh-day-Adventist like myself, still count the Sabbath from sundown to sundown.

"But that's the Jewish Sabbath"

"Well yes honey, Jesus kept the seventh day Sabbath that way. It was His custom as it had been for centuries for most of the Jewish nation and was for His disciples and apostles thereafter. So you're right about that, He was Jewish."

"Someone told me that when Jesus died on the cross, those laws were done away with"

"Well, if you're right, and there's no indication of that change written in scriptures anyway, why wasn't the law about not killing, not stealing, not committing adultery, honoring your parents and God, done away with as well? The seventh day Sabbath was part of those ten commandments so why would the fourth commandment be done away with and not the others?

In these discussions about my odd ways, there was never an argument, just a silence as it must have seemed strange to him . Since these brief exchanges never went beyond the above, I never pushed to burden Gene with adopting "my peculiar ways". I merely answered as I was asked. Sometimes I'd rattle on about ancient secular history, as best I knew, about the circumstances surrounding that change. I never knew whether he thought I was out of my mind, seriously thinking about what I was saying or about which curve to throw to Duke Snider.

At times, though, when he really seemed to be listening, I'd continue on with my secular history lesson. I would explain how in the fourth century, Constantine, the Emperor of the Roman Empire, who had recently converted to Christianity and was anxious to amalgamate his divergent populace. Because the sun worshippers' day to keep holy was Sunday and because Christ had been raised from the tomb on that day, Constantine made a brilliant decision-one that united his empire. He decreed in 321 A.D. that Sunday-the holy Day of the Sun-would be the day to worship the Lord Jesus. So we, as Christians, have inherited a Sunday "Sabbath."

We had a terrific time with both Gene's parents and my Mother. At Gene's, some reporter and photographer would always mysteriously show up at the Conleys. Gene's Mom would joke that Les must have been busy on the phone. He was understandably proud of his son; and I know that deep down his mom was too, even though she would try to downplay his success.

My Mother had moved to Bend Oregon, to be near her sister and husband on a ranch between Bend and Madras where my paternal grandparents had homesteaded along the Dechuttes River in the late 1800's. My aunt had married a "hunter" and he along with other folks were getting ready for the hunting season to begin. Gene, not wanting to be left out and inspired by all the tall tales told by these rugged "woodsy" types, purchased a 30-30 rifle in preparation for his first big game hunt. He had hunted rabbits on horse back in Richland, Washington but these fellows sported beards, wore flannel shirts, had wide suspenders to hold up their woolen pants, and carried hunting knives. These were serious hunters, laying in deer, moose and bear meat for the winter. They spoke with disdain of "the greenhorns"-those gentlemen hunters who shot their prey but were unable (or had no knowledge of how) to slit the animals throat, bleed it out and gut it so as to let the entrails spill out before the meat became "gamey".

So it was on this cold Autumn morning, this motley crew set out to go "huntin" with Gene in tow. He had even found a red jacket large enough for his 6'8" frame-with appropriate hat and along with his brand new rifle and stock of ammunition, felt suitable to be in the company of these bold warriors. As they climbed to the top of a steep forested hill, it wasn't long before they spotted a couple of deer leaping over the next rise ahead of them. Gene was first to take aim at a "forked-horn" and brought down "poor Bambi" with his first shot from his first high powered rifle. Running and unbuckling his brand new hunting knife in one hand, his rifle in the other, he proceeded in haste to imitate his contemporaries' vivid stories by getting the deer into position to slit its throat. His adrenaline was pumping but trying not to show it, so as not to be labeled a novice or worse yet, a "greenhorn", he failed to put the rifle's "safety latch" on. With his knife in one hand, his finger on his gun's trigger with the other, he quickly manipulated the deer's head, only to have his gun fire, barely missing his toe and badly cutting his hand.

This whole experience left him with the conviction that this would be his first and last hunting season. His rifle was mounted on a gun rack along with a b-b gun and a couple of bats for eternity. It was time for basketball.

After safely depositing the babies and myself in our brand new apartment, Gene flew off to Boston to join the Celtics for exhibition games in Maine. Mr. Perini, the "Braves" owner was quoted as saying, "I have nothing against basketball but playing it is a dangerous thing to do". Mr. Quinn, the general manager still with the Braves was quoted as saying, "I don't think with a year off from playing basketball, that Gene will be able to make the team". This was a new tack they were taking. It was obvious that their past threats didn't do the job so perhaps they really believed that Gene couldn't make the team. In any case, there wasn't going to be a monetary compensation offered. This hadn't been what Gene had in mind anyway. He really wanted to play basketball. He had been offered a PR job in Milwaukee with a brewery and an offer to sell insurance but these weren't even considered. He really loved the game. Auerbach and Brown were counting on his ability to get the ball off the boards as Red always said, "you have to get the ball before you can put it through the basket".

Gene was getting into the groove and by November, just before the season opened, he had sent us tickets to fly back to Boston. He said that he had a place for us to live. It was all hugs and kisses at the airport but as we were leaving for our new home, he began his tale of woe, or at least it was woe for the children and myself.

We were to stay in a house with a Celtic fan. She was a young dear person, not quite 4' 10" and terribly crippled but it didn't dampen her enthusiasm about her beloved Celtics. I never found out whether she had inherited this little cottage in Revere, Massachusetts, rented it or had purchased it but it was located near the Boston Garden. The price was right. There was a bit of a catch, however. The space she was renting us included not only herself- it was to be shared also by Ed Macauley, his wife and two toddlers. Not only that, it was an upstairs duplex and had only 2 bedrooms and one bath. In other words, five adults and four children sharing a space that, as I remember, couldn't have measured 1,500 s.f. I hadn't remembered meeting Ed and Jackie back in the '52-'53 season so naturally, I don't imagine they were too thrilled with the fact that we would be occupying the second bedroom and sharing the kitchen and one bath with another four people. The bedroom measured a little under 12' x 12'. This compartment was to be our home. Our hostess would be sleeping on a couch in the tiny front room. It was cold, it was dark and from its close proximity to the Atlantic ocean, it was damp. The Macauley's were as hospitable as possible under such circumstances, and made supper for the rest of us.

All four of us bedded down that night, with little Kitty in a box and Gene Jr. on the floor. Gene and I were engaged in fearsome combat for the bed was only double-sized. The battle waged on through the night while baby Kitty wailed herself into a real crying jag. This chaos went on until the sun faintly shown in the eastern window, our only window. So on the eve of the Hoop Opener, we composed a press release that explained why Gene was going into Basketball retirement.

"It is with deep regret that I announce my retirement from Major League Basketball and the Boston Celtics, to concentrate fully on Major League Baseball.

During the past week I have had the opportunity to review my short career in both basketball and baseball. After many pro's and con's, I have made the decision to retire as a Major league basketball player.

The reasons for my decision are many:

1. I have my family to consider - my wife and two children. During the baseball season, I seldom see any of them. The basketball season is even worse.

2. In respect to my Celtic teammates, Mr. Walter Brown, and coach Red Auerbach, I feel that I would be doing them an injustice by not being able to concentrate 100% on two major league sports.

3. I sincerely feel that I may be cutting my baseball career short by continuing the rugged 12 months schedule of two major league sports.

My decision to concentrate on baseball alone does not arrive from any difficulty whatsoever with the Celtics owner, Walter Brown, or the team's coach, Red Auerbach, or any member of the team or organization. I have been treated wonderfully in every respect by the Celtic organization and hate to leave the team and the city of Boston." Signed, Gene Conley.

We know that both the owner and coach were unhappy with this new and sudden development. Mr. Brown and Red had counted on Gene for rebounding and he had been slated to start the opener as their center. He had had a remarkable exhibition series. We both felt guilty and disappointed about it for we knew Gene really wanted to continue. It was just an impossible situation. Kitty's all night expression of unhappiness with having to trade her warm cozy and comfortable crib for a makeshift box in a strange cold and crowded room, marked the turning point. I knew that Gene and Ed would be on the road most of the time so they were set but not knowing Jackie, our gracious hostess at that time, I felt intimidated and wasn't sure I could handle it. Moreover, I hate to admit it , but knowing that we had a very comfortable apartment with central heat waiting for us back in Milwaukee helped change our minds as well. It's true, what can I say, I was and am a certified wimp.

Like a vulture seizing his opportunity, John Quinn attempted to swoop down for the kill. John asked for a meeting with Gene to sign his 1955 contract. Gene was as innocent as a lamb and anxious to have this formality out of the way for he had anticipated a substantial raise. When he came to the Braves in 1954, his contract as a rookie was for only $10,000.00. So naturally, being rated number two in earned run averages in the League, making the All Star squad his rookie year, and despite having an interrupted season, had managed 14 wins with only 9 loses, he felt his raise would be substantial. Regardless, his euphoria soon evaporated when he found just how powerless a MLB player really was, despite his talent or accomplishments. He was being schooled by one of the best. This exercise in futility was merely a stacked deck. Mr. Quinn's so called raise was a joke. Gene became 1955's earliest "Hold out". Basketball, he found had been a valuable asset and without it, he had lost his leverage. Baseball owners had no authority over other sports, but in their game, they were lords.

Gene found if you can't beat 'em, join 'em; after returning to Milwaukee, Ben Kerner, the owner of the Milwaukee Hawks Basketball Club, hired him to be their PR director. He became a team official. (at least for the season) Then all heck broke out. From the Boston Herald, under the headlines of "Brown May Prevent Conley From Taking Front-Office Berth"

"Gene Conley is a lanky rosy-cheeked young man with a boyish face and an innocent demeanor that apparently conceal an unsuspected flare for subtlety and intrigue. First, he defied the Braves--for whom he had a 14-9 record last season and said he would play basketball this winter. Then he went to Brown and mentioned the salary he expected from the Celtics.

'But that's exorbitant', protested the owner. 'You didn't play at all last season. You played only a little two years ago.'

'But I'm funnier now,' argued Conley with a boyish grin."

The story went on, "Maurice Podoloff must wonder how he stands being president of the National Basketball Association. 'Here we go again', said the little man around whom rages the pro basketball whirlpool', speaking over the telephone from his New York office.

'Here is this Conley. What is he trying to do? I am told by Walter Brown that he is suspended by the Celtics but wants to work for Milwaukee. Can he do this? I don't think so'

'Brown was saying no, last night. At least it sounded like no.' He said, 'Conley will work for me or nobody else.'

Strange how a little four month old infant can change not only its parents' lives but can exercise the emotions of those who live in that very visible glass bowl known as the sports world.

Spring Training, 1955

Gene Jr.   Gene Sr.

CHAPTER 16

DAY OF RETRIBUTION

Spring training, 1955 brought us back to our little grass shack on Anna Marie Island, which was not far from the mainland and the Milwaukee training base in Bradenton, Florida. Gene still hadn't signed his contract, even after a few short meetings over the winter.

John Quinn, the general manager, was having a great deal of difficulty signing many of the Brave's players. Lew Burdette, later to become the World Series hero against the Yankees, a unique and cagey character, would meet Mr. Quinn at local bars for his contract talks. This was brilliant thinking on his part as during contract negotiations, the general manager was known to lose it at times. The pressures of being a general manager could account for that, as they were a one man show in the mid century. He was having trouble signing Eddie Mathews and Bob Buhl as well.

We were to have a "Camp's Cottage" birthday party for our son on Gene's return from his contract talks with Quinn. With all the infinite preparations, there was still time enough to rehearse our determined stance regarding what we honestly thought Gene was worth to the club. Just before his appointment to do battle that day, we made a pact. Our resolve was, that if it looked as if Quinn absolutely refused to accede to a $20,000.00 contract, he would walk, no matter what. We knew what this meant, it wouldn't be an idle threat, it would mean, no baseball this season and Gene would have to look for employment elsewhere. Nervous but determined, we both went about our assignments. We had invited about 40 guests and there was a great deal more to be accomplished. Gene made his way to the Dixie Grande Hotel. Gene was going up the stairs at the Dixie Grand as Eddie Mathews was coming down.

"How'd you do Eddie?"

"The damn s.o.b."

Gene took it he didn't sign.

"Hello Mr. Quinn".

"Gene, so glad to see you, how's the family"?

This phrase was always used by John. When addressing players for whatever reason, this was his standard phrase used for all occasions. For that reason, it had become an inside joke with all the Braves players. When asked by another player how it went with Quinn, they would always add, "and did he ask you about the family"? Something endearing there somewhere.

On the table was a fifth of whiskey and some glasses. Mr. Quinn invited Gene to sit down and have a drink. Gene was in no mood. "Gene, I've talked it over with the owners and feel that we can offer you a substantial raise." With a broad smile, anticipating Gene's approval, offered $3,000.00 more.

"Well, Mr. Quinn it's like this, I quit basketball to concentrate on baseball. I've made "Minor League Player of the Year" twice. Even with an interrupted rookie year, I was able to win 14 games and was chosen as an All Star. At the time I was asked to go on the disabled list, I was ranked second in the National League with an E.R.A. of 2.84. I was runner up for Major League's "Rookie of the Year" as well. I don't think $3,000.00 is going to do it".

"But Gene, you had trouble with Philadelphia".

"Mr. Quinn, Philadelphia is the League's last place club. I beat Brooklyn, the best club in the National League, five times".

Then Gene dropped his bomb shell. "The way I figure it, I'll sign a Braves contract for $20,000.00."

It was as if Mr. Quinn had been mortally wounded. He had been drinking before their meeting and the two to three glasses since, did nothing to temper his anger.

"Gene, you must be joking?"

"I'm deadly serious Mr. Quinn."

"Listen Gene, you're never going to play in the Braves organization. My advice to you is to rejoin the Celtics as that is where you are going to be playing....if.....if you can make their team."

"Is that your last word sir?"

"Yes, I'm deadly serious as well, go play basketball."

"Okay, Mr. Quinn I will go play basketball, it's a great game." Gene got up, walked across the room, opened the door and...

"Gene, you get back in here and sit down!"

"All right you'll get the $20,000.00 but I'm telling you now, you're not worth it!"

Nothing like a vote of confidence.

The next day as Gene made his appearance at the park, making his way through a few newspaper men, noticed John Quinn sitting in the front row. Not knowing what to expect, the General Manager stood up, shook Gene's hand and said, "Gene, it's good to see you, how's the family?"

Gene's progress that spring was phenomenal, as if he were trying to prove he was worth his contract. He was the first pitcher to go nine and won each time he went to the mound. Bob Wolf the Milwaukee Journalist was predicting 30 to 35 wins for Gene.

Pitchers hardly make that many appearances during a season. "Look" magazine did a special feature on Gene, and Grimm was going to start him for the season opener. It didn't quite turn out that way and as a matter of fact, against St. Louis, after two batters hit home runs, he lost his first game of the 1955 season.

A pitcher is only as good as his last game so he didn't let that be a habit and began to win, thanks to his batting abilities combined with decent pitching. Sometimes there is an early spring season when nothing is going right for a team. The pitchers were off and the best the sluggers could manage were averages in the low 200's. By May 17th, however, Gene had only lost one and was being hailed as their "stopper".

By the time he had won 6 in a row, he had climbed up a notch by being tagged the Braves' "Ace" before he faced Carl Erskine for the second time. They had locked into a 12 inning stint just four days previous to this outing with Gene winning the game 2 to 1. On May 31, however, his next 12 inning duel with Erskine ended with a win for Erskine (same score, only reversed). Years later Carl said he wasn't the same after those two drawn out games.

Gene's success was nothing short of spectacular and with the endorsements, commercials and featured articles splashed across pages in national magazines, my equilibrium was starting to be affected. I can't say that Gene succumbed to pride but sorry to say I was letting it get to me as if it was some sort of an accomplishment I had achieved. I had done a couple of commercials on radio, pictorial newsprint commercials, modeling assignments and the weekly television show, "Play Ball". My ego was way out of proportion and I didn't see it coming.

It was one of my last appearances on the "Play Ball Show", which halted my self perceived importance along with a change in Gene's actual superiority. The show had gone well. Embarrassing to relate, but I felt that I had been both witty and charming. My parents had tried to instill modesty in my character with certain values, living within the grace of God and His commandments. To be careful about the hours of the Sabbath was a tradition in our family, having done all our work and preparations by Friday night sundown. This was a natural way of living for me. Saturdays were spent in church and afternoons in fellowship with the congregation or maybe a nature walk and if time permitted, bible study or related articles read. Gene didn't interfere or comment about my lifestyle, he seemed to understand.

The TV show was to be over by sundown Friday night. Our friends were taking care of little Gene and Kitty and I would be home before sunset. The other Braves' wives were so much fun and so bubbly however, it was always difficult leaving them. The director was going to be taking everyone out to eat after the show and then on to the game which meant I would be involved after the Sabbath began.

After a good deal of coaxing, I had succumbed to dinner and even though I felt uncomfortable, gave into my peers' urging to watch Gene pitch. Because I had given into the dinner invitation, it left me without a car so it was only a matter of convenience, I rationalized, in order to have a ride, I would simply have to wait in the stadium until Gene had finished.

The game was against the lowly Phillies and Gene was expected to win. I squirmed in my seat as my conscience began to bother me. What followed was a series of events that brought an end to Gene's spectacular mastery over his opposition and also brought an end to my conceit and carelessness. I had always accepted the protection and the blessings for granted I suppose. I was never flagrant about going against what I had been taught or what I perceived to be true. However, little by little I was letting vanity into my life where it had laid dormant for years. The principals I had held sacred all my life had never been sacrificed before.

Most would call it pure imagination caused from an overactive or guilt ridden conscience but it seemed as if a protective shield had been lifted to release all kinds of hell. The Phillies players were just barely catching a piece of the ball that were landing just beyond the reach of our infielders. Then, an ominous substance floated onto the field in the form of little black specks like a plague of locust. In the grandstands people were going berserk. Bob Trenary of the Milwaukee Journal explains it best under the headline:

"SIDE ACTS ENTERTAIN"

"In the matter of side interest, the game was particularly fertile. Around the fourth inning, there was this fall of soot from the soldiers home smokestacks that set the crowd of 27,759 churning like an ant hill, and there was a rouser of a fight between two fans in the left field grandstand in the eighth."

This, I had reckoned was **my** "Day of Retribution"!

As this evening of doom descended from the dark skies and as Gene threw his next pitch, there was this horrible sound of something snapping or cracking that even our catcher, Del Crandall heard from his crouched position. "Gene, what was that?"

"I don't know, Del, something in my shoulder snapped." It was obvious from this point on, he needed to call it a night.

Even though he was able to win his next outing against the Pirates, 2 to 1, his next duel with the Dodgers' pitcher, Don Newcombe, caused him to leave in the fifth. Don had hit a hummer right through the box that struck Gene's right shoulder that was still tender from whatever had happed in the Phillies game. He told the manager that he was all right to continue. It was obvious he was not. He was unable to lift his arm high enough for a wind up.

Were these portentous series of extraordinary events based on faith, coincidences or superstition? In my case, I had some serious repenting to do and besides, it doesn't hurt being humbled. It only adds character.

Gene's 1955 All Star Victory
Joe Nuxhall and Stan Musial

CHAPTER 17

THE 1955 ALL STAR GAME AND BEYOND

From this point on, I would never again know the luxury of taking for granted the dominance Gene usually enjoyed against his opponents. His successes would not be based purely on Gene's athletic abilities alone as these were now impaired.

It pained me each time he took his rotation as I felt the guilt of my own making, at least in my own mind. The writers and fans at this time were not aware of a problem. Gene had a family of four to provide for and his obligations to that end, made it impossible to admit anything was amiss. Agony was taking its toll as he continued throwing, tearing away at injured ligaments a little more each time. In his next outing against the Chicago Cubs he managed a three hit victory for his tenth win. Even though his next game against the Cincinnati Reds was rough around the edges, his bat more than made up for his lack luster pitching. *"He singled once, sacrificed once and survived once on an error which left him running around the bases like a Ty Cobb",* Bob Wolf of the Milwaukee Journal wrote. Luck and pure guts shared in this, his 11th victory before the All Star Game of 1955.

In the fifties, there were only 8 pitchers chosen for an All Star berth, one from each team usually. Gene was one of them for the second time in the Majors in as many years. The other Milwaukee Braves chosen were; Henry Aaron, Eddie Mathews, Del Crandall and Johnny Logan. County Stadium, the new franchise's ballpark was to be the setting for the 1955 All Star Game. The All Star players from Milwaukee had the most players chosen from one team. There was "standing room" only.

This would be an exciting affair, a once in a lifetime event. My mood was quite tranquil as I prepared for the game that day, secure in the knowledge that Gene had just pitched two days before and would not likely be chosen to pitch in any part of this celebrated affair. I was composed and serene as my Mother, Little Gene and myself settled in to enjoy the festivities. Previous to this game I had been a little spooked and hadn't returned to the scene of that fateful May evening when Gene's rotator cuff snapped and that black pall settled over County Stadium. The only anxiety lurking in the back of my subconscious was that he could still be required to warm up sometime during the game as I knew what torment he would have to suffer.

As always the Milwaukee fans filled every seat and were ready and anxious to voice their enthusiasm at every move on the field. To say that the Braves' fans were partial is putting it mildly. I think it was because the players were as green as they. Milwaukee's fans weren't as jaded as say, the Dodgers' fans, as they hadn't the span of time indulging their reliance on tried veterans as did the Dodgers. The Dodgers had won time and again, winning three games to the one they would lose each year. They played with an arrogant, impersonal assurance. They expected the winning play when the occasion demanded. They had daring, they conferred and consoled and encouraged each other with a nonchalant impertinence toward the feelings of the crowd or their opponent. They always kept up a steady grinding pressure against their competitors. The Milwaukee club of the fifties were young, anxious, untried and unsure. The fans desired a successful outcome but were never certain, merely surprised when the home team showed signs of brilliance.

There were over 400 reporters, columnists and editors at this gathering as well as the electronic media. The weather was one of those rare days in July when the humidity was down and the sun blazed high against a very blue sky. There was red, white and blue bunting strung in corners, walls and rafters as well as the Brave's Indian Chief logo. The opening ceremonies were both entertaining and moving, bringing one almost to the point of tears. The cheering was thunderous and enthusiastic, especially when the Braves players were announced. Milwaukee had done a very credible job for their first All Star Game.

The game in the seventh looked very much like a victory for the American League as the score was 5 to 0 in their favor. In the eighth inning, with the American League still leading by a score of 5 to 2, with two out, it was almost a certainty they would win the 1955 All Star Game. By now I was feeling even more relaxed and almost giddy, anticipating the end of the game, despite a feeling of disloyalty for not rooting for our National League entry. Gene only had to warm up for two more innings and with only one more to go, he would not be challenged nor his arm and shoulder injured further. My comfortable complacency was shaken, however, when there were two errors committed by the American Leaguers. Along with a couple of hits, the score was now tied, 5 to 5. Gene continued to labor in the bullpen for the Nationals as did Frank Sullivan for the American League. At that time, they were the tallest players in the Majors. They labored in the bullpen through the seventh, eighth and ninth innings but still the game remained tied. My anxiety began building but there was still a chance Gene wouldn't be used as Joe Nuxall was doing so well. The game remained tied into the

10th as Frank and Gene continued their private game of warm up. In the 12th inning, the public address system blared out the depressing and chilling message; "And now coming in to pitch for the National League, Big Gene Conley of the Milwaukee Braves".

There was the most thunderous ovation I had ever heard. The Milwaukee fans were ecstatic, rising to their feet, shouting and cheering their support and approval. I was in a state of shock. The sound level was deafening. Everyone was up except Mom, myself and Little Gene who had climbed up onto my lap cupping his little hands over his ears, trying to avoid the noisome crowd. Hiding behind Little Gene's head, I slumped down and exclaimed, "Oh Mother, no Mother, please...........not Gene". I knew he had a crippled arm. I knew that millions would be watching on TV. I knew the capacity there at County Stadium. I knew of all the media present that day. I thought of the humiliation Gene would face and after last year's loss, I imaged this would just about kill him emotionally. The fans were ecstatic as they couldn't figure out why Durocher hadn't pitched him earlier, a writer was to report in the Journal the next day. They had no idea of the condition of his arm. At the time I didn't think of the possibility that TV cameras could be pointing in my direction as if they did, they saw a very dastardly exhibition of cowardice.

"Oh, Mother, this is just terrible".

"Now honey, we're all going to sit here and just pray about it and he'll do just fine".

I had, from living with my saintly Mother, learned to trust her faith so that is exactly what I did. We prayed silently that things would work out while all around us pandemonium reigned. The nerves were present but the fear was gone.

For Gene, the encouragement of the fans supportive cheering, melted away the pain and ended apprehension before it began. The familiarity of the fan's cheers, the stadium and his little domain, that little pile of dirt, filled his soul with assurance. He was home. Stan Lopata came out to discus the complicated signs. Years later I said what were these complicated signs and he says, "one, two and three".

"What do you mean? What was one?"

" Fast ball".

"What was two?"

"Curve ball"

"And three?"

"Slider, only I didn't have a slider so we went with only one or two fingers", Gene laughed. So much for complicated signs. Today, pitchers have these mastered in Little League and by high school, they've added spitters, fork balls, palm balls, split finger fast balls, screw balls and excellent baseball coaches. In the Minors or college, video cameras film the game in real time and in between innings, the pitcher and coach are able to confer with one another, evaluating problems or execution of mastery over their opponent.

Three record setting players were ready for battle that late afternoon as Gene made his final warm up pitches on the mound. Al Kaline was the league's leading hitter; Mickey Vernon twice the league batting champion and Al Rosen, twice the leader in runs batted in. Micky played 20 years in the majors, made 7 All Star Games, Rosen made 4 All Star Games in his career and was the Most Valuable Player of the American League in 1953, Al Kaline had 22 years in the

Majors, making 18 All Star Games, had over 3,000 hits and in 1955, won the Batting Title, subsequently making Baseball's Hall of Fame. They made up a formidable trio.

Holding Mom's hand and hugging Little Gene tightly, we watched and prayed as to our amazement, one by one the three batters went down. Gene had struck out the side! More applause and another standing ovation. I had learned my lesson in May. Humility, mixed with gratitude kept me from standing or applauding. All I could manage was a faint and nervous smile as we might have to go another inning as the game was still tied.

This was a chance to vindicate his last All Star appearance when he lost by loading the bases and without a run scored nor an out made, he had shamefully left the mound. He had stumbled back to the team dressing room, his face wet with tears then.

When Stan, the Man, Musial went by the dugout, he said to Hank Aaron, "Hey, Henry, do we get paid for overtime?" Henry replied, "no Stan, we don't".

Stan was like that. He always talked when going to the plate. Yogi Berra once said, "I don't know about Stan's sincerity. One time he came to the plate and asked me how the family was and before I had time to reply, he was on third base".

In the bottom of the 12th inning, Musial came through with the most beautiful home run I have ever witnessed and is still one of the most significant events mentioned in Major League history's All Star Classics. When recalling or listing All Star highlights, Stan's home run is always brought up. Stan never knew what that home run meant to the Conleys. This home run meant that Gene was the pitcher of record and the winner for all time, but to me, it meant an answered prayer and more importantly, even if theologically flawed, I felt the proof of acceptance.

As expected, there were telegrams with glowing congratulations, articles, interviews and just plain notoriety. Later, at Ebbetts Field, young fans who had been begging Leo Durocher's wife, the popular actress, Lorraine Day, for autographs, quickly turned away when Gene made his appearance on the field. His coaches and teammates perceived that Gene was his old indomitable self and he was used a few more times. Even though fielding errors caused a lot of his problems in those games, by the time he had pitched in three more, the opposing players became puzzled. Lou Chapman in an article in the Milwaukee Sentinel quoted some of the Dodgers comments: *"The giant 6 foot 8 inch pitcher was the special bogeyman last year for the Dodgers, who fell victims before Gene's booming fast ball and variety of curves. Gene held the same magic powers the first two games of this season, but apparently has lost the formula of late since he has now dropped three straight to Brooklyn's pacemakers, that is, counting Friday night's 8-4 setback.*

The right-hander was such a soft touch for his former Dodger cousins on this last outing that some of them wondered out loud after the game whether or not he had an ailing arm."

'What's the matter with Conley?' Jackie Robinson asked: 'Has he got a sore arm or is there something wrong with his back?'

"Catcher Roy Campanella voiced the same thought but pointed out, 'Gene loosened up later in the game and showed some good stuff.'

'Our boys have such a deep respect for Conley's pitching.' Robinson came back, 'that they all wondered what was wrong with him the way our hitters

cut loose at his pitches early in the game. Gene's given us so much trouble in the past, the question of a sore arm or perhaps ailing back came up.' "

It took four more outings, and three more loses for Manager Charlie Grimm to come to terms with Gene's problems. Even a three week rest made no difference. It was decided that with only five weeks more until the end of the season, Gene would be put on the disabled list and sent over to the Mayo Clinic for a complete examination. In the fifties, Medicine was still in the dark ages. He was pronounced a fine and healthy specimen but it was determined that he must have pulled some ligaments under the shoulder cap. They suggested that he purchase a punching bag to use in order to strengthen those areas and some physiotherapist used diathermy, whatever that is, to ease his pain. Well, he purchased the punching bag and installed it in the basement. That's about it. For Gene, athletics were natural. Working at it seemed abnormal so our newly installed punching bag extraordinaire, has remained the centerpiece of our basement work out room for fifty years. The diathermy was pleasant enough though.

Gene assumed that with complete rest, his pain would disappear and with basketball not even considered, the winter of '55-'56 became another round of family fun. Our financial status was limited but not our imaginations. Returning to the west, we visited first Gene's family and then settled down at my Mother's place in Bend, Oregon. They had no television access in those days so we hiked a great deal with our pre-school kids in tow around the mountain trails of the Cascade Range. We explored log cabins that were mostly abandoned second homes, water falls and swift rivers.

My sister had skis we had purchased for her the Christmas when Gene played basketball for the Celtics in 1952. That was our extravagant Christmas giving year when we purchased evening wear for our Mothers, and sweater sets for

Gene's sister at Bonwit Tellers, and then had to borrow to get to spring training. When the snows came to the mountains around Bend, Gene purchased a pair of skis for me. Back then manufacturers couldn't or wouldn't make ski boots large enough for a kingsize guy, so Gene was assigned the daunting task of keeping our two, plus my sister's little girl, from killing themselves while my sister, Patti and I played at skiing. I say "play" at it as in that era of skiing, in order to fit a prospective skier properly, they measured the ski, at the length of a person's height plus the reach of ones arm held high over the head. This would enable a skier greater speed which made it almost impossible to gain real joy from the sport. With fear and intrepidation, we would trudge up Mt. Bachelor in order to ride down in abject terror. Mt. Bachelor only had a tow rope then and since we did not have the price of a ticket nor the desire to try it, we hoofed it. Just before Christmas this particular year, we "put down" on a 14 foot travel trailer. It looked like great fun as we had just heard that Disneyland had recently opened in Anaheim, California. Having eighteen month old Kitty, three year old Little Gene, plus nineteen month old Debbie, my sister Patti's little girl, we felt that this would be a perfect mode of transportation for us all. My sister was a single parent, attending college and would be off during the three week Christmas vacation.

It seemed so quiet and still, driving over the pass near Crater Lake in the dead of winter. The forest that had been dressed in dark green velvet this past summer had now transformed itself into a sparkling white frost. We all anticipated a marvelous adventure.

Going slowly over the icy pass, pulling our little home, we came upon one of the strangest sights in our travels. Along the side of the highway, a bearded hunter was awakening from a night's sleep between two mattresses. These mattresses were resting on an entirely made up iron bedstead. Our stretching bearded hunter was out under the open sky, oblivious to vehicles passing by only a few yards from the highway. His attire of fire engine red long johns were not an embarrassment to him at all as he picked up his trusty rifle. It was true Americana Rustic.

Being movie aficionados, my sister and I wanted to see every movie star's homes once inside the city limits of L.A. Dragging our mud splattered 14' home behind us, we traversed the hills of Beverly. Towards evening, we came upon the Beverly Hills Hotel where there seemed to be some sort of glorious event going on as all the ladies were dressed in full length ball gowns and furs as they alighted from their limousines. I remember being so excited watching as we drove by slowly. It was difficult to see much as the entrance was so far from the main road so Gene, being Gene said, "you guys want to get a better view?" Yeah sure. But before I had time to respond, Gene had turned our caravan up the main entrance drive with Patti and I screaming, "Oh, Gene no!!!" We were totally embarrassed as he laughed in glee. He was thoroughly enjoying the scene. We must have been a bizarre vision. Maybe some writer or producer got his inspiration for that "Sit Com", "The Beverly Hillbillies" from that sight. We were dressed in jeans and on the floor board, in plain sight, lay piles of baby bottles and discarded diapers. The doorman bowed as he opened my side of the car for all to view. I was humiliated but Gene couldn't contain himself from the pleasure of it all.

"May I help you?"

Gene said, laughing, "No sir, my wife and sister-in-law just wanted to get a better look". The doorman smiled and acted as if nothing unusual was occurring.

Patti and I were mortified as we drove away from the Hills of Beverly to the Valley of Ventura to find respite in an RV park.

I loved the smell of the summer or at least, spring-like weather in December. After more sightseeing, my sister and Gene thought it a grand idea to go to a nightclub of all things. The only one we had ever read about was "Ciros" which is only history today but then, it was "the" place to see and be seen by the stars in their natural habitat so I begrudgingly agreed. It wasn't exactly the proper place for a straight laced or uptight tea totler to be, but I was out voted. Obtaining a baby-sitter to watch our little clan, we dressed as best we could and headed for the bright lights of Hollywood.

Valet service took care of the car. We made our way nervously into the darkened club. I spotted a dancer who had appeared in musicals of the day. I believe his name was Bobby Van and then actor Dick Egan and actress, Lorraine Day. Just as I spotted her, Leo Durocher spotted us and rushed over to greet Gene. He was so cordial and kept asking us where we were staying as he wanted us to come up to his place for cocktails that night or later on during the week. Gene, never a loss for words said, "Oh, Leo, we'd just love to but the kids haven't seen Disneyland yet and we have to get back to Bend before Christmas Eve."

"Oh, that's okay. Gene, why don't you just give me your number and the name of the place where you're staying, where are you staying?"

"Well, Leo, it's just a little place in the Valley," still not coming clean with the whole truth.

Gene was just too vague for Leo but he continued asking where we were staying and that he could send someone to pick us up during our stay in L.A. However, Gene remained indefinite, saying but not saying as to where we were staying. I think Leo just wanted a baseball person to talk with as show business people have their own agenda and language. He really wanted us to come up to his place that night as they were having a party but as flattering as his invitation was, we knew we had three forsaken little children, alone with a stranger and should be returning to our little habitat.

Gene knew the Security Chief at Warner Brothers, Walter Glover. He was at Pullman's Washington State University before moving to L.A. He was very accommodating and introduced us to many stars of that day. James Dean had just been killed and many people on the lot were in mourning. He had recently finished his parts in the movie, "Giant". That day they were going to shoot the last scene, the scene where Elizabeth Taylor and Rock Hudson were comparing their two grandchildren, two pre-schoolers in a playpen. They were shooting just the kids that day and Walter got the wild hare to see if one of our kids would qualify. This was a little off the wall which proved so later as they had already hired a couple of cute kids. It was just another fun afternoon's adventure. However, over the next three or four years, Walter would continue to call Gene whenever the Braves were in town to invite him and any other player on the team to meet whoever was shooting at the time. During this period Gene met Bette Davis, Alan Ladd, Hugh O'Brien, Robert Taylor, Jimmy Stewart, Glen Ford, James Garner, Richard Todd, Barbara Rush, Pier Angeli, and producer Mervyn LeRoy, and oh yes, the gate guard. They probably were just as unimpressed with him as he was with them. For he would have to feign knowledge of them and their work for he cared little for movies. The only actor he could relate to and who had knowledge of Gene and his profession was James Garner who also hailed from Oklahoma and had been a high school and college athlete.

After the Disneyland experience, we hitched up our little abode and headed back up north to be in time for the holiday with Mom. However, that was the winter of 1955 and not to be as flooding separated us from the highway. We spent Christmas Eve eating in the only restaurant open this side of the deluge, a

Chinese Diner. Sort of a typical "Conley" holiday as bizarre Christmas/New Year's celebrations became the "norm" with us.

Milwaukee Braves Starters — 1955

Bob Buhl   Lew Burdette   Gene Conley   Warren Spahn

CHAPTER 18

GLOOM TO GLORY

Gene was anxious to get to warmer climate that early spring of 1956 and as usual we left for Florida early. Hope springs eternal and in this case we were hanging onto that virtue with anticipation, that with concentrated physical conditioning, he could work out the stiffness that remained aching in his damaged shoulder. He had used the pool at Milwaukee's new Jewish Athletic Club to try and stretch out the lingering shoulder problems and felt his arm troubles were behind him.

Spring training had its usual bright spots and all was going well but in Waycross, Georgia, as the Braves made their journey North, a reoccurrence of Gene's arm problems started to plague him. Joe Reichler of the Milwaukee Sentinel wrote: *"Pennants, as a rule, are not lost in March but that is exactly what may have happened in the case of the Milwaukee Braves when Gene Conley, their ace right hander, suffered a recurrence of his chronic back and shoulder miseries.*

Milwaukee must have a sound Conley if it is to make up the 13 and 1/2 games that separated it from the pennant winning Brooklyn Dodgers last year. If Conley cannot take his regular turn and contribute the 15 to 20 victories expected of him, the Braves will be lucky to do as well as last year when they finished second.

Charlie Grimm, their manager stated, "We've never had Conley a full year. He was out three weeks in 1954 and six weeks last season. If he's right, he's a potential 20 game winner."

Once more Gene was put on the disabled list and left behind in Jacksonville Florida to work out with their Braves farm team until he felt he was ready. He worked hard and along with intensive therapy, he began to heal. Each day we would listen to our Braves win again and again. It was phenomenal! Every pitcher they were playing was winning which was great for the team but did nothing for Gene's chances of working into a regular rotation again.

It was June 4 before he was worked in as a starter. In late May, he had been used in relief against the St. Louis Cardinals, pitching six innings to win his first game of the season. *"He looked like his arm was well," said Musial. All of us thought so. We were talking about it on the bench. There can't be too much wrong with him if he can throw that hard right away (Conley had pitched to just one batter previous to Monday night). . I sure hope he's all right, 'cause he's young and he's got a great future ahead of him."*

"If his arm is sore, I hope it never gets well," added Schoendienst. If it does, we'll never get a hit off him. He looked even faster than he was before he hurt his arm."

"Jackie Robinson, watching him pitch batting practice one day remarked, 'He's now throwing with a free and easy motion'. "Conley's reply to all this was, 'I wasn't sharp at all', he explained, but I figure to be after the long lay-off I had. My arm felt okay and I threw harder as I went along."

The next three games Gene started were either a draw or a loss. He had flashes of brilliance but it didn't coincide with the breaks of the game. He went the full nine innings his next time out, winning his second. Charlie Grimm noted, *"Conley is the key man. He's a potential 20 game winner, and if his arm's all right we'll have as good a chance as anyone."* The Braves were back in the lead. Looking back on 1956, Gene said, even though he was throwing good enough to make the pitching rotation, it wasn't fun anymore. The uncertainty of not knowing when his shoulder would be a problem plagued him each time he approached the mound.

By the time Gene had won his 4th game with a shutout, the Braves were still leading the National League but Fred Haney had taken over for Charlie Grimm as manager. He inherited a very talented group of ballplayers. He had five starters with era's in the low threes: Warren Spahn, Lou Burdette, Ray Crone, Bob Buhl and of course Gene. Managers today are only too happy to have two first rate pitchers, Haney had five. Gene's fifth win over the Giants was a shutout. His control seemed to be getting better but he had also managed to lose 6 games. The Pennant race would heat up as the Dodgers made their run. By September 10th we were leading by one game. The Milwaukee Braves had never been so close to winning their first pennant. Warren Spahn had won his 20th but so had the Dodger's Don Newcombe. The stadium was packed at each home stand. You could almost hear the fans holding their breath with every pitch. Finally, it came down to the last game of the season with the Dodgers and the Milwaukee Braves in a dead heat.

The Braves were followed to the airport by cheering fans. They were to play the St. Louis Cardinals and if they won, would go into a playoff situation with the Dodgers, always the team to beat. Everyone in Milwaukee listened intently, maybe even prayerfully but to no avail. They lost! One would think that everyone would go into mourning but not the Milwaukee fans. They were the best ever. In a few short hours the highways and byways became long lines of humanity leading

173

to the airport. The Braves' wives were told to park their cars at County Stadium, and large lighted buses would drive us to the airport to meet....no...not our winners, but our heroes. There wasn't a dry eye on that bus. We marveled at the way the fans responded. It truly was a miracle as out in that darkness, tens of thousands were forming. The hour was nearly midnight by the time the players taxied out in front of the terminal.

At first, the players, came off looking dejected but when confronted with all the cheering, the flash bulbs, and the music, lighted faces soon replaced despondent ones. It was just too much! You'd think we had just won the World Series. They appreciated the excellent efforts of these 25 men. The love exhibited between fan and player that night was mutual. After a couple of television interviews, we were off in those same lighted buses so that the many out there along those darkened highways could get a glimpse of their boys. In that bus, that night, there was a new found resolve.

Gene's earned run average wound up being the sixth best in the National League even though he had only eight victories. He had also saved a few as well so for a three month plus season, he really hadn't done that badly. He was encouraged that he could still pitch a pretty good ballgame. John Quinn didn't quite see it that way as Gene was one of the last to sign but out of stubbornness, his contract remained the same. Nineteen hundred fifty seven was to be a banner year for the Braves.

In spring training, sensing that this may be the year, players were more in tune with each other. They had been untried and inexperienced during the past three years but a new confidence and a greater desire to bring Milwaukee, not only a pennant, but dare we dream, a World's Championship?

Warren Spahn tried unsuccessfully to help Gene with his wind up. Gene, strangely enough, never had the opportunity to gain tutelage from a knowledgeable coach. In high school when his family moved to Richland, the high school was brand new and so was the coach. In college, even though the team made it to the National Collegiate finals to gain second place in the Nation, his coach's experience in coaching baseball was playing football as an undergraduate. In the minors, he experienced retired Major League batters for mangers and after making it to the Majors, a pitcher was expected to already know how to pitch, so there was no effort made to try and improve his basic skills.

Gene's windup was contrived, it was long and it was drawn out and by the time his arm came around to release his pitch, he was throwing all arm, with no body leverage. He toyed with the idea of going with a no windup throw to preserve his shoulder. Gene was convinced that this would not only reduce the stress on his shoulder but he would be in a better position to utilize his body with each throw. It wasn't that he didn't have the grace during a full windup but he wasn't able to exploit his elongated frame to advantage. However, his manager, Fred Haney, after observing his efforts, suggested he lose the new idea. Not wishing to be contrary or odd, Gene kept the old conventional windup.

Utilizing a five man rotation plus having a number of early spring rains caused many delays in getting the needed work the pitchers desired. A five man rotation wasn't working. The next three games Gene participated in were low scoring, but along with appalling bad luck, he and the Braves were losing. The press began calling Gene the "hard luck pitcher" but still, in all, Gene was carrying a .400 batting average. Small consolation. It looked as if this wasn't going to be the Braves' year after all. It was the middle of June before Gene won his first game as opposed to four loses. Pitching in and out of relief assignments afforded little in the way of consistency. The good news was, the Braves were winning again and not only that, leading the league.

Gene's next outing was against the Dodgers and it was a great night for him, pitching a 4 hit shutout along with hitting a single that brought in the only run of the night. There were 45,840 people in attendance, the largest in the League up to that date. Gene had now managed six wins out of seven contests.

The Braves were now leading by half a game.

His seventh victory came at an auspicious time for our family. He had taken me to Milwaukee Hospital's "Women's and Children" on the morning of August 7th. Just two hours before Gene took to the mound, Susan Kelly Conley made her debut, weighing in at a mere 7 lbs., 13 ozs. I say mere, as son, Gene was 9 lbs. 3 ozs. and Kelly's sister, Kitty, had been a robust 8 lbs. 11 ozs. at her coming out party.

In St. Louis the weather went over 100 as Gene won his eighth and as Journalist, Bob Wolf cleverly commented in the Journal: *"At this moment too, it's a question as to what is hotter, Conley, the Braves or the St. Louis weather. Any way one looks at it, it's sure to end up in a dead heat."* Against the Cardinals his next time out, he pitched 9 perfect innings in relief of Juan Pizarro. Juan had been brought up from triple A for the run at the pennant. All Gene received for his fine effort was exercise as after nine innings, he was relieved.. It was lost in the 12th.

Then just as suddenly as the Braves' luck had come, it turned and made a mad dash out of town. Adversity struck in the form of errors, combined with our leading hitters' inability to get the ball out of the infield which further eroded our lead. The hitters were averaging only about 2 runs a week in September and concurrently we slipped behind winning only 3 games out of 9. The Braves were feeling the pressure. They hadn't "choked" but they were tight. Haney used Gene a lot in relief during that period and as a matter of fact, on the night they clinched the pennant, Gene had relieved Spahn. In the tenth with the score tied 3 to 3, Henry Aaron, coming out of a batting slump, hit a home run that clinched the pennant and gave Gene his 9th win of the season.

To go to New York was tantamount to nirvana. It called for a new hat, so off to the Boston store, dragging my three, I tried balancing baby, hats and toddlers while making my selection. Frustrated, I turned to ask my five year old son what he thought about my choice when to my horror, he wasn't there. He wasn't anywhere. He had quietly disappeared. I was in panic! The sales ladies were frantic as well, and called the police. I somehow got through to the dugout to talk or shout to Gene about little Gene's disappearance. There were sirens screaming in the background as I cried inconsolably. A motorcade drove up with Gene in the lead car. As the motorcade pulled up to the store, a detective jumped out and came over to the little blonde curly headed boy standing patiently by the department store entrance. Following, Gene gathered up Little Gene into his arms in relief. The detective asked him why he had been standing there. His logical answer was that he had lost his Mother, and was waiting for her to come out the same door as they had entered.

Gene's little namesake was showing the beginning signs of an independent thinker, much like his Father. Later, rather than doing the usual four years of high school, college, medical school and a residency, he did only three years in high school, three years in college, three years in medical school, and then finishing, doubled up on two "specialty" residencies at the same time.

Little boy lost made a great human interest study in the papers the next day, but I was never so angry at him, all at the same time, dismissing his disobedience with grateful relief!

History recorded the Milwaukee Braves of "Mudville", (as the eastern pundits liked to call Milwaukee), winning the World Series that year or should I say, Lew Burdette won the World Series that year, with 3 out of the 4 wins against the Yankees. The Milwaukee fans didn't disappoint them with their planned celebration, as during the parade that followed our cavalcade, every band from middle school to Wisconsin's colleges performed. At the end of the parade, the governor, mayor and assorted politicians, along with the Braves families stood on a balcony high above city hall while the population of Milwaukee and beyond cheered and sang and played. It was a most beautiful day and no one was inclined to leave. I don't believe I have ever witnessed such a happy event so enjoyed by so many.

CHAPTER 19

ALMOST OBSCURITY

Nineteen hundred and fifty eight would be a turning point for Gene. The Braves were expected to have a repeat performance. They were abundantly crowded with a fine group of pitchers; Warren Spahn, Lou Burdette, Bob Rush, Joey Jay, Carlton Willy, Juan Pizzaro, Bob Buhl, Gene Conley and Bob Trowbridge and they were all "starters". I believe in every pitcher's life, a little rain must fall, and its name was Fred Haney. Probably there were many reasons one could account for Fred's problem with Gene. There have been some who felt Fred had a "little man's complex" but such a label is too nebulous to explain away this mystery. One does not have to be told by a teammate or media type that the manager was reacting as if he were unaware of his gentle giant. Hank Aaron used to refer to Gene as Haney's "Bo Bo" in jest. Everyone was aware of it. Perhaps he hadn't been preprogrammed to appreciate Gene's talent. This is understandable as Fred hadn't been present when Gene had his phenomenal successes, joining the Braves about the same time Gene had been left behind with a sore arm in spring training. That, coupled with the fact that Burdette and Spahn were having their own phenomenal successes now. Having an abundance of pitching talent afforded him the luxury of not having to struggle through with a sore armed pitcher. He probably saw Gene as being helpful to him in a relief capacity. No one will ever know for sure. Gene had never been a reliever and had been used only that way when it became absolutely necessary to hold a crucial lead. Now, being used

NEW YORK, April 28 ...Brave Killers ... Gene Conley, second from left, Milwaukee Brave pitcher, is congratulated by teammates in Polo Grounds dressing room yesterday. The happy warriors are, left to right, Bobby Thompson, Conley, Danny O'Connell and Hank Aaron. Thomson, O'Connell and Aaron hit home runs, 1955.

sparingly, combined with pure misfortune and disregard, Gene's confidence was slowly being eroded. In one of these fiascoes, after an afternoon of errors and bloop hits, (which once again denied him victory), Gene stormed into the clubhouse where buckets and assorted paraphernalia were kicked and strewn about. Finally settling into a full blown "frump", he noticed that Lew Burdette, while the game was still in progress, had walked in. Lew said, "don't worry Gene, it's only a ballgame, you'll get 'em next time". His sympathy so moved Gene that tears welled up in his eyes, which he remembers with gratitude even to this day.

The more Fred kept him on the bench, the more he found solace with the guys at the many bars and clubs on the road. It was during the All Star break, in the middle of one of those protracted hot and humid summers which had just about worn everyone down, that we thought of the perfect escape. Since few homes came equipped with air conditioning in those days, (certainly ours wasn't), we thought it an excellent idea to travel north to Lake Geneva.

The lake was refreshing and we all luxuriated in its cool waters and afterwards, finding a beautiful old Inn, we settled in to have dinner on its large verandah. As if it were beautifully planned, a sudden rush of cooling wind blew in from Canada to transform the heavy oppressive air into blessed cool perfection. Unfortunately we woke a little late that next morning. The previous ten nights had been fraught with sleeplessness because of the heat and humidity. Mr. Haney had called a practice that morning which meant that Gene would be a little tardy. He called to speak to Fred so as to explain his soon to be, late arrival. Mr. Haney wasn't available at the time so he spoke to Joe Taylor, the Braves Club House supervisor. He asked him to relay the message that he was with his family at Lake Geneva and might be a little late but not seriously late. Not even dropping us off first, he rushed into the clubhouse to suit up. Joe said, "Gene I hate to say this, but

Fred said to tell you, not to suit up as he didn't want you to practice or to be on the field today and that it would cost you $50.00".

In other words, he didn't want Gene nor was he going to be using him in the near future.

This only produced more apprehension. Gene always showed mental and physical toughness when the circumstances demanded it but this was new, being rejected by one's own manager. Rather akin to being dismissed from ones own family. A player can take a blistering reprimand from his manager but being ignored hurts, hurts a lot. A player in the fifties was totally dependent on his manager and looked to him as an almost godlike figure. Thus, in an attempt to make it all go away, especially the bad breaks and infrequent starts, a serious drinking problem began to emerge. Which came first, the drinking which caused the bad breaks or the bad breaks which contributed to his drinking. Whatever it was, it only exacerbated his problem with Fred. These were the beginnings of the days of wine and roses.

Statistically, if you are fortunate enough to get around forty starts per year, chances are, if you are a decent pitcher, you will win your twenty. That year, Fred's philosophy was to use nine starters, only giving Burdette and Spahn their 38 and 40 starts. Four of the starters were given anywhere from sixteen to twenty starts. Bob Buhl and Gene were given 10 and seven respectively during the entire summer of 1958. In the middle of summer, headlines meant to shock and amaze, blazed across most of the papers in the country. I suppose I should have been stunned or suspicious but I remember being only slightly amused. The story was out of Hollywood but the wire services carried it back to Milwaukee.

"Braves Playboys invade Hollywood mansion". "Starlets thrown into the pool by 'Braves' Playboys." "Police were summoned".

This debacle started one afternoon in LA with a day off. Del Rice, one of the Braves' catchers, commandeered Red Schoendienst, Frank Torre, Lew Burdette, and my all time favorite hero, Gene. Some Hollywood producer who lived in Beverly Hills had invited Del to his home for a luncheon and had asked him to bring any or all of his teammates. Road trips, especially travel days, are rather boring for the player, contrary to the lurid tales reported by gossips then and now. After seeing the LaBrea Tar Pits and watching the races at Santa Anita, there really wasn't that much else left in LA to see so this diversion sounded just about right. As it turned out, it was a party resplendent with a number of starlets accompanied by their agents.

Boys being boys, one thing led to another as the afternoon wore on. Outside, someone had thrown one of the "wanna bees" into the pool. This wasn't the only problem the host had. At the same time, Gene had already found mischief of his own in the living room. Some big clown had challenged him into a full Indian Wrestle. This was equal to offering candy to a baby. The two combatants took their positions on the floor next to the producer's light colored antique grand piano. As Gene explained it, they struggled for a short while and then when Gene pitched this big guy up, over and into the piano leg, the force caused rather a large chunk to be dislodged which in turn, seriously compromised the piano's stability. The break caused the rest of this nine foot beauty to come crashing down at which point the gendarmes were called in to restore peace.

Our delinquents made haste in Del's "rental" realizing it wasn't prudent to remain. I can't imagine that their welcome was still valid in any case. Dreading Haney's wrath and after imbibing that long afternoon, Gene began to berate himself inside Del's "rental". Out of frustration, he hit the dashboard with such force, his right hand and finger sustained hairline fractures. The dashboard didn't look so good either. Del Rice told the leasing agent that someone had tried to break into the car. The agent looked it over carefully and finally said, "looks to me like someone was trying to break ***out*** of the car".

The affair had been great PR for the starlets but bad news for the World Champion Braves. Today, this sort of event would've been fodder for every sport's talk show in the country, even CNN and certainly ESPN but in the latter part of the fifties, this sort of thing was hushed as sport's writers respected the player's privacy. They were frequently part of such episodes as players and media shared a common camaraderie. These two institutions were socially inclusive, drinking shoulder to shoulder, with the celebrity was a common occurrence for the print media. This was before free agency and money separated these two entities.

But Fred was not amused.

As mentioned before, this couldn't have come at a worse time for Gene. The little manager couldn't really rake Burdette, Schoendienst, Rice or Torre over the coals as these were the seasoned heroes of the World Series but Gene, being the youngest and already in the dog house, was "meat". The next day, whether he was aware of Gene's injury or just his hangover, perhaps with vindictiveness, Fred decided to use him in relief which only fattened his earned run average as his hand and head were in no shape to help anyone.

Gene didn't see another "start" the rest of the season and to humiliate him further, he was used in batting practice. Whether this was Fred's idea of "tough love" or his just being a dolt, Gene had made up his mind never to play for him again. Gene kept his six losses without a victory and the Braves lost the World Series to the Yankees. And the bizarre Hollywood incident was only one of many, Gene often found himself involved in.

Quite innocently, he became part of many odd occurrences which put him in the wrong place at the wrong time. In 1956, Red Murff, a 35 year old seasoned minor league pitcher, in the middle of his rookie year in the Majors, had just lost a 12 inning game in relief, against Brooklyn. (Red later became the scout who signed Nolan Ryan and wrote about this incident in his book, ***"The Scout"***.) Gene was only 26 at the time but had heard about a late night Italian restaurant on one of his previous trips to New York. Meaning to cheer Red up a bit, Gene invited him to an early breakfast around 2:00 a.m.

After alighting from a cab and on entering the vestibule of this large restaurant, three thugs were actually punching and kicking some woman who was cowering in the corner. The maitre d' was just standing there motionless.

Quoting from "The Scout", *"Hey what are you doing there?", Gene yelled, "you don't do that"*.

Looking up at the 6' 8" giant and Red's 6' 3" frame, the three, in shock, stopped suddenly as the woman escaped into the night. That dispatched, the two found a booth and settled in to devour their huge order, thinking that was that.

"Youse guys shouldn't have stuck ya nose inta sumthin' thet wuz nun uh ya bizness" the tough guy growled as he made his way to their booth."

Gene doesn't remember doing it but in Red's book Red said,

"Gene stood up slowly, stretching like a monolith, almost to the ceiling of this Italian joint. He towered over his accuser and stared down into his beady little eyes, Conley appeared poised to take this guy apart."

"You shouldn't beat up a woman," he drawled menacingly."

Red went on to say, *"About that time I noticed the slender guy putting his hands in his pockets. I decided these three were gangsters and fingered the smallest one as the group's hired gun. So being the brash country boy I am, I walked over to the supposed triggerman as Conley and Mr. Tough Guy continued their less than amiable conversation."*

All Gene remembers about the incident was that when Red informed him of the guy's holster and gun protruding out from under his jacket, he was so rattled, he was barely able to swallow the rest of his scrambled eggs.

Gene does remember Red saying something like, "Look here you guys, we play for the Milwaukee Braves baseball team and Mr. Perini wouldn't like it, you threatening us, nor would the Gambino Family". That last statement rather took them aback and they retreated out onto the street.

The maitre d' who had previously been frozen, told them that the little guy with the gun was "Johnny D", one of the biggest enforcers in town. He suggested they call a cab as the gangsters undoubtedly would be waiting out there and it wouldn't be healthy walking back to the hotel.

This was a whole new world to Gene. It was a common occurrence, especially in New York, that on the days he pitched, he would usually get a call asking how he felt that day. Being naturally friendly and obliging would tell them, whoever they were. Later, finding out they probably were gamblers, learned to hang up.

He has had his history with the Mafia. A few years out of both baseball and basketball, in the early 70's, headlines and TV news announced that Gene, Bob Cousy of the Celtics and Babe Pareilli of the "N.E." Patriots, were accused of fixing scores when they played.

As most mature readers of sports and political news will probably recall, in 1972, Joseph (Barbosa) Baron, the "animal", strongman for organized crime, had been testifying before the House Committee on Crime. They were investigating the underworld's influence in sports. He also implicated Frank Sinatra as a "front" for Raymond Patriarca of Providence, RI in the ownership of several hotels, along with implicating a Providence construction company.

In the Providence Journal of May 25, 1972, it quoted from Barbosa's testimony, *"Tameleo met late 1964 or early 1965 with Gene Conley, then a center for the Boston Celtics basketball team, and Babe Perilli, a quarterback for the Boston Patriots football team, at the Ebbtide, a night spot in Revere, MA. Immediately after the meeting Baron said, 'Tameleo told him that the Los Angeles Lakers were going to win a scheduled game with the Celtics 'by four points.' Baron followed Tameleo's advice to bet on the game, the Lakers 'won by four and Baron won $100.00, he said.'"* It was also quoted that *"Bob Cousy who was then a forward for the Celtics had meetings with Tameleo."*

Bob Cousy retired in 1964 and was never a forward. In 1964 and 1965, Gene was working as an executive salesman for a company in New York so he couldn't have been involved with shaving points. His last year with the Celtics was 1961, finishing up with the NY Knicks in 1964 and as Gene recalled in the American Record, *"Even if I was still playing, four points wouldn't have helped the Lakers in the playoffs as the Celtics won all three games in Boston."* He was at that time, however, entertaining clients and company officers at Celtic games. He does remember going to the "Coliseum" an after hours club near the Garden for a bite afterwards but never to Revere. The Coliseum, he found out later, was allegedly Mafia owned and operated.

Red Auerbach was interviewed by George Sullivan, then with the Boston Herald Traveler and his remarks were adamant, *"This whole thing is ridiculous. I know Conley as well as I know anyone, and his integrity is beyond reproach. He's a happy-go-lucky guy, always joking and perhaps a bit naive. And if he indeed talked to this person as has been claimed, then Gene obviously didn't know who the guy was...simply a case of somebody saying, 'Hey, I want you to say hello to a friend of mine'. That happens all the time to people in sports...everyone wanting you to say hello to some friends of theirs. If it turns out that person is an undesirable, you can look bad in a strictly innocent situation. So this is a terrible slap in the face to one of the great all-around athletes and nice guys of our time, and it disturbs the hell out of me."*

Channel 5 came out for an intensive interview as did newsprint people. Our phones were tapped for awhile, and most people accepted his protestations but as always, there will be those who hang on to such scandal as gospel just because it was in the papers.

Barbosa, anxious to get out of prison any way he could, used any high profile players in the New England area he could think of at the time.

Getting back to nineteen hundred and fifty eight, this indeed, was turning out to be an interesting year, if not unquestionably the most disappointing. As it had been in 1957, when Gene pitched the game in relief that clinched the pennant, Gene was in relief when the Braves cinched it in 1958. However, unlike 1957, at the end of the 1958 season, he was in the negative with 6 losses and the Braves lost to the Yankees in the World Series.

CHAPTER 20

THE DAYS OF WINE AND ROSES

"They are not long, the days of wine and roses: Out of a misty dream Our path emerges for a while, then closes. Within a dream."

Ernest Dowson

There was a bright side to 1958. Starting from the bottom, left only one direction in which to go.

Winning Baseball's World's Championship in 1957, had left us in a state of euphoria. Though we could have been delusional, we felt our four room luxury apartment, perfection. The other three couples in our building didn't share our contentment.

Having one child had barely been tolerated but after Kitty came, the responses to our light-hearted greetings were not exactly met with the same degree of cheer. We could handle that but with the arrival of Kelly, our third edition, made it unbearable for them. Our landlord gave notice.

So it came about that by the end of that 1958 summer, we had almost completed our first real home in Elm Grove, Wisconsin. The landscaping and the planned porch off the glass sliders were still missing but we had managed the mortgage. Now, our hearts were failing us for fear. The mortgage and all the accompanied mysteries of home ownership brought about a new dimension to our

189

John Lang (batting practice pitcher),
Jimmy Stewart (on location
"The FBI Story"), Gene and
Mervyn Leroy, Director - 1958

lives. The certainty of a cut in contract, the uncertainty of remaining with the Braves, the building costs exceeding the builder's advertised quote, along with the disappointment of losing to the Yankees left us floundering and very nearly broke.

We had promised Mom, during the Series, that in appreciation for her baby-sitting duties we would show her Mackinaw Island in Michigan's upper peninsula. I had been so involved with the children and the domestic side of life that I was oblivious to the possible doom that could engulf us. Looking back on this period, I can almost visualize this little black cloud hovering over us wherever we journeyed.

We had traveled about a hundred miles from Elm Grove when Gene, in one of his rare silent moods, suddenly stopped the car. He got out and went to a phone booth which had Mom and I understandably bewildered. After a short conversation he came back and said, "Katie we can't go anywhere, I'm going to Boston to play for the Celtics".

Okay. When Gene speaks, everybody listens in this family. We turned around, took Mom to the airport and Gene packed his foot locker. This meant the children and I would maintain the home in Elm Grove while he set up residence in Boston.

One important detail Gene had left out. Red had informed him, during that short phone conversation, that he didn't need him and that he doubted he could make the team after his five year layoff from basketball. Not only that, he now had Tommy Heinsohn, who had just won the NBA's "Rookie of the Year", Bill Russell, Frank Ramsey and Jim Loscutoff. In other words, Gene's positions were sufficiently filled. He reluctantly gave into Gene's "try-out" but informed him in no uncertain terms, that he not only had to pay his way to Boston but, if he didn't make the team, he would also have to pay his own way back. His sudden departure

Eddie Mathews, Gene and Joe Adcock
Another Braves Victory - Ed and Joe Hit Home Runs
Gene received the victory - 1957

back in 1954 hadn't endeared him to Red for sure. When he arrived at Logan, he grabbed a cab to the Garden, foot locker in tow. Upon reaching Mr. Brown's office, he took that foot locker and shoved it across the floor and then walked in to find Mr. Brown and Red.

"Well, Red, it looks as if Gene is planning on staying".

However, Gene knew he had a long way to go. His legs were soon suffering from shin splints and his feet were starting to form blisters the size of silver dollars again. As it had been in 1954, the trainer worked his magic with his trusty needle and black thread weaving in and out of open blisters providing room in which body fluids could ooze each night. In the morning, an antiseptic and patch would be applied to begin the same routine until the threading commenced once more. A little primitive to say the least. His past experiences before the 1952 and 1954 seasons proved to him that it would finally work but the pain was no less intense. Jock Semple ran him through another season of accelerated training. Gene forced himself furiously to run up and down the steps of the Garden over and over as this time, his competition was much keener. With only eight teams in the NBA, if a player wasn't exceptional, he was out. His feet continued to bleed and as it had been in previous late training schedules, his temperature would rise each night and soup again, became his sustenance. There were four hungry mouths to feed besides his own and now a house to finish so it had to be accomplished.

His new residence was the Hotel Lenox where Red had and did live, during several seasons. Red's permanent home was in Washington D. C. This wasn't anything novel for Red, he thought it quite normal to live away from home.

Some people move away from discouragement and challenge. I honestly believe that some, like Gene, need "challenge" to enliven their talents. Being held down as he had been for much of the '58 baseball season just made him more determined to succeed in basketball.

Red took him along when the team traveled to Pittsfield, Massachusetts for an exhibition game. Gene scored seven points without a warm-up, surprising even Red and a reporter asked Gene, "Are you thinking about quitting baseball?"

"You kidding? I'd never quit baseball. My arm never felt better this year. If I had arm trouble I might have given it some thought but I haven't and I want to get back to baseball next spring."

"Conley who has been out of basketball for five years, remarked, 'My legs were good and sore. I've got to get back in shape.' "

Again, in another article, *"Baseball pitcher Gene Conley of the Braves contributed eight points as the Boston Celtics beat the Cincinnati Royals, 100-85, in a National Basketball Association exhibition game Friday night at Franklin, Massachusetts."* Followed the next day by the headlines, ***"Braves to Consider Conley Cage Pact."***

After that, they hounded General Manager John Quinn much as they did five years before. *"John Quinn reiterated Friday that the club had not given Conley permission to play basketball but had told him it did not approve."*

'What our action will be regarding Conley's flouting of a section of his baseball contract will not be determined until Joseph Cairnes (president), Birdie Tebbetts (executive vice-president) and I have had a chance to discuss the matter thoroughly', Quinn said. 'To my knowledge, there never has been a similar case to set a precedent'.

Quinn went on to say, '*Conley has a standard "uniform player's contract" with the Braves, which presumably is valid until January 15, 1959. One clause reads: "The player and the club recognize and agree that the player's participation in other sports may impair or destroy his ability and skill as a baseball player. Accordingly the player agrees that he will not engage in professional boxing or wrestling, and that, except with the written consent of the club, he will not engage in any game or exhibition of football, basketball, hockey or other athletic sport."* It would be very difficult to prove or disprove the club's assertion or their credibility as there had never been a contract copy given out to the player during this era.

In reply, Gene was quoted as saying, *"I'm certainly not going to make an issue out of it. I feel great now. As far as I'm concerned, NBA basketball is the best in the world and I think the Celtics are the best basketball team in the world."*

Coach Red Auerbach declared that, *"Conley looks fine thus far but lacks experience while away from the game these last five years. Gene can make the difference on this team. Conley would be in the Celtics line-up when they open their National Basketball Association season against the Knickerbockers in New York Saturday night."* This was the first time he had heard he had made the team.

Back on the "Braves Ranch", John Quinn was replying to all of this, *"He hasn't asked permission and I would not give him permission if he asked. I don't believe baseball and basketball mix. I don't like to see players in whom we have investments take part in anything where there is a risk of injury."*

The nature of this controversy waged on, *"Conley reached by telephone said, 'I agree with Mr. Quinn, when he told me he didn't think the two sports would mix. I don't think they do either if you play both full time, but I just want to play basketball this winter. Considering how little I pitched the last two and a half months of the season, I think it's the best thing for me. The Celtics have given me permission to leave on February 15th, in plenty of time for spring training."'*

The Milwaukee writers questioned the Braves' star catcher, Del Crandall, about Gene's inability to win during the shortened 1958 season. *"Strange as it may seem, big Gene was faster this year than any pitcher on the Braves' staff--I'd have to hand it to Conley. Why didn't he have a good year? You tell me.*

Whenever the big guy was called on to pitch, he got beat every way imaginable. I don't think he got a good break anytime out there. But wait until next year. He's got a very good chance of coming back, because he has the stuff to do it."

Gene's remarks on this issue, *"In my mind I'd be wasting time if I didn't keep active in one or another over the winter. I never felt so good in my life as I did in '53 after I played with the Celtics the last time. I had my best year, too, with 23 wins and 9 loses with Toledo."*

"Conley pointed out that he had not signed a contract with the Celtics. 'I haven't even made the club yet', he added, "Remember this is the team that won the world championship two years ago and finished second last year."

"Conley who will be 28, November 10, played 39 games with the Celtics in 1952-53. He quit after the training season the following fall. The 1958-59 campaign will open Sunday."

"Big pitcher Signs to Play in NBA Despite Objections of Baseball Club".

Amid all this confusion, the Braves decided that since intimidation hadn't worked with Gene, they'd make the best of things as in the papers the next day after the Celtics signed Gene to a $20,000.00 contract, *"Why was Gene Conley permitted to play pro basketball in violation of his baseball contract? Someone wanted to know." "Conley is an exceptional case," Birdie replied promptly. "He had his greatest season in baseball the year he played basketball. He feels he'll be a better player this year for having done the same thing."*

Then out of the blue,

"GENE CONLEY EYES BIG BROADWAY ROLE"
by: George Clarke

"The complicated career of Gene Conley, six-foot-eight-inch addition to the Boston Celtics and the principal in a recent tug-of-war between the Celtics and the Milwaukee Braves, for whom he pitches betimes, has now been further involved by what looks like a first rate chance for him to become the star of a new Broadway show.

Gene, who probably thinks that Stanislavsky, the Russian master of the drama, is a town in Siberia, has been informed by a reputable New York theatrical agent that he is being considered for the principal part in "THE TALL STORY", newest comedy from the pens of Howard Lindsay and Russell Crouse, two top men in the theater.

Admittedly considerably confused by the whole thing, Gene has been in communication with the agent, has been told what it is all about: and even as you read this, is waiting for the next move.

What will happen after that, with contracts in force with both the Celtics and the Braves, remains to be seen.

However.... First inkling of what is going on came in a letter from JoVan Patten in the office of Kenneth Later, one of the most important agents in show business.

The letter informed him that he had been suggested for the part of the hero in the comedy, which has to do with an over-size country boy, self-conscious because of his height, and who plays basketball for a small college. The suggestion had been taken up with the authors, the producer and the director with a favorable re-action, and would he please get in touch with her.

Gene was inclined to dismiss the whole affair--after all, he has just come out of that wrangle between the Celtics and the Braves, who, for a time, refused him permission to play basketball during the winter months--and he felt that he had had enough of such matters.

Such was the situation when Your Reporter encountered him at a pre-opening get-together in the new Red Garter Room at the Lenox and EXPLAINED ROLE TO HIM:

When it was explained to him "that if he got the role it could mean a year (two years), even more on Broadway for more money per week than he had ever received: that Lindsay and Crouse are the authors of such all-time hits as "Life With Father," Arsenic and Old Lace," "Call me Madam," and, last season's "Happy Hunting," he began to take notice.

He called Miss Van Patten on the telephone.

She was pleased to hear from him. Confirmed all the facts in the letter and told him to wait for further word.

"But mam", said Gene, "I can't act!"

"That," said she, "is exactly the kind of a young man we're looking for!" Elated, but still confused, Gene went off for an afternoon nap explaining: "We've an inter-squad game tonight in Framingham, and I'll be chasing Bill Russell around all evening...and I need my rest."

Broadway, for the time being, at least can wait.

This journey into Never Never Land had a short shelf life as Bob Wolf of the Milwaukee Journal reported three days later, *"Gene Conley who spends his summers pitching for the Braves and who currently is playing basketball for the Boston Celtics has passed up a chance to add acting to his list of accomplishments."*

"On radio station WRIT, Joe Taylor, sports director on his daily radio sports show confirmed this with Mrs. Conley. 'Gene was thrilled by the offer', she said, 'but if he accepted it he would have to stay out of sports for two years more. He also thought about the hassle involved and decided it would be best to forget about the idea..he had been inclined to dismiss the offer even though the authors, producer and director all consider him fitted for the part.' "Miss Van Patten was especially enthusiastic as she had told him that Conley's Oklahoma accent was 'just beautiful'.

Just after signing his contract, Red was reported in the evening paper, *"Conley would be in the lineup when the Celtics opened their National Basketball Association campaign Saturday night at New York against the Knicks. Conley who can jump higher from a standing position than can the fabulous 6'*

10" Bill Russell, has been jumping center and tapping the ball to big Bill in exhibitions. If it works the way it has been, the Celtics have a potent new weapon in setting up their plays."

In the papers the next day, Frank Ramsey added his observations, *"If Gene wants, he can be the best ball player on our club."* In actuality, Gene was used primarily as a "role" player and always took a secondary position. This was fortunate as this proved the only way he managed to survive both sports, not to mention that seven on that Celtic team are in Basketball's Hall of Fame, and three were chosen the NBA's top 50 players of all time.

From almost the beginning, Gene gained a new nickname with the Celtics. He had already acquired the handle, "Stretch" from Henry Aaron. Under the brooding shadows of the "L" train, stood the old Boston Garden, grungy with years of caked on grime as was anything that came in contact with it. The "scalpers", mostly of Italian descent would yell out, "Hey Gino" as he approached for each practice and game, knowing full well that "Gino" would return their greeting. Johnny Most, the Celtic's gravelly voice sportscaster took it a step further and christened him, "Jumpin' Gino".

With the publicity concerning the Braves/Celtic controversy along with the added attraction of the Broadway offer, the television industry started picking up on his celebrity and the children and I were able to see "uncle daddy" on the networks. "Uncle Daddy" was the handle Bill Russell amusingly referred to him. He was on "What's My Line" and "To Tell the Truth", two very popular game shows of the late fifties as well as the Gillette commercials of the early sixties. Mr. Brown remarked to Gene one day, "Gene you get more publicity than Ted Williams in this town."

These were the days before the phenomenon of the sport's agent. Gene received calls from companies like Gillette and with each solicitation, a compliant sport's personality responded cheerfully. His affirmative reaction was always the same, from corporate marketing executives, to charities, to print/electronic media types down to the local boy scout troop's weekly meetings. Restaurants called offering dinner and cash just for his appearance. However, one time was enough as eating proved to be impossible. Even Gillette's offer of $500.00 for a series of televised shaving commercials on "Friday night Fights" was a little weak, even for those days. There truly is a place for sport's agents, just for the athlete's protection as the player was taken advantage of and would be today, without them. Though Red once remarked, soon after agents first came on the scene, "I'll never let an Agent see the light of day in my office!" Later on, when John Havelchik and then Larry Bird, brought theirs into the Celtics' offices, agents became a common denominator.

Along with the lucrative Celtic contract and the extra commercial monies, that little ominous black cloud that had been traveling along with us for most of 1958 was starting to dissipate, but, alas, not for long.

It was difficult financially, Gene in Boston living in a hotel and the children and I keeping up appearances in our newly acquired chateau in Elm Grove, not to mention the emotional toll which in some ways, was more devastating.

However, we seemed to be coping. Then the other shoe dropped. Red came to Gene one day soon after some of the notoriety had died down and said,

"Gene, what did you do to Walter Brown?"

"What do you mean Red?"

"You took advantage of Walter, this club can't afford your salary. We're going to have to let you go."

On Christmas Eve of 1958, Gene was cut from the squad. Merry Christmas. His instructions while letting him go, were to keep in shape. The media reported that at least, Gene would continue to draw his salary (completely fabricated of course) and that the Celtic's attendance had been down. In the late fifties, attendance was always "down" no matter how superb the club performed.

Gene's sudden arrival Christmas morning stunned me as I hadn't a clue up to that point that things like this could happen. Not only that, I had just purchased numerous gifts to put under the tree.

"Don't worry Katie, Red will be calling in about three days. And so it was as if on schedule, Gene received his orders three days later, to report immediately but that his contract would now be cut in half. We were in no position to quibble as half was better than none.

We both learned a valuable lesson from this experience. We had never had anything like this happen to us before. I'm sure that in the early days of baseball, this sort of thing had been common as well, but we had never experienced it before. With a young and struggling NBA, we reasoned that our philosophy would have to be adjusted accordingly and before signing anything from now on, we would have to expend a great deal of thought and precaution before signing another NBA contract.

Actually, 1958 had many lessons to benefit from. During those long months of being part of a baseball team, not being able to play, had built up a great deal of pent up emotion. The culture of that era, especially in baseball, was to see how "macho" a man could become. There were stories of past players like Babe

202

Ruth, Ty Cobb, Paul Waner and those of that ilk who played hard and partied hard. Their lifestyle was admired. Paul Waner who is in the Hall of Fame told Gene a story about their road trips to Chicago. Most ballparks had night games which allowed players a late morning wake up call but not in Chicago.

One day, "Big Poison" (Paul Waner) came to the plate barely able to function. Gabby Harnett (Hall of Fame catcher who played 19 years for Chicago), said "P, turn around and look at me." Paul swung around, squinting through slits where his eyes should have been. "Oh, Hell, you've been out all night and you'll for sure get 4 for 4".

Gene had been a two fisted drinker before 1958. College was just one round of drunkenness. During the '58 baseball season, it seemed that every time he pitched, every "baseball way" to lose a game, came to pass. This didn't improve his drinking habits as he was being prevented from redeeming himself with his athletic prowess. His imbibing was only of longer duration. On the "road" Gene's notoriety was being established as well as embellished as he was starting to put everyone under the table. The famous broadcaster, Curt Gowdy, years later was attending a banquet of some sort and said to Gene, "you know Gene, you must have been the strongest athlete that ever lived".

"How's that Curt?"

"Well, Gene, no one could have played both of those sports at the same time while drinking the amount you did." Suffering from hangovers on the field was the norm.

With the Celtics, however, he knew he had to keep a lid on it. With all the publicity he garnered wherever he went, he still had to produce and to prove to Red and his teammates he was a legitimate contender. This forced him to rethink his former philosophy. Gene respected Red as the team's leader, everyone feared Red, each Celtic knew that this was a dictatorship and felt confident that he was at the helm against the competition. Gene would have done anything to garner Red's respect and during this period, Gene learned to be an aggressive player. Rebounding was Gene's forte. He certainly could score but there were about nine other guys who could as well. Red's theory was that you couldn't score unless you got the ball. He has always made a point in conveying that the Celtics never had anyone, during his reign of championships, who "placed" in the top ten in scoring. So Gene was a credible asset. Every game during the season was like a playoff game as with only eight teams in the NBA, each was talent laden and the second team could easily hold any lead gained by the starting five. There were no "blow-outs" in the league. The games were not decided until the final seconds. The Celtics disliked playing in Syracuse as it was a tough crowd. This only produced a tougher Red. He intimidated, he agitated, he irritated.

One time during a tight and ferocious fray in Syracuse, one fan got so infuriated with Red's haughtiness that he made it onto the floor and slugged him which brought every player to his rescue. The Celtics each took turns pummeling this poor audacious fan who countered with quite a lawsuit. The arena was so small the crowd was able to touch the players as they ran off the floor. Frank Ramsey had worked up the Syracuse crowd to the point of riot one time. As Frank ran through the tunnel to get off the floor, one fan leaned over and grabbed him around the neck and held him there in mid air. Without thinking, Gene slugged the fan as it was clear the fan was determined to kill Frank which brought on another lawsuit. St. Louis was no better, pelting Red with fresh eggs. When departing the floor once, an enraged St. Louis fan yelled at K. C. Jones, "you dumb nigger". Red stopped everyone, looking up at the fan said, "You want a piece of him?" "Come on down and have at it." Needless to say, there was no challenge that night.

Red's reputation has followed him to this day. On the brink of tying his record for most NBA Championship wins, Phil Jackson, coach of the L.A. Lakers, talked with glee about besting Red's mark as it would have pleased his old Knick coach, Red Holzman, recently deceased. In our struggle to gain a NBA pension for those players who played before 1965, we used to get letters from the NBA Oldtimers venting their hatred of Red. Red was a brilliant "baiter" and their anger had not abated in all those years. His opponents absolutely despised Auerbach's arrogance but his players luxuriated in his supremacy. Opposing players especially hated his audacious habit of pulling out a cigar with a grand flourish as the Celtics pulled ahead and then smoked it with relish as they fumed. The referees were in his pocket as well for any call against the Celtics brought on foot stomping, expletives and name calling which embarrassed and intimidated their psyche no matter how tough their demeanor seemed to be. I believe that Red had an odd sort of love for his players in the locker room but once on the floor he turned into one of the world's greatest thespians with his unfeeling manner.

DADDY WAS UP AGAINST A BIG HITTER

Gene Jr., Kelly, Katie and Kitty
Celtic Play-Offs - Boston Gardens - Watching Wilt Chamberlain's
Philadelphia Warriors - 1959

CHAPTER 21

NEW BEGINNINGS

Up until the start of the '58/'59 NBA season, Gene had merely played the games. Auerbach's mastery at managing players changed a less than aggressive athlete into a more resolute performer. He was among giants of the game figuratively and physically. For the first time he was comfortable with his contemporaries. Their size and their intelligence encouraged the competitive side of his personality and inspired him to push the envelope. Every individual on that team was an energetic and vigorous machine. They didn't saunter to the scorer's table, they ran to it.

There have been stories reported that Gene was Bill Russell's "back-up" which has begun to have a life of its own and its basis, pure fabrication. If a reporter worth his salt would think about it, if Bill averaged 46 minutes per game, a game being 48 minutes, that would mean Gene averaged 2 minutes per game. Since Gene averaged approximately 7 points and 7 rebounds per game, that would mean that Gene would have had to be some kind of phenomenal genius to do that in 2 minutes. His average playing time per game was around 18 minutes. Usually, when playing with Russell, Gene would take the post position and Russell the corner or forward position when the Celtics were on defense, especially when Chamberlain came to town. Chamberlain's average was 50 points per game. It was Gene's job to try and position himself in front of Wilt, (which was a battle in itself), in order to prevent one of Chamberlain's teammates from lobbing the ball over to him. A routine pass to Chamberlain gave Russell or Heinsohn the time and opportunity to intercept the pass and be off and running. It was a foregone conclusion that if Gene failed to gain that position in front of Wilt, it was an automatic two points for Wilt, as he simply turned and dunked. On offense, Russ and Gene would reverse their positions.

The referees seemed to concentrate on this baseball player trying to play basketball. Gene's role was to play tough and get the ball at all costs which added up to an unusual amount of fouls, sometimes when he wasn't touching anyone or even near the play.

On one such evening at Madison Square Garden in New York, playing against the Knicks, Russ, playing center, Heinsohn and Gene at the corners on defense, Tommy, trying desperately to intercept, cut across the key and ran into a Knick who had possession of the ball. The whistle blew and a quick foul was called on #17, Gene's number. The Ref pointed in Gene's direction. Tommy's number was fifteen. Gene was at the opposite corner holding the loose ball.

Mindy Rudolph, running over to Gene said, "Gimme the ball!" Being quite innocent this time and getting tired of being used as a scapegoat and constantly harassed by eager referees, Gene protested, "I wasn't even in on the play, I was over here".

"You give me the ball or it's a Technical".

Once again, Gene protested, "No, I wasn't near the play".

Okay that's it, you've got the Technical and you're out of the game, give me the ball".

"You want the ball? Okay, here's the ball" and Gene made a motion as if to hand it over to Mindy but instead, pulled it back and made a forward pass into the upper balcony, never to be seen again.

By the way, the Celtics must have taken care of the fine as it never was taken out of Gene's paycheck and Red never commented on the incident. If anything, Gene felt it had pleased Red.

Basketball seemed to free Gene. It's a reactionary game. Baseball is a cat and mouse activity, not much room for the combativeness of raw emotion. In basketball, though, there's opportunity for less than sanctioned moves that can infuriate players to take extreme measures. In college, usually, you don't run up against such raw experiences of brazen effrontery that you find in the NBA so you either adjusted or got a day job.

Being baby faced and affable, I believe Gene was baptized early on with challenges which were not expected to be returned in like manner. Also, it could have been that being a baseball player playing their game, may have caused a little resentment with some.

On one such occasion, a Detroit player by the name of Wayne Hightower actually held Gene's arms behind him so as to prevent him from making a play. It wasn't caught by the ref but there was no need. Gene, who quickly whirled around, meaning to punch Wayne's lights out, missed and merely glanced a fist over his shoulder. Then, the ref noticed. Gene was asked to leave the floor.

Years later, when Gene was in the ABL, his New York Tapers were playing a week in Hawaii. The referees were a little less stringent and often let the players mix it up without calling too many fouls as it slowed up the game. Gene was at the foul line leaping up to tip the ball in after it had been missed, when 6'

11" Fred Sawyer, determined to impede this action, doubled up a fist and hit Gene square in the middle of his chest!

Gene came up from having the wind knocked out of him and let go with a flurry of fists. Fred had the reach on Gene, but not the passion, and finally, Fred fell to the floor. The other players actually formed a ring around them, shrinking away from the confrontation while the photographers flashed away. Finally, the refs discharged their duty and sent both players off the court. The team called in a Japanese doctor to examine Gene's right hand as that poor fist had met an immovable force that night. He sustained a fine hairline fracture across the top of his hand. The Japanese doctor kept shaking his head and saying, "why do you Americans always use your fists, you should always turn the open hand and strike on the outside of it as then it will not fracture so easily."

Just as they were discussing their ride to the hospital, Big Fred was in the door frame and growled, "Conley I want more of you". The doctor backed away and fists again flew until Big Fred, once again, lay on the floor. Gene was instructed at the hospital to wear the cast for six weeks. Playing with a full cast proved to be too annoying and one night, under warm running water, the cast became history.

In that same league, Bill Spivey who had been an All American from Kentucky under Adolph Rupp, who had been barred from the NBA for taking part in point shaving while in college, proved much too hazardous under the boards. His favorite was elbows to the chest. Not heeding Gene's warning to desist, Gene finally had enough and knocked him to the floor. Another Kodak moment was immortalized on the front pages of papers across the country. As Gene used to say, borrowing "Ali's" famous quote, "I float like a butterfly, sting like a bee", as Bill's blow had not been returned or at least, not landed.

Once, while Stan Studtz was coaching the Tapers and Gene was still with the Celtics, Red agreed to a scrimmage just before the Playoffs to sharpen their competitive edge. Leroy Wright of the "New York Tapers", who later became a great friend of Gene's, was being a bit over zealous about his performance. He was giving Russ a hard time so Red put Gene in and it wasn't long before Gene pushed him back and when Leroy's temper got the better of him, blows were struck. Red yelled to Heinsohn to break it up but Tommy's response was, "Red, I'm not getting in the middle of that". Later Red vowed he'd never again agree to having his players subjected to guys outside of the NBA.

Ray Felix, a New York Knick was a player that liked to mix it up and as it was with a lot of players in their last years of competition, had a number of "tricks" that irritated most centers in the league. His favorite, rather than go up for the ball on a "free throw", as his opposition jumped up for the "tip", would elbow his man severely in the chest while he was in mid air. Such was the case one night as Gene made his leap, Felix struck with such blatant force, Gene chased him all the way down the court, turned him around and struck him in retaliation which brought us another Kodak moment to digest in the papers the next morning. As the children and I hibernated in Milwaukee, I was starting to cringe each time the Milwaukee Journal was delivered.

Gene never started a confrontation but Red's preaching was not lost on any Celtic and each knew never to back down from bullying on the court. Walt Bellamey who was with the Chicago Zephyrs at the time, knocked Gene in the chest so hard once, he was floored for lack of breath and wasn't able to move until the teams had run back again. Another confrontation ensued after a chase. Woody Sauldsberry had developed a foul little habit of grabbing his opposition's arms as they tried to set up a pick. In Boston, he tried it with Gene as he tried setting a pick for Sharman. Gene warned him not to try it again but when they played the

Warriors the next time in Philly, Woody once again repeated this same move which brought immediate retaliation. However this time both Gene and Woody escaped being asked to leave as each sustained a double foul.

We didn't see much of Gene that winter or the subsequent winters for that matter but when they played at Milwaukee that first year following his Celtic return, it was with much anticipation and joy! Each time it was accompanied with a little dread as well. We cringed to see Gene's face, sometimes rearranged. Gene carries a little permanent bump on his well turned Irish nose, his little finger is permanently deformed from a tug of war with Bob Pettit and on various places on his hands and fingers, he carries calcium deposits from past breaks while playing? When I hear players talking about the "good old days" while playing in the NBA at All Star Weekends and Retired Players Association gatherings, I have to laugh watching all these players who so fiercely battled one another now hugging as if they had been bosom pals.

As the 1958/1959 season was drawing to its close, it was obvious that the Celtics were going to be in the playoffs. February 15th had come and gone, and the Celtics' broken promise of letting Gene leave on that date, was not lost on the Braves' organization. Gene had been staying with Frank Ramsey, his wife, Jean and their children in Newton. Lucky thing too as he contracted strep throat and if he had been alone in the hotel you wonder if he would have survived as his temperature shot up to 105 degrees one night. They called the team doctor who gave him shots and told him to rest and drink plenty of fluids, of course. This was just too much for Red who said he would give him only two more days to get back on the court. He did, carrying a temp of around 102 degrees, but report he did.

That same year, February 27, 1959, the Celtics, against the Minneapolis Lakers set a record that Gene was involved in (as was most the team). The Celtics defeated the Minneapolis Lakers, 173 to 139 which, to my knowledge, still exists as the highest scoring game ever played in the NBA. It wasn't long before the Braves Manager, Fred Haney was quoted as saying in disgust, *"What is he a baseball pitcher or a basketball player?"*

In Bradenton, the Braves' spring training headquarters, Mr. Perini, owner and CEO of the Milwaukee Braves was quoted as saying, *"We're so 'stacked up' with pitchers that he wasn't worried about the National League Champions' lone holdout, Gene Conley."*

"Who's worrying about Conley?" Perini asked, *"the only fellow who should be worrying about Gene is Conley himself."*

This controversy raged on. At the Giants spring training camp, Willey Mayes was quoted as saying, *"They say we (Giants) could win the flag if we got another good right-handed pitcher. If anybody asked me, I'd say we ought to get Gene Conley from the Braves. Everyone says he doesn't throw hard anymore, but I know that every time he faced me last season, he threw hard enough to get me out."*

At the same time, Bob Cousy was quoted as saying, *"Gene has shown great improvement. He's rapidly picking up confidence and has been learning fast. It's too bad Conley didn't stick with basketball. If he had, and lived up to his potential, he'd be a top player now."*

Back in National Baseball Land, *"it was reported that rival clubs had shown a surprising amount of interest in the unhappy right-hander who has ignored the lure of Florida sunshine to continue playing basketball with the Boston Celtics. General Manager John McHale who had just been made the new Braves General Manager was impressed".*

After that, Birdie Tebbits, the Braves' Vice President called Ramsey's home to talk with Gene.

"Gene, we're ready for you down here".

"Well, Birdie, I feel obligated here. It looks like we're going to be in the Playoffs."

"If you're not down here right away, you're out of a job."

Gene met with Red.

"Gene we need you, you can't go now, tell those baseball people to go to hell. Tell you what Gene, we'll give you an extra $2,000.00 to stay and with the playoff money and hopefully, the championship, you'd be making more than you would in baseball." (not quite but it would make up for a little of the $10,000.00 cut from his original basketball contract or the cut expected in his baseball contract) Frank Ramsey was in the kitchen when Birdie called again.

"Gene, why haven't you made reservations?"

"Well, Birdie, it's like this, the Celtics need me so bad that they're willing to give me $2,000.00 to stay on and along with the playoff money, that would translate into around $6,000.00 so I can't afford to be there for three weeks."

Frank's eyes were widening as in those days, owners and management were to be respected at all costs. As the story goes, Frank always signed his contract and told Mr. Brown, the Celtic owner, to just fill in the amount.

"If you stay for those playoffs, you won't be down here."

"Birdie, if you're saving a big bed down there for me, you better give it to someone else."

By then, Frank's mouth fell open as this just wasn't done in Kentucky. "Gene, I can't believe you said that to Mr. Tibbets!"

So that was how he was traded to the Philadelphia Phillies.

Since Gene wouldn't have wanted to play for Haney again anyway and would have had his salary cut a full twenty-five percent had he gone, was able to make Red happy by staying, the Celtics won the World's championship, which made all the Celtics happy, and Philadelphia was so happy that they picked up his previous year's contract without that salary cut. It was a wise financial move all around. Funny enough, it was John Quinn who had just been fired by the Braves and hired by the Phillies that made that trade to sign Gene.

Back at the ranch, before the playoff money or the promised $2,000.00 bribe, I was having a battle all my own. I was robbing Peter to pay Paul. One late winter day, our neighbor, Gladys Ronke was visiting me in the kitchen. There was a knock at the door. It was the telephone repair guy to take the phone off the wall. This was one of life's most embarrassing moments for me. It's bad enough struggling to keep things going in private but to play out your agony in front of one of your upscale neighbors is more than that, it caused actual pain. When Gene left to play for the Celtics that fall, we felt confident that with the $20,000.00 contract we could not only maintain but be able to save for the first time or finish the porch in any case. When Red cut the contract in half and with us having to live separately, we were put in serious debt.

Long distance communication caused our phone bill to skyrocket. It was difficult to cut Gene down to a few short sentences. These were the days when the actual phone instrument was rented from the phone company. My face must have blanched as our telephone repairman, sized things up at once and announced that since "you are leaving for more than a month, we have a policy that we remove the instruments from your walls and then when you return, we replace them". Well, that took care of my shame and Gladys, who went along with it, bless her soul, (whether she believed him or not), never mentioned it then nor has she since.

Just before the Playoffs started, Gene left instructions for me to pack for winter and spring, take Gene Jr. out of second grade and Kitty out of Kindergarten and fly with them and Kelly to Boston and then on to Leesburgh, Florida. The prospect of being with Gene, seeing the Celtics during the Playoffs and then flying down to Florida conjured up all sorts of excitement. I did as I was told with pleasure. I brought Little Gene's books and assignments with me to homeschool him for however long it took.

Boston in February, was like spring compared to the icy cold of Wisconsin and the children and I relished our long walks into the city from the Kenmore Hotel. The final Playoffs were so great ! Gene saw a great deal more action during the playoffs. We must have been quite a novelty act as each paper, of which there were five, had their own photographers, snapping pictures of the children and I watching Gene, the baseball player, play out this game of basketball. This felt rather bizarre, as not knowing the other wives and the thoughts that must have been running through their minds, made for a most uncomfortable feeling for me as their husbands were all "well established" Celtic players.

The famous World Champion Celtics' break-up dinner was another stranger than fiction event. It was held in some small dinning room of the Lennox Hotel as I recall. All the Celtics were present with Red, Mr. Brown and the other owner, Mr. Pierri. The team's wives' were invited as well and, as I remember, about two representatives from the media. That was it!

Another surreal moment. There were a few comments from Mr. Brown and Red and then, one by one, each player was asked to give their testimony. I say, "testimony" as religious testimonies of which I have been witness to, couldn't have been more heartfelt. "It is a thrill to be part of such an extraordinary organization or honor or whatever......" It was all so serious, almost spiritual as it was so quiet and reverent. Then, it was time for the media to have their say, all two of them. It went something like this, "well, I'm really a hockey man myself and I don't know much about this game of basketball...but I congratulate you all for being World Champions". I believe one covered baseball from the Christian Science Monitor.

A little disappointing as just a short year before, when the World Champion Milwaukee Braves had their break-up banquet, the huge hall was bedecked with flowers, an orchestra was playing, and just about every reporter and media personality in the midwest was present to mark this glorious occasion. The Braves, the following day had been feted with a cavalcade of open convertibles resplendent with bands, ticker tape and shouts from thousands of fans. I believe the governor, mayor and all the Politicos of Wisconsin were in attendance overlooking Lake Michigan.

Within a little over a year, Gene had World Championship rings in two major league sports which, so far has never been equaled.

Elm Grove, Wisconsin - 1960
Gene, Kitty, Katie, Kelly and Gene Jr.

CHAPTER 22

COMEBACK

At warp speed, bright and early the next morning after that bizarre "World Championship Banquet", the Conley Clan boarded a plane for Leesburgh, Florida.

All smiles and glowing from all that had transpired; the "trade" to Philadelphia, the Championship, prospects of an informal spring training, (as baseball season had already begun), just being together without strict scheduling held out promises of sorts. This type of adventure however, had never been tried. There was no guide book to direct our way. At the end of the basketball year in '52/'53, Gene had made baseball's spring training on time as his rookie year with the Celtics had been played out as a minimal role player. Not only that but the Celtic's run for the championship had been short lived. We hadn't a clue, in 1959, how this was going to work, nor did we realize that the next five to six years would prevent, not only a normal family life, but the luxury of training in both sports. Reporting late for each regulation year in both basketball and baseball meant shortened performance records. It would also prevent Gene from having a day off from this point forward until the end of his playing days unless, of course, as it is in baseball, the game would be rained out. It always amazes me now, to read in the papers how, in mid season, an athlete requires a week just to calm his nerves from the rigors of one year's season.

Two sport stars of the last couple of decades, have combined football with baseball as it is a logical proposition. The lag time between the end of the football season and baseball's spring training gives the athlete time to regroup, rest and prepare mentally as well as physically. With the recent lengthening of the basketball seasons as well as baseball's, I can't see how any future athlete will be able to replicate Gene's record in these two sports of twelve successive seasons in six years.

Gene was part of a brand new team but not part of their timetable, nor had he met his teammates, outside of Robin Roberts. Robbie had been a teammate on two previous All Star teams. Gene had this clean slate on which to write his new story line. This shortened period of time, preparing for another long hot baseball season meant not only missing regular spring training, but without teammates to practice with or bond to, no manager or coaches to learn from, no trainer to treat aching muscles, nor a traveling secretary to inform you, you were left entirely on your own. The locations for these private training sessions were below Major, or for that matter, Minor League caliber with only yourself to depend on. This was a "throw back" to when Gene, as a boy, would knock on doors to field a team. With all the injustices rampant in baseball at the time and being very close to being an indentured servant, he now realized that there had been a comfortable sort of security in that structured world of conformity. It was not only difficult to adjust to the idea of not being a "Brave" anymore but strangely enough, being without a media to critique what you were doing was a little disconcerting as well. We were let loose, lost at sea, our expectations, a mystery and for whatever fate had in store, we had to "just do it".

Leesburgh was an old, yellow, rotted out, moldy motel for the kids and myself as we didn't have a car or bus to transport us any place else. Their tiny pool in front, looked like the retirement home for every toad, frog and assorted vermin that had come to die. The weather was nice but keeping three active little people busy and happy was work! Gene was picked up each day by Andy Seminick, a former "Philly" who was to catch Gene each morning at the local park. Others drifted in from nowhere, just to be around an active Major League Player I presumed. The park was on the edge of a swamp and if the ball was hit too far into the deeper reaches of the outfield, Gene was warned not to retrieve it. This boggy area was known only as Alligator Alley, brimming with that species, only too anxious for a tidbit of hand or foot. Nine days couldn't go fast enough to get back to civilization.

Once again, the children and I were sent home. Being a professional ballplayer's wife had not changed much from the previous eight years of married life. By the time we returned to Milwaukee though, spring had done its magic and home, mortgage and all, was a beautiful blessed relief! Something was missing though. Being traded from the hometown team left a gaping hole in my heart. No longer did the Milwaukee Journal report the happenings of my favorite player. There was nothing about the Phillies, only the box scores. The Braves players' wives must have felt my pain as they planned a luncheon in my honor, a farewell luncheon. I was given a gold "charm" for my "player's bracelet". (Gold charm bracelets were mandatory jewelry for player's wives in those days.) It was inscribed, "we'll miss you". Enough to bring tears. Ah well ...

When Gene joined the Philadelphia team, it was already May, a little over a month into the season. The atmosphere of the clubhouse was warm and reassuring. The Phillie's manager, Eddie Sawyer, was quiet, dignified, and intelligent, and players like, Robin Roberts, Curt Simmons, Richie Ashburn, Harry Anderson, Gene Freeze and his old Milwaukee Brewer teammate, Wally Post, made him feel right at home. Most of these players were also Basketball fans which made it easier as well. They really wanted to know about the NBA and teased Gene with mock challenges to take him in the post. Eddie used Gene in relief in his first appearance. It was obvious he would have to earn his starting position. Against the Chicago Cubs team, he pitched nine shut-out innings, fanning eleven, two short of a Philadelphia record but had nothing to show for it but self-satisfaction as the team had already lost it in the first inning when he was brought in for "relief".

He got his "start" next time out in Pittsburgh, and adding to his previous 9 shutout innings, added another 8 scoreless innings before giving up a single and double for the lone run, striking out 7, walking none and helping his cause by driving in a run, scoring a run and hitting a pair of singles, winning it, 8 to 1. His first win of the season!! Only one problem, he came out in the ninth, being hit by a Smokey Burgess line drive through the middle. His index pitching finger was cracked and swelled so badly, he wasn't able to finish the last inning.

Drama time; his next outing was against his old teammates in Philadelphia. Many writers were busy amplifying the issue all out of proportion as they wondered how a last place club with a cast off pitcher would fare against the World's Champion Braves. I was still in Milwaukee, praying as usual. It was a magnificent game. Gene shut out his old teammates and immediately the reporters and photographers were like bees on honey.

"The new ace of the Philadelphia Phillies pitching staff could have hardly helped being happy after beating a club that had cast him away two months ago. But he also was cautious. 'Let's face it,' he said, 'The Braves have a great ball club and I'll have to go out against them again, so I'm not popping off. It's a good feeling just to win.' "

"They asked him if he had tried harder against the Braves than he might have against another club, Conley insisted that he didn't know. He did say, 'I

wouldn't say I slept as well last night as I usually do - I felt keyed up.' Aaron's comment was, 'He moved the ball real, real good, he was in and out, up and down. He hardly ever gave us a good pitch to hit.' Johnny Logan offered a different observation. 'He pitched good ball, all right, but his biggest asset was his desire to beat us.'" The telegrams we received after the two All Star games and World Championships were nothing compared to those we received after this particular game. I think the baseball fan, maybe all sport fans, love an underdog who gets his just desserts. We received telegrams from family members, our neighbors, strangers from Oklahoma, Washington State, Florida, Pennsylvania and even Milwaukee. Western Union joined the crowd by sending one that was signed, "Western Union Conley Fans" of all things. His most prized was one from Red, *"Good luck old boy. I'm rooting for you. Hope you have a great year. Call Russ Wylie K136303 Philadelphia as soon as you can. Regards, Red Auerbach."*

Much of the season, Gene was pitching fantastic ball. His teammates were so "for him" and they tried so hard behind his pitching. To be a part of this, I would drive our station wagon filled with our little group of enthusiastic little people, Gene, age 7, Kitty, 5 and Kelly, 2, all the way from Milwaukee to Philadelphia each home stand, staying at the Valley Forge Motel. Some of the players from the Philadelphia team would drop by just to spend the day and swim with us in the motel pool. It was such a loose group of former "Whiz Kids" who had won a World Series in 1950 and an entirely new group of cast off players like Gene. They were a last place club but "most interesting".

These were not ordinary players. There had been instances of downright legends told about some, one or two who carried revolvers on the road. Thus, the "Dalton Gang" moniker. Pranks of others; one, was to wait inside a hotel room until the sound of a key turned in the lock, hopping into a filled bathtub, face up, in a death trance, eyes wide open. This always invoked shock and panic as the unsuspected player tried to revive a deadpanned roommate until he broke up in laughter. The story of one disgruntled pitcher, not being used, being egged on by the other pitchers and players after a game, went in to Manager Sawyer's office to find out just why he wasn't pitching. He came out laughing, "You know what he told me when I asked him, 'Just what am I to this club anyway?'. He said, 'Best he could tell, I was the clubhouse clown.'"

"Gene Conley's selection to the National League All Star team gave the pitcher more satisfaction than he was willing to show on the surface. Ignored as a member of the champion Milwaukee Braves last season, when he was used infrequently and wound up with an 0-6 record, the 6'8" right-hander was determined to prove manager Fred Haney was wrong for not pitching him more often. To the big guy's credit, however, he never publicly criticized Haney. The fact that Haney, who will manage the National Leaguers, had the final say in picking him for the team, undoubtedly made Conley feel he has proved his point."
--- Allen Lewis, Philadelphia Enquirer.

Once, I had mentioned to Gene about some particular grievance Fred had perpetrated against him, he replied, "yeah, but I was a pain in the neck to Fred too. It was mainly my fault," referring to his bouts of inebriation. In spite of his regrets, in his third All Star game, he managed two perfect inning, striking out three, including the much famed hitter, Ted Williams in the process.

By the middle of July, he had his third shutout, blanking the Cards 11 to 0 and winning his seventh game of the season. At the end of July, he had won eight and had been listed with eleven other pitchers in the league as a possible candidate for the coveted "Cy Young Award". His hitting was as hot as his pitching records and by August, had recorded his 12th victory, a three hitter, but at a cost.

"Conley, the crane-tall pitcher, scored an expensive victory. Twisting to escape a pitch thrown by Glen Hobbie, he was slammed on the back of his pitching hand."

"The hand was swollen after the game and x-rays were scheduled today. Conley belittled the injury. 'I couldn't pick the ball up, so threw my hands up instinctively. The hand began to stiffen up during the game, so I was throwing to spots, mostly breaking stuff, sliders and curves--slow curves I've got to admit.'

It was an amazing performance for a guy with a hurt hand. After yielding back-to-back doubles to Tony Taylor and George Altman in the third, he held the Cubs to a single by Al Dark the rest of the way."

Another article appeared the following day, *"How Gene Conley managed to pitch through six innings against the Chicago Clubs Wednesday night with a broken right hand was explained today by Phillies' trainer, Frank Wiechec."*

'All it took,' he said, 'was a lot of guts.'

"The Phillies agree. They also say the amazing part was the fact that Conley not only stood up under the pain and torment after being hit by a Glen Hobbie fast ball in the third inning, but held the Cubs to one useless single through those six innings in posting his 12th victory, 4-1." 'Big Gene was hurting,' was Carl Sawatski's comment. "Carl was doing the catching at the time." 'But he wouldn't even think about leaving. All he said every time I talked to him was, 'I'm going to try and hang in there.'

"Upon examinations at Temple University Hospital, Gene learned that his middle metacarpal bone on his right hand had revealed, a half-inch fracture. Weichec kept spraying his hand with a solution for deadening the pain during those six remaining innings but he couldn't get any finger pressure on the ball.

Conley, as unassuming as he is tall...passed off the feat with his customary modesty."

'I gave them (the Cubs) the junk ball treatment' he said. 'My slow stuff got slower and slower.'

"Since metacarpal injuries usually require six weeks to heal, this means the big fellow is through pitching for the season, and that, according to Phillies' general manager, John Quinn, 'is a shame' Conley left for his home in Milwaukee."

Afterwards, we received several glowing articles about Gene's possible "Comeback Player of the Year" award.

Stan Hochman's column, under the headlines, *"Season Ends for Raw Courage Kid" "He defied Brave executives by playing pro basketball with the Boston Celtics last winter."*

'We didn't need a name,' Coach Red Auerbach says belligerently when asked about the use of Conley, 'we had plenty of names in Cousy and Russell and Sharman. Conley was a good basketball player, one who made the team on his merits.'

"But a nagging premonition of disaster colored his answer whenever you suggested that basketball might be the proper way for a pitcher to prepare."

'This is a long season,' he'd sigh, 'and anything can happen.'

"Now the season is over. It ended after he'd scored his 12th win with a team smothered in the basement for much of the campaign."

"Trainer Frank Wiechec, as parse with words as he is generous with pills, tape, gauze and diathermy, calls Conley's performance the other night 'raw courage.'

"His catcher, Carl Sawatski remarked, 'we were all in on his little secret. He'd tell us 'I just want to win 15, I want to have my best year.' And now the year was over."

4/9/59 - Minneapolis
Coach Red Auerbach of the Boston Celtics carried on shoulders of
Sam Jones, Jim Loscutoff, Tom Heinsohn and Gene Conley
Won World Championship, 118-113

CHAPTER 23

UP FROM THE ASHES

On returning to the home we had struggled to keep, we both realized that paying state income taxes in Massachusetts, Pennsylvania and Wisconsin didn't make a whole lot of sense so we put it up for sale. Even though we weren't sure where we would live on a permanent basis, we knew being separated as we were, was just too ridiculous, both financially and emotionally.

On September 21, 1959, Gene signed his Baseball contract for $20,000.00 before dawn and at noon, signed a two year contract, guaranteed, with the Celtics for $20,000.00, the same amount that had been cut in half the season before. He was told, at that time, no one had ever had a multi-year contract in the NBA and certainly not a guaranteed one. This may or may not be true. At a Celtic reunion recently, in celebration of a "Red's Tribute" party, Ed MaCauley was amused to hear one of his teammates from the fifties remark that Mr. Brown had told him at that time, that no one on the club received more than $8,000.00, knowing that he had received a little over twice that amount.

"Conley Captures Coveted 'Comeback Player' Award"

"Gene Conley's basketball team won the world's professional championship last season. His baseball club finished in the cellar.

"Today, October 23, the lanky Philadelphia pitcher himself came out on top in the voting for the National League Comeback Player of the Year by the Baseball Writers' Association of America."

Within a year and a half, Gene had been on a World's Championship team in baseball as well as a World's Championship team in basketball, receiving two very brilliant rings. Also, during that time, as a member of the Braves, won two National League pennants, had been voted on the National League's All Star team and won the National League's 'Comeback Player of the Year Award' as well as being rated the sixth best pitcher in the National League because of his low earned run averages.

Up from the ashes of despair, had come triumph.

In the Philadelphia paper, under Sandy Grady's column: ***"Man About Sports",*** ***CONLEY PROVES HIMSELF AS A BASKETBALL PLAYER-TAKE IT FROM WILT.***

Donald Eugene Conley is the most versatile invention since the safety pin. Given enough time, Mr. Conley certainly could play end for the Eagles, race at Indianapolis, score respectably in the U. S. Open, and shoot a snappy game of nine-ball on the side.

He had been hoorayed when he pitched 13 wins for the Phils. Last night the Convention Hall mob gave him a lustier ovation when he left the floor, a loser in Boston basketball underwear.

This was the same crowd -- 12,343 with four thousand rejected by a weeping Eddie Gottlieb -- that booed when Bill Russell was announced out with a tender ankle. Since the populace had paid to see the first clash of Wilt vs.

Russell, it was like the Burr - Hamilton duel without Aaron Burr. Two hours later, nobody felt cheated.

To Conley goes some credit. He proved a willing, aggressive rock-and-roll partner for Wilt, performed doggedly for 42 minutes, showed a deft hook shot to lead the Celts with 24 points, and never lost his deadpanned poise when Wilt soared like a flapping albatross to dunk a shot.

*Pretty racy stuff for a fellow fresh from Eddie Sawyer's caravan of masochists -- and a guy who is rarely called to play more than ten minutes by the Celtics. Maybe Conley's ferocity didn't surprise two spectators named Harry Anderson and Robin Roberts, who've seen Gene's competitive juices at close range. But it impressed Wilt Chamberlain. ____ **Did real good'**, Russell says*

For the first time in his pro career, Wilt left the court to shake an opponent's hand when Conley fouled out. Why the tribute? "Because he played a damn fine game," said Wilt. "I was relieved to hear Russell wasn't able to play - - but that Conley, he was a lot rougher on me physically than Russell."

Conley's technique of guarding Wilt was primitive as a fast ball down the middle. Usually he leaned wildly against Wilt like a man trying to push a car out of a snowbank.

He embraced Chamberlain, locked elbows with him, spinning always to stay between Wilt and the backboards. They were like two giraffes in a grotesque, bruising square dance.

"I thought Gene did real good," said Russell, who was a dapper observer in a brown suit and green Tyrolean hat. "Next time my ankle's gonna be okay and I'm gonna try my new tactics on Wilt. Maybe I'll carry me a Derringer." He laughed hugely.

231

The Warrior clan, pleased to have humbled Boston two nights in a row, also spoke approvingly of Conley. Conley's heroics may seem over-inflated when you note that Wilt set a new Hall record with 49 points. But as Neil Johnston points out, "A lot of them came on fast breaks -- and after all, Conley's only human." (actually Gene fouled out with six minutes to go and twelve points of those 49 were not his responsibility.)

Wilt's strength Impresses Conley

Conley, boyish and elated with the same small-town joy he shows when he wins for the Phils, toweled off his dark hair wearily. "Pitching a 12-inning game never pooped me like this," he said. "I'm not used to all this action, and two nights in a row of it really wears me out." "Hey, you looked pretty good," said Harry Anderson, the outfielder and beauty contest judge. "Horse, I made six or seven mistakes against that big guy," Conley said seriously. "When I'd go for the rebound instead of trying to block him, he'd just go over my head. Next time I'd handle him differently."

"If you play all season against Wilt, grinned Anderson, "you'll report to us in good shape."

"Well, I told the Celtics I'd finish the season with them, no matter what happens. But at this rate my heart won't hold out."

Over in the Warrior digs, Wilt had admitted he enjoyed watching Conley pitch baseball. "I'd like to swing at that ol' fast ball of his, though," jabbed Chamerlain. "Man I'd pop it 400 feet."

"He probably would," said Conley, inspecting his bruised physique. "Wilt must be the strongest man alive."

When Donald Eugene Conley hauled his suitcase out the door, he was smiling. The pitcher in him was undoubtedly thinking: Gee, what a strike zone.

From Boston, Phil Elderkin wrote:

Gene Conley who plays basketball as if his life depended on it, has few friends among his Boston Celtic teammates during practice sessions.

"Will somebody tell that Conley this is only an intra-squad scrimmage?" remarked Tommy Heinsohn, trying to hide a grin.

Naturally rough but without meaning to be and with a lumberman's physique, Conley cuts quite a figure at six feet, eight inches and 230 pounds. Gene smiles whenever his teammates kid him about his aggressiveness, yet he never lets up.

"It's just one of the things," said Boston Coach Red Auerbach, "that I like about him. You never have to worry about getting less than 100 percent from Conley."

"We want him because he can help us. I just wish we'd had him regularly since the 1953 season.

"The fact is that most pro basketball fans don't understand how important a fellow like Gene (who can get you the ball) can be to a club. They think a man isn't helping you unless he's scoring a lot of points."

"If you've got four scorers like Bob Cousy, Bill Sharman, Tom Heinshohn and Bill Russell, your fifth man can be a fellow like Conley who - even if he never does any more than get you the ball--poses a real problem for the opposition."

Gene played forward most of the time, **with** Russell, not in place of him, except in some instances during a "jumpball" situation, as his talent was not only his strong rebounding efforts, but his leaping ability.

Selling our home in Elm Grove was proving more difficult than we had imagined so we continued to be without "Daddy". The Boston homestand was to be played at the Garden during the playoffs so our little group and I boarded a 727 for Logan.

Attending the playoffs with the children made for another media rush. One writer asked Little Gene, *"Are you going to be a big league pitcher like your father?" "The youngster retorted, 'No sir. I'm going to be a basketball player.' Walter Brown and Auerbach immediately staked out the boy on a regional basis, although he is at least 14 years away."* By the middle of April, 1960, the Celtics had won the World Championship again, making it two in a row. Another break-up dinner but this time, rather than two lonely reporters, we now had managed to attract a few more but the format was much the same, another moving testimonial from each member present. The following day, we were in Leesburgh for another short spring training as it was already the middle of April. After pitching two innings against a class D Florida team, Gene declared himself ready.

In the Milwaukee papers, it was reported that the Milwaukee Braves were willing to have Gene back. We hadn't sold the house yet, maybe......... John Quinn, the former Braves' General Manager who had been fired by them and hired by the Phillies in 1959 was featured in an article that spring about his last year's acquisition of Gene for Stan Lopata. *"Stan, who had caught 25 games and hit .104 while Gene had won 12 for Philadelphia, approximately a fifth of all their victories which was Quinn's very first deal in his new job. If the Braves had kept him, they would have won the '59 pennant instead of losing to the Dodgers in a playoff. 'That was most unfortunate, wasn't it?' said John Joseph Quinn, his cheeks damp with tears, 100 percent crocodile."*

Rejoining the Phillies that season, renewing a few acquaintances, he was surprised how many strangers there were. Their beloved manager, Eddie Sawyer, had decided to retire. Along with the Phillies' new manager, Gene Mauch, Mr. Quinn had been active during the winter. Except for Robin Roberts, The World Series Champions, the "Wiz Kids" of 1950 were mostly gone; players like Curt Simmons, Richie Ashburn, Gene Freeze, Granny Hamner as well as Wally Post would be sorely missed but Mauch had a vision. He would be going with youth, a new rebuilding plan had commenced. Robbie and Gene were now roommates, and about the only veterans left.

Gene's first win was very interesting and very strange. May 15, 1960 is a date that will live in infamy. It wasn't all that serious except to the Manager and Billy Martin, shortstop of the Cincinnati club. It was Gene's second outing and they were leading by a wide margin in the eighth inning. The opposing relief pitcher, was Raul Sanchez, who had already hit two Phillies' batsmen when Gene came up to bat. Raul's next target was Gene's hip. It stung but after giving Raul his most menacing scowl, took first with pleasure but it did not set well with Manager Gene Mauch. He came out from the dugout as if shot from a cannon. Mauch had retaliation on his mind which cleared both benches. He was furious as he had been short a pitcher anyway, and he didn't want to lose another. Gene, no stranger to confrontation, went to cover his manager as Mauch was no match for the opposing pitcher. Gene felt a blow from behind his ear. Whirling around, without thought or malice, socked Billy Martin in the jaw. It was a gut reaction. Everyone was into the fray. Even cool heads, like Robin Roberts and Frank Robinson were duking it out in another corner. Later Roberts apologized to Frank as he had said things that were not appropriate. Martin, who was taken to the hospital, found he had a broken or cracked jaw. He swore vengeance, even if he had to take a bat to get justice the "next time" out. Since Billy was known for his combative personality and compulsive behavior, Gene did wonder about it, but "next time" proved uneventful.

Two games later, after having two successful outings, that episode caused him to give a little more attention to that injury as during batting practice, his leg gave way to excruciating pain. The doctors treated him with shots of medications to calm the sciatic nerve and bed rest was ordered. The play-offs in basketball, necessarily had taken away a month from his season of baseball and now, powerless, he lost another month.

Mauch, cautious about starting Gene after his long layoff, put him in relief against his old club, the Milwaukee Braves in Milwaukee. His two innings were perfect, striking out two, giving up nothing. Up until that time, the Phillies were trying hard to live up to their "cellar" position as they set some sort of record, hitting into three double-plays and one weird triple-play. It was always a dramatic occasion when Gene played against his old teammates, and this game was no exception. The Phillies, were losing the game by two runs when Gene came in to pitch. When it came time for Gene to bat in the 10th, there was already a man on first and with two out, another "Philly" batter had been walked intentionally to get to the pitcher. Gene guessed right and sent a Don McMahon pitch into the leftfield seats, hitting a three-run homer to win the ballgame. It was a sweet victory but knowing it was already the middle of July, it didn't look like a record year.

Gene was rooming with Robin Roberts on the road and Robbie could see the struggles that Gene encountered and the stresses of playing the two sports. Where the "seventies" was the era of mind altering drugs, baseball in the "fifties" and "sixties" had almost supported the use of alcohol as the drug of choice. After every game, there was the usual case of beer in the clubhouse to ease the player's excitement and injuries. The problem was, where most players could relax and enjoy a couple of beers to calm jangled nerves after a victorious win or a disappointing loss, it only initiated a long evening of bars for Gene.

Every spring training, whether the regular kind or Gene's short week of it, there was this determination that this year was going to be different. He would vow not to have another drink of alcohol and would be successful during the process, probably because of our presence. It wasn't long, however, usually by the first road trip, the pressures of major league competition or loneliness would disturb all those resolutions. Inherently apprehensive, Gene is more comfortable in a social setting. He requires an audience. Even though you eat, sleep and play ball with each other, the player is necessarily subjected to isolation. With only eight teams in each sport, your position of employment is tenuous at best. You are not only in competition with your competition but with your own teammates as well. There is a certain "coolness" amongst your own kind. Gene thrives on telling yarns and generally having fun in a relaxed atmosphere of humorous bantering and with the use of intoxicating beverages, this was accomplished with ease. This endeavor didn't start in the "Majors". It was acceptable behavior in both high school and college and continued throughout his professional athletic life. It could have been a genetic predisposition, being both Cherokee and Irish but in any case, he noticed it was becoming a problem.

Everyone, even including Fred Haney, tried to curb his penchant for alcoholic obsession, as people really cared about him. His amicable spirit was easy to love. Major League Sports then, were in a position to ignore problems such as his. Players were expendable. There was a vast minor league system which could be called on to replace a player when a "major leaguer" was having difficulty. Now, in the twenty-first century, with twenty-nine teams and a much leaner minor league system, major league players are given much more attention. In the sixties, as long as the player produced, he remained a problem only to himself.

On this night of comeback, winning so dramatically with that three run homer in his old Milwaukee "digs" where manager and new general manager had dismissed him with little remorse or regret, brought pure satisfaction. Rooming with Gene all year, Robbie was cognizant of Gene's struggle with alcohol. As soon as the reporters left, Robbie took Gene aside and said, "Gene, you're going to really savor this victory, we're going to go back to our room and just think about what you've accomplished this night". Gene was so taken by Robbie's concern, plus his admiration for him, that he obediently followed his instruction. This was one of those special nights which will be forever remembered and treasured.

CHAPTER 24

SO LONG PHILLY HELLO BEANTOWN

Because of his successful outing in relief, Gene Mauch didn't lose any time in starting Gene once again. In the middle of July, 19,541 fans were at old Connie Mack Stadium to watch a defensive duel between Vernon Law, the winingest pitcher in the National League and Gene Conley. Happily, it ended in a four-hit, 2 to 1 victory for Gene.

In the Philadelphia Inquirer the next day, the writer, Ray Kelly, remarked, *"While the Phillies are idling, the thought occurs that this town has never fully appreciated the athletic prowess of Gene Conley. He's a remarkable man."*

"The six-foot, eight-inch giant spends the winters playing basketball with the world champion Boston Celtics. Then he takes a couple of days off and swings into the baseball season with the Phillies. This has been going on for three years."

I don't know how he does it," said teammate Robin Roberts. "The travel time big Gene puts in alone would wear out an ordinary person."

Another Phillies player mused: "I wonder how many ball games he'd win if he rested up during the off season like other pitchers?"

1961 - April

GENE CONLEY CONGRATULATED BY CELT TEAMMATE
Bill Russell, son Buddha, 3, visit at Fens. (UPI)

SOX AND CELTICS congratulate Gene Conley after he won his first assignment for Red Sox with a 6-1 victory over Washington. Relief pitcher Mike Fornieles (center), who hurled ninth inning and catcher Jim Pagliaroni (right). At right, Celt mates Bill Russell and K.C. Jones (right) congratulate Conley, who shakes hands wil Bill's son, Buddha.

At the moment, the skyscraping right hander has the best log among the Phillies' starting pitchers. (6 and 4)"

It didn't go quite as smoothly for him the next three outings. The excuse could be logically made that Philadelphia's lowly position in the standings could account for it but Gene wasn't looking for excuses. He felt that spending more time anesthetizing himself was preventing him from a clear conscience and the circumstance of blessings. He began to theorize that if he could just overcome this idiocy, he could reclaim his mastery or at least put in a decent performance. Going for his eighth win, he was pitted against the wily Lew Burdette, his old friend. Fidgety Lew, who had an excellent "spitter", had been the World Series hero in 1957, a 20 game winner and an all star. When the dust settled, he was a "no-hit, no run" winner and Gene had a 1 to 0 loss against his former teammates. Gene was among the first to congratulate Lew. He grabbed the phone as soon as he could get into the clubhouse.

"Lew, congratulations, how could you do that to me?"

"Gene, I had to pitch a no hit, no run game, you only allowed one run". Gene's catcher said to Gene, *"you stayed good all night tonight, buddy, so don't feel bad. It ought to make you feel good to know you can pitch that well."*

It did and he won his eighth, a four hitter, against the Chicago Cubs the next time out, and then losing one to the Dodgers. A Philadelphia error had caused that loss but brought no consolation to Gene. He was starting to feel a little like a yo-yo, winding up the year with an 8 and 14 record, striking out 117 men in 183 innings while walking only 42. The Celtics were always in the playoffs which caused another late start and then with his hip or leg injury, it cost him almost a month or so of "starts". The old specter of whether he should continue playing both sports loomed in the wings as the season ended. The magazines and papers theorized that he should choose one or the other to be an effective player.

It had been a lovely fall day in Elm Grove, Wisconsin. The Journal had come out with a photographer to get a story before he was to report to the Celtics, late again of course. We all looked relaxed, like a calm normal family enjoying the crisp clean air on our front porch that day. Little did we know what fate had in store for us.

Soon after the Journal folks left, the phone rang. It was for Gene. Mr. Bob Carpenter himself, owner of the Philadelphia club was calling.

"Gene, this year has been a tough one for you hasn't it?"

"Yes, Mr. Carpenter, it has been."

"We've had a meeting and we've decided that you shouldn't be playing basketball anymore".

"Well, Mr. Carpenter, it's like this, I need the money and the Celtics are paying me $20,000.00 a year and I figure I've got about three or four more basketball years left. Besides, Mr. Brown and Red have been very fair to me and have let me know they really need me."

"Gene I believe we could pay you an extra $20,000.00 not to play, how's that sound?"

"I don't know, let me speak to my wife."

Gene and I had a short conference. He had accepted money for not playing before but the circumstances were different now. Not only were we making more money with Gene playing both sports but, he was really feeling like he had reached his potential in basketball. Winning world championships was pretty "heady" stuff and knowing he could do it for three or four more years had to be taken into consideration. True, basketball didn't have the benefits that baseball did then, nor the history and status that baseball had but Gene truly loved the game.

We thought about that cattle ranch we had come across on hikes into the mountains of Oregon and the imaginary "Circle C" brand that we had fantasized about at times. It would take about $25,000.00, after tax money to realize that dream, so that was the figure Gene went back to negotiate for.

After hearing this figure, Carpenter lost it.

"Gene, why I'd never consider giving you that much, tax free"

"Well, that is what it would take."

"Listen here, Gene, if you couldn't play sports, you'd be nothing but a truck driver!"

"What's wrong with being a truck driver? It's an honorable profession, what's wrong with it?"

"Conley, you'll never wear a Phillies uniform again."

"Mr. Carpenter, I'd never put on a Phillies uniform again."

All Gene heard then was a loud "click" as Mr. Carpenter had enough. Upon relating this story to Red a couple of days later, Red was so angry he could spit. "What the hell, he was born with a silver spoon in his mouth. He's never earned a thing in his life."

Three weeks before this confrontation, Gene had bought a 65 foot mobile home so that we could be with him more and not have to travel back and forth from Elm Grove to the Resort in Valley Forge, Pennsylvania each long homestand. It was great fun stocking it with bedding and dishes before I left to enroll the kids in school back in Wisconsin. We had looked around at the homes in and around Valley Forge and had fallen in love with the area but because we had difficulty selling the home in Elm Grove we had been prevented from purchasing another. As things turned out, that was a blessing as we would have had to sell again before moving in.

True to Mr. Carpenter's word, by December, in the middle of the Celtics' season, Mr. Quinn, the Phillies general manager was able to trade Gene for Frank Sullivan, the Red Sox 6' 7" right-hander. They had both been in the bull pen during that memorable all star game back in 1955 which Gene had won. Frank was one of baseball's wittiest players.

His comment afterwards was, "it was baseball's biggest trade". He also quipped, referring to himself, "I was in the twilight of a mediocre career anyway".

It was awesome news to us. It meant Gene would be playing baseball and basketball in the same city!!! We could almost have a normal existence. We had the mobile home trucked up to the Boston area between semesters, put our furnishings in storage and left our home in the hands of a local Elm Grove Realtor. The only town that allowed mobile homes at that time and the closest town to Boston, was Foxboro. We were to live in Foxboro for forty years. It was joked to have more horses than residents at the time. Foxboro was country for sure, but also had that country charm. The children were a little thrown as at that time, in Foxboro, they taught French from Kindergarten up, another new experience.

As one of the Celtic owners had also owned an arena in Providence, Rhode Island, several games were scheduled to be played there. Being located halfway from Boston to Providence, some of the Celtic players would stop by to have tea before those games. The Boston writers were amused by a ballplayer living in a mobile home and couldn't wait to write a feature on this oddity, complete with photographic spread.

It had been rumored that Gene left the Phillies in a huff after the 1960 season and Auerbach was asked about it. Quoting Ken Mudler of the Boston Globe: *"I was shocked," replied Auerbach. "I don't know the details, but I can tell you this much: Gene Conley is as fine a gentleman as I have ever met. He has never caused me or the team a bit of trouble. And I've never coached a player who gives more of himself than Conley. He puts out 100 percent whenever I use him."*

"Gene can center with anyone in the league," said Auerbach, "and that includes Chamberlain (Wilt) and Russell (Bill). And he's also tough on defense.

"I can't blame him for playing baseball, though. With this expansion business cropping up, he could pitch another ten years, though his lifetime in basketball may be only two more years."

Auerbach was quoted in another article, *"I'd say he's the most incredible athlete in the country. The average athlete would crack under that strain in a hurry. He thrives on it. Why he stayed out of basketball for five years and then came back to be a standout: I never knew or heard of another player who was able to do that."*

'How much longer can he keep it up?'

"Not indefinitely," He's strong enough physically to go on taking the gaff, but he's bound to become weary mentally in time. I'd say he had another season or two of good basketball left in his system and maybe five or six years of baseball."

It wasn't long before Dick O'Connell, general manager with the Red Sox, asked Gene to come by for a talk. We didn't have a phone yet, so the Massachusetts State Police pulled up to our trailer home to inform us. We only had one car so I took him to Fenway Park which was a "first" for me. The exterior had an all dark green appearance which seemed to be lacking in architectural elegance and a little antiquated. Although, later on, coming up into the interior where the whole scene could be taken in, I was amazed at how it took your breath. I was impressed with the tranquil peace it produced. Perhaps it was because of the peace of emptiness that gave reason to this, but still there seemed to be an ethereal beauty that couldn't be explained. That certain shade of grass combining with the darker green seats and walls produced a phenomenal calm. I can't imagine anyone ever disturbing this historic outdoor building. I understand now why they originally christened it Fenway Park. I circled the block waiting for Gene to return from his conference.

Reflecting on my visit inside Fenway, it suddenly occurred to me that I had never seen the inside of Connie Mack Stadium. Each time Gene pitched, I would wait in our station wagon, listening to the game on radio while our kids romped about in the back of the wagon until he was through for the night. We both thought Mr. O'Connell's desire to see Gene, was to sign him to a contract. This would mean that he would become the only player in American sports' history to play for two professional major league teams in one city. (actually, he has played for three; the Boston Braves, the Boston Celtics and the Boston Red Sox) Dick O'Connell knew what he made last year and as a starting point, offered the same. I believe that Gene was so thrilled to be playing both sports in the same city, he more or less agreed, but didn't sign anything. When Gene returned to the car, he remarked how nice Mr. O'Connell had been and how he thought he was going to like playing for the Boston Red Sox. As he drove around the block, he suddenly stopped and said, "I believe I sold myself short, I'm worth more than that. So we turned around and once again, Gene went into the Red Sox offices. "You know Mr. O'Connell, I believe I'm better than Sullivan and I think I should be getting $25,000.00." All right Gene, it will be $25,000.00." When he got back into the car and related his conversation, I said, laughing, "Gene, you should have asked for $30,000.00!"

The next day, a press conference was called. Mr. Brown of the Boston Celtics was coming over to join Gene and Mr. O'Connell. Posing for photographers at the signing, it suddenly occurred to the media that never before, in the history of American sports, had two officers (one an owner, the other, vice-president and general manager) of two different sports, ever appeared together for the signing of one athlete. It was very unusual in that era and in the climate of today's hot sport's business, not likely to happen again.

Obviously Gene was finally, very comfortable being welcomed by both the two different kingdoms of basketball and baseball in one city! It was obvious by this time, after four years combining the two sports, that this city and its media representing it, could tolerate a two sport athlete. Baseball had enjoyed a long history of dominance in American sports. It carried with it, a certain dignity and cache. It was obvious that the institution of baseball was so well established in this country, the mere mention that anyone entertaining the thought of playing another sport, brought on reactions of sarcasm and insults that made an athlete feel guilty of some sort of sin. Managers would often, if feeling disgruntled on a particular day, say things to Gene like, "why don't you just go play basketball" or "why don't you make up your mind, are you a basketball player or a baseball player" and other indignities too numerous to list. Gene was a two sport athlete. He loved them equally. Baseball, it seems, was a monogamous union. It had, in the past, demanded full allegiance of its employees, and even the slightest hint of revolt or perceived mutiny might set their guardians into a threatened mode. He had found a home. Boston, our home, sweet home!

One reporter asked him, "how can you go on playing basketball and baseball?"

Gene replied, *"It's easy. I've got a wife and a family. They all have the same habit. They like to eat."*

In the playoffs with the Celtics, Gene was making "double-doubles" and enjoying an especially fantastic Philadelphia series, playing along side of the fabulous Bill Russell. It was an honor to be a Boston Celtic, to once again win another World's Championship. Once they had conquered Philadelphia, he was so confident the day before they wound up the world championship, he had already bought our tickets to Ocala, Florida to start his abbreviated spring training. Nine days later, he was not only starting his baseball season but was the starting pitcher against the Washington Senators.

It was the latter part of April in Boston and as most people residing in New England know, the weather can have a mind of its own. In order to know which inning to pick up Gene during his first outing, I drove around Fenway, praying and listening to the car radio as a combination rain/snowy mist swirled in front of me. Going into the ninth with a shutout, he gave up a couple of singles which brought in a relief pitcher and his first win of the season. To add to this satisfying win, was the fact that the Celtics' Bill Russell and K. C. Jones took the time out on that cold N.E. day to be in the stands to cheer him on. This honor was another memorable moment for Gene. The tide was beginning to turn between Boston's basketball and Boston's baseball attendance as nine days before this performance, there had been a "sell-out" crowd at the Boston Garden to see the Celtics defeat the St. Louis

Hawks, but only *"2,748 paying fans, 1,000 sailors and a lamb in the stands"* were there to observe this joyful day at Fenway

Joking after reading this in the papers the next day, Gene quipped, "I was really a draw, wasn't I?"

His comfort level was being met, having the calm Red Sox manager, Mike Higgins in the summer and the Celtics' determined and talented coach Auerbach in the winter all within a subway ride. However, this prospect was short-lived as "expansion" in the NBA had already started its greedy march through the country. The Chicago Bulls, was the new entry. They were allowed to choose one unprotected player from each NBA team. Each NBA team was allowed only seven "protected" players and the Celtics protected Russell, Cousy, Heinsohn, Ramsey, their newly acquired draft choice, Satch Sanders, Sam Jones and K.C. Jones. The logical draft choice then, would be Bill Sharman who in 2000, was voted one of the greatest 50 players ever to play in the NBA. Bill decided, rather than play for the Chicago franchise as expected, he would accept the offer to coach for the Los Angeles Jets, the new American Basketball League's entry out west. Sharman was raised in southern California. Knowing that he was always a question mark as to whether he would discontinue playing basketball for baseball each season, Gene felt pretty sure he wouldn't be chosen and that Jim Loscutoff or the young Gene Guarillia would be the logical choice. However, this was not to be. Chicago drafted Gene Conley. Many felt, including Gene, he might not accept Chicago's draft next year. Disrupting the kids twice in one year wouldn't be fair to them so he felt like he would just fade away like an "old soldier" when basketball rolled around that fall.

Meanwhile back at the Sox ranch, Gene notched his first defeat of the season but then went on to pitch a marvelous 1-0 victory on 4 singles. Many commentators asked Gene when he first joined the Red Sox what he thought about the Red Sox' "country club" atmosphere as compared to the other two National League teams he had been with. When he was with the Braves, every player was clearly focused on being in first place with dreams of being in a world series. The two years he was with the Phillies, they supported the rest of the league from the cellar and made the best of it. There was character, layers and layers of character and some future hall of famers but their glory days had ended long before Gene arrived on campus. The Red Sox were mostly at a comfortable mid point level and were not known for their power hitting. In comparison, the Braves were praised for their power hitters with a nice mixture of intense, talented veterans and rookies, their pitching was deep and always placed at the top in the National League standings. The Phillies had their Dalton Gang, (as some in the media had labeled them for some of them had been reported to have carried guns). Mostly, they had very talented veterans who cared about each other, and were enjoyable to be around. Other than the Red Sox seemed more relaxed than his previous teammates, he really hadn't been aware of anything especially unique about them, unless, of course, you'd call their habit of playing cards in the club house right up until game time, unusual. This, Gene had never experienced as most major leaguers zoned out the mundane to prepare for the game. Bill Russell, before a game of importance, could be found retching in the clubhouse privy.

CHAPTER 25

ROUNDING THIRD GOING FOR HOME

From this point on, it appeared that Gene would be destined to inherit new ingenious ways to lose ball games. Even so, flashes of his old uncanny ability to come through in the clutch, enabled him to keep his starting rotation status. Not only that, but his hitting abilities were winning ball games along with accumulating two home runs for the season.

He had been to Yankee Stadium before. As a teenager, he had hit a home run and pitched shut out ball to win the National Hearst All Star game and was given the Most Valuable Player trophy. His next sojourn at Yankee Stadium was when the Braves won the World Series in 1957 and again in 1958, where, from the bullpen, he watched the Braves lose a World Series to the Yankees. He was anxious to do battle with Boston's hated rivals. He most always pitched good ball against the Yankees, but the Yankee pitchers did well too. In the Boston Globe, on May 25 of that year, under the headlines, "YANKEES APPLAUD CONLEY", *"You fellows made a hell of a deal", said Yankee Manager Ralph Houk to a group of Bostonians after today's 3 to 2 tingler, here.*

"Conley sure pitched a real good ball game," Houk continued , "I've got to say he pitched a lot better against us today than Frank Sullivan has for the last couple of years."

Dick Radatz, Bill Mombouquette, Gene
Pitchers - 1962

"It looks as if we're foul-pole bit and not snake-bit." Gene said after the game. The reference of course, was that today's was the second foul pole homer off Boston pitching within a week."

"When Roger Maris hit the foul pole on the Conley fast ball, it ended 13 consecutive scoreless innings by Gene" 'There had been so many close calls on foul balls down the lines here that a few year's ago they doubled the height of the foul poles to the stadium roof. It was done to help out the umpires. It's a good thing they did it. For if they hadn't, I'll bet ten to one they'd have called Maris' home run today a foul ball.'

No wonder the Yankee's 1961 team was deemed the greatest Yankee team of all time. It took only 295' to notch a home run in right field at Yankee Stadium and since they had two of the strongest left handed-pull-hitters of all time in Mantle and Maris, it doesn't take a brain surgeon to understand why the Yankees led the league during this era.

Of course, short fences and foul ball poles were nothing new to Gene where, in the National League, at the Polo Grounds, it took only 250' to left and 257' to right, (even less, if hit up into the overhanging decks) to count for a home run. Then at Ebbets Field in Brooklyn, it was only 323' to the left field stands and 297' to a 10' wall, topped off with a screen, to produce a "homer". Now, those parks were challenging! Today, the media, pitchers and visiting teams make a great deal out of Fenway's "Green Monster" which is a short 302' away. The "Monster" can indeed look tempting to a right-handed pull hitter but right field has many a left-handed pull hitter smirking in anticipation as well. The tall white foul line pole is only a short 320' from homeplate and if hit, counts for a home run.

The box seats which extend out further and are at ground level serve as another "trap" as if the ball is hit into the short stands here, the pull-hitter, even hitting a low line drive, could have a home run. It is so low there that many a Boston fan has made the mistake of interfering with a low line drive by merely leaning over from his box seat. This interference with the play is counted as a ground rule "double". Strangely enough, there is an advantage for a pitcher at Fenway, as center field is long and wide and if he is "on" and his arm obedient, his fielders alert, he can keep the visiting team at bay. Gene loved pitching at Fenway.

Preparing to win and do well against the Yankees though, was always inspirational as it meant so much to the Boston fans. No matter how well Gene pitched against them, though, the outcome did not advantage him that year. Then again the Yankees had an excellent pitching staff. There was only one game against the Yankees that Gene did not do well. This was the year Roger Maris broke Babe Ruth's record for most home runs in a season. Two of those home runs were off Gene. This was no surprise as this was also the year that Gene was keeping a dirty little secret. His old injury to his rotator-cuff had paid another call. (Perhaps from rushing from basketball into the baseball season without a spring training??) Gene broke a record of his own. He gave up more home runs that year than any year previous to that or after, coming mostly in the later innings. It was especially hard for a strong athlete like Gene, as before that injury, he could stand flat footed, and without winding up, throw a perfect strike into a catcher's mitt from the farthest point in center field.

His first three outings had been impressive, before the pain started. In his debut, he held the Senators to one run. In his next start in Detroit, he went the distance against the league leading Tigers and beat Jim Bunning, 1 to 0. In his lone relief job, with two men on base, nobody down in the ninth, he struck out two batters and got one out by a simple fly ball to center. By the middle of July he said he had pitched his best game of the season, beating the Baltimore Orioles, 2 to 1 but he was now carrying a 4 and 7 record. Mother was visiting us for a few weeks the middle of that summer, and being a nurse and a believer in home remedies, spent hours, soaking heavy towels in hot water, applying them to his ailing shoulder and then covering that with a plastic coated pad trying to break up the soreness. In spite of her good intentions, the pain stubbornly remained. To divulge this information would explain or give excuse for his late inning fatigue but it could also mean an end to a career and after all, his arm had healed on its own before. He persevered in agony.

Even with a sore arm, he managed to win games against the Kansas City Athletics, Minnesota Twins (where Gene hit a home run and completed his game), then stopping the Cleveland Indians, 8 to 0, (in addition to hitting his second homer of the season) and by August 23, had 8 wins by defeating L.A. In twenty decisions, he had won nine, most times by his own hitting. Mike Higgins was quoted in the Globe as saying, "I would like to use Gene as a clean up batter but everyone would think I was crazy". Gene's last game and victory came against the Orioles and reported by the Globe's, Roger Birtwell, "Conley never was faster for the Red Sox. He struck out 10, held the Orioles to five hits and permitted only three runners to advance to first base." By the end of the season, he had won his 11th game.

We were looking forward to a winter off. Secretly, though, Gene was disappointed that the Celtics hadn't protected him in the draft that fall. The family had been together in the Boston area now for almost a year. Chicago wasn't an option. With Little Gene in fourth grade, Kitty in the second grade and Kelly finally adjusting to being away from her favorite "white house" in Elm Grove, Wisconsin, Gene wasn't about to disrupt us so soon.

Peace and contentment suddenly came to a crashing halt with a late night phone call from a Paul Cohen, president and owner of "Tuck Tape". He persuaded

Gene to play in the new American Basketball League with his Washington Tapers. He was only too happy to offer the same contract the Celtics had given him, promising that he could fly home to Boston on days off. I remember not being overjoyed at this prospect but it proved much later, to have been fortuitous.

Gene really did love playing basketball and the competition was challenging. Most of the players were "All Americans" and when the league folded the following year, a great many went into the NBA. It wasn't the Celtics though. Mr. Cohen had forgotten to mention another small motive in employing Gene. On the team's road trips, his request was that Gene accompany Stan Stutz, the Tapers' coach, and Tuck Tape's sales manager, on sales calls to some of the larger corporations. His "day's off", it seems, were used as days to sign "buyers" to national sales contracts for Tuck's industrial tapes, sometimes entertaining them as well.

Entertaining, was an euphemism for getting "stoned" out of your skull in order to nail down a million dollar deal. Not only that, but their other center, who they had depended on to play most of the time, didn't. Gene played nearly all the game, every game and the wear and tear of alcohol, traveling, not only from coast to coast, but to Hawaii for games as well, began to show up in angry confrontations with the competition. The results of that fight in Hawaii left two metacarpal bones fractured. It was his left hand but the injury was not really set, nor was he given rest, so Gene played on, and on, and on....

Late one afternoon during that basketball season, I received a call from a San Diego doctor. It seems that Gene's drinking had reached a crisis stage. Gene had an anxiety attack that had him shaking and scared. He went into a hospital emergency room in San Diego where the doctor, who had taken care of him, called me. He was very concerned. He had given Gene a tranquilizer shot and left him in an examining room to calm down. When he heard Gene scream, "hey, hey, there's black spiders all over the ceiling," the emergency room doc realized then that this strong healthy looking guy wasn't the healthy specimen he appeared to be, and basically put him completely out with another shot. Knowing who Gene was, and after Gene had been there awhile, thought it best if he took him to his home for the evening. Better not to have hospital personnel share this information with media. Gene called and asked me to take the kids out of school and catch the next plane out.

Arriving in San Diego worried and nervous, I was surprised that Gene seemed so calm and healthy. I had expected an emaciated crazy person, I guess, from the seriousness of the doctor's voice and Gene's urgent pleading. Instead, I found him smiling and happy and not only that, he had rented a car and wanted us all to drive to L.A. to take the kids to Disneyland! Being uninitiated to anxiety, or near mental breakdowns at the time, I didn't recognize that Gene might have taxed his strengths to the limit. It is a long drive through an ugly desert of cactus from San Diego to L.A. and Gene began unloading while the children mostly slept. It had been a long journey from Boston. It was good for Gene to have this time to talk. He explained about this side job of selling tape, while playing. He hadn't been home in a very long time, and this stressed him even further. With his questionable arm problems, he was almost on the verge of quitting both sports. By the time we arrived in L.A., we decided that Disneyland was not on the agenda, (much to the chagrin of the kids) and headed to the airport. The team had moved, in the middle of the season, to Long Island, NY, and he needed to get back. The only redeeming factor here was that he could now start commuting from Boston to the home games.

In December, Joe Cashman for the Boston Record American wrote, *"Since it is his left hand which he broke in a basketball fight, the injury won't affect Gene Conley's pitching...But what about his hitting?...That's something for the Sox to be concerned about...Baseball's tallest player and only two-pro-sport participant was the most dangerous hitter on the Fenway staff last season..He made more hits, knocked in more runs, scored more times and got more extra-base blows than any of his mound mates...Included among his barrage of blows were two home runs...For the greater part of the season, Gene was batting close to .300."*

The American Basketball League season ended without playoffs, which enabled the Conley Clan to enjoy the first real spring training in three successive years, and Arizona was a pleasant relief to the snows of the New England landscape. I gathered up all the children's schoolwork assignments for the next six weeks and joined Gene. Nineteen-hundred-sixty-two was going to prove a very, very interesting year.

Gene had determined once again, that alcohol would remain buried in his past. The results were enjoyed by the whole family as he had a wonderful spring training. Lew Burdette, who had been a Milwaukee Braves' teammate, good naturedly used to say, "never give an Indian firewater". Lew was like that. Some would even label him a "character". He used to drive umpires, managers and players nuts. He so spooked batters with his "spit ball" pitch, that even when he wasn't using it, they were so focused on it, and so confused, they were easily fooled. More than one time, as Lew released a pitch, he would excitedly yell, "look out!!" and the batter would bail out for a strike three!

As the Celtics were winding down their "playoffs", the 1962 baseball season was starting to become a favorable experience for Gene. An article in the Globe, under Jerry Nason's column titled, *"C'S ALMOST BLEW TITLE BY LOSING CONLEY IN DRAFT"* read, *"The front office almost sabotaged the championship for them last Spring by putting Gene Conley's name on the open-draft list, then asking Bill Russell to play 84 games without a stand in.*

As a result the Marathoner of the Week was not a Finn entitled Oksanen. It was a basketball player named Russell.

He played seven play-off games with 260 pounds of elbow action called Wilt all over him...then seven more against Los Angeles. He was practically walking on his knees by then. Russell totaled out 672 of a possible 675 play-off minutes."

Gene's success with the Sox this year was partly due to a sober Conley, partly having a full spring training, and partly because the Sox were scoring. If he had still been with the Celtics this time of year, he would have missed hitting another home run, and his two wins.

He was having the time of his life, winning his third with a double and a single, each driving in two runs. Then against the Tigers, he doubled for his fourth win with many thanks also to Dick Radatz, one of the Red Sox all time great relief pitchers. Henry McKenna of the Boston Globe wrote, *"Big Gene Conley went the route for the fifth time as he gained his fifth win. Gene also inserted a one-run double that missed being a homer by inches, if that.....Gene's E.R.A. was only 2.39. Then the Yankees came to town!*

The Boston Globe's Roger Birtwell writes, *"How do the Yankees do it? Consider the case of Gene Conley. In the eighth inning yesterday at Fenway Park, he had a 1-0 shutout over the Yankees. With two down in the eighth, and a runner on second, he struck out Yogi Berra on three pitched balls.*

Yet later in that same eighth inning, the Yanks tied the score.

And in the ninth..without a hit...the Yanks won, 2-1.

It was a pitching duel Between Conley and Bob Turley. In the second inning, Geiger had stolen second base and became the second and last Red Sox runner to reach second all afternoon.

But Conley was pitching superbly. Even against the might of the Yankees, the single second-inning run seemed sufficient. Until the eighth inning, only three times did a Yankee batter reach base.

As luck would have it, when Gene struck out Joe Pepitone, the ball bounced off of Pagliaroni's glove into the grandstand which was recorded as a "wild pitch" and gave the dreaded Yanks second life as Tresh doubled to bring him in.

Against the Athletics, errors figured in another loss. It was obvious that he was not being blessed or was it just the breaks of the game?

On the road, Gene's harmful little habit of visiting bars was starting to shake his confidence level. In Lord Alfred Tennyson's poem, "Sir Galahad", there is this line that is almost biblical in implication, "My strength is as the strength of ten, Because my heart is pure", (Going against his conscience prevented that secure feeling) Going against oneself, is not being true to what you perceive to be right. Dulling the mind merely delays the commitment for awhile. You're still left straddling the fence and worse, physically shot. The nagging pain in his shoulder came back to complicate his internal conflict.

On "homestands", when a game happened to be on a Saturday, he would join the family at the Boston Temple which was only a block and a half away from Fenway. So after services, he would walk over to the Park to either pitch or workout. He would gain inner peace while at church. It also started another round of theological questions.

At this moment though, he needed more than spiritual answers, he was once again in need of physical healing. He was pitching regularly but the nagging pain that he had struggled with the previous year had returned. This time, he sought an orthopedic doctor of stature in the Boston area, a Dr. O'Neil. He had previous cortizone shots before but not many and Dr. O'Neil seemed to hit just the right spot before Gene deplaned for Detroit and the Tigers who were leading the league at the time. He was overjoyed when he called me after the game as his shoulder hadn't given him a twinge of pain. Best of all, he had another 3-0 shutout. As Hy Hurwitz of the Herald American wrote, *"It was a night of sixes for the six-foot, eight-inch Conley. His sixth complete game as well as his sixth win. He held the Tigers to six hits, all singles. He walked five batters but the Tigers stranded 11 runners as Gene was at his peak in the clutch."*

He had won nine games before facing the Yankees at Fenway. Your percentages are better if your arm is feeling good and you're in rotation but you still have to have runs to win. Luck is, at times, a deciding factor. As the Brave's Lew Burdette used to say, "I'd rather be lucky than good". Against the Kansas City A's, Gene had pitched scoreless ball for eight innings but left in the ninth for a pinch-hitter. For his efforts, Gene merely came away with exercise. I was disappointed, not about failing to gain another victory but suspicious that perhaps he might be going against himself again.

Fenway was packed to the rafters that hot early July day. At least 1,000 fans were turned away at the ticket window. Ralph Terry, the Yankees' "ace" of the Yankees' pitching staff was going against Gene. Hy Hurwitz writing in the Herald

American, *"Conley had outpitched Terry for seven innings. He kept two singles widely separated.*

He opened the eighth by rubbing out Bill Skowron. Hecktor Lopez lined a single to left to set the stage for the games only score. He advanced to second as Clete Boyer dropped a broken bat single into center field. When Terry popped out to short right field, Conley was one out away from maintaining his runless hurling......but rookie Tom Tresh then singled into right field and Lopez beat Lu Clinton's throw home with the games lone run."

Another quote, *"For Conley, his was another nightmarish effort, marking the fourth time the Sox have failed to get him a run.*

"In addition to the New York game, he (Gene) lost a 3-0 game to Baltimore and a 4-0 start to Los Angeles. Also, he's dropped two 2-1 games, one to Washington, the other to New York, both on unearned runs." (Roger Birtwell reporting)

By now, it was becoming frustrating. Gene couldn't win for losing and the All Star game selections were only a couple of weeks away. Larry Claflin wrote, *"Boston's Gene Conley may have earned a place on the American League's second-game All Star team. At least, Yankee and AllStar manager Ralph Houk last night said he is considering Conley."*

Hy Hurwitz wrote, *"Gene Conley has been a steadier pitcher than Monbouquette this year with the Red Sox. In fact, Gene has a better record than Billy as Conley has pitched more innings and has turned in more complete games.*

Just before the All Star selections, however, the Yankees played the winning card that sparked one of the most bizarre and storied yarns in baseball's history.

I had met and become friends with a couple at the Seventh-day-Adventist church in Boston. Bud was a medical doctor teaching Pathology at Loma Linda Medical School. He was in Boston on Sabbatical, doing research at Harvard. Lolita, his wife, was so full of life experiences and vitality, you couldn't help but fall in love with her. Many told us then and have since, that we looked and acted like sisters. We each had three children. Their ages and temperaments were compatible so it was only natural that we all bonded. It was her bright idea that we should experience Junior Camp at Lake Winnekeag, a church run summer camp in Ashburnham, Massachusetts. We should volunteer our services as "counselors" in exchange for our children's tuition for about nine days and since Gene would be on the road for that time, I reluctantly agreed. As things turned out, it was a very wise decision.

It was a busy time for us. Each morning, bright and early, 5:30 a.m. to be exact, that we, as counselors, were called in for morning worship and scheduling before waking our girls. After a days' activities of swimming, riding horses, crafts, excetera, and as the sun set over Lake Winnekeag, the night was topped off with campfire, stories, and song. After soothing our little homesick charges, Lolita and I would begin our evening conversations in this tiny room between the two wings of bunk beds where our 8 to 11 year old girls tried to sleep. Our whispered chatting sometimes lasted until 2:00 a.m. It was soon becoming questionable whether we would make the nine days allotted.

One night, after an especially animated and extremely interesting discussion, one of our little girls pleaded with us, "Mrs. Hirst, Mrs. Conley, would you please be quiet so we can sleep?" Bless her heart. We were guilty as charged.

CHAPTER 26

"GOODNIGHT PUMPSIE GREEN WHEREVER YOU ARE"

It had been an especially humid day and late afternoon wasn't promising any relief. The cabins were "Rustic Americana", without air conditioning. The camp was very isolated. No television, no newspapers and only one lone telephone, "for emergencies only". This was purposely planned in order to exclude the outside world and enhance the awesome beauty of Mother Nature in its purist form. Nevertheless, I had begged off the afternoon crafts' session. Everyone was moving in slow motion anyway. My mission was clear, finding a radio station that carried the Red Sox/Yankee game. I had smuggled in this cheap little portable radio as Gene would be taking on the Yankees at Yankee Stadium that hot and sultry afternoon. I could have saved myself a lot of grief, had I not found that station.

The scratchy reception was as uncomfortable as the antiquated bunkbed's lumpy mattress but I was very anxious to follow the game. After all, Gene's last three outings had been promising so surely after his "no decision" game against Kansas City where he walked none and allowed only five hits for seven innings before being relieved for a pinch hitter, seemed like a good omen. Although that disappointing game against these same Yanks had me a little insecure. And then again, I reasoned, that heartbreaker against the Chicago White Sox surely meant he was "due", as they say in baseball. Even though the Red Sox weren't hitting and

Gene pitching at Fenway

errors were made and wins eluded Gene's grasp, the papers had been reporting his possible berth on the All Star team again. Wouldn't that be neat, I thought, being chosen for All Star games in both leagues?

Searching for the Boston station and shaking uncontrollably, my heart began racing even though he usually pitched his best at times of greatest stress. The Yankees of 1962 with Mantle, Maris, Skowron, Tresh, Howard, Lopez, Boyer, Berra, Kubek and Richardson made up the strongest slugging team in their history. Pitching, it has been said, however, is seventy-five percent of the game and the Yankees had some beauts; Ford, Terry, Turley and Stafford. In 1962 the Yankees finished first. In 1962, Boston finished eighth.

"Billy Gardner went without sleep, Carl Yazstremski went without his sunglasses and Gene Conley went down to defeat as the Yankees broke open the Red Sox, 13 to 3, at Yankee Stadium yesterday.

Gardner missed a double-play and Yaz missed a fly ball.

A horrendous third inning gave the Yankees three out of four in the series and sent the Red Sox to Washington mumbling to themselves.

The elongated Conley appears snake-bitten as far as Yankee games are concerned.

He pitched two scoreless innings and then Boyer opened the third with a single. And that's where the Gardner and Yastrzemski angles came into the picture.

After Bouton bunted Boyer to second, Tresh singled, with Boyer holding third. Now Richardson hit to Frank Malzone, who threw to Gardner, slightly slow on the play.

Tresh was forced, but the relay to Pete Runnels for the double-play was tardy, although Runnels did argue that the throw was on time. Boyer had to hold third.

Conley thought he caught the corner with a 3 and 2 pitch to Mantle that would have retired the side.

That, as in the case of the missed double-play, would have ended the inning without a run.

There wasn't any faulting Elston Howard's double, but then Dale Long lifted a routine high fly to left field. Yaz lost the ball in the sun and in came two more runs, making it 6 to 0. Boyer added to the horror with his homer. " (Hy Hurwitz, Boston Herald American)

That, they say, was that and the pitcher or pitchers that replaced my hapless hero added kerosene to the fire which produced seven more runs. It was just a "Bad Day at Black Rock"! I couldn't believe this comedy of errors! It was good to give up, turn off and get on with the program. Craft city awaited my talents.

What I had just written off as just one of those things, wasn't so easily dismissed. The following events have taken on legendary proportions that have become one of the most misunderstood baseball tales told, retold and questioned about from that day til now. There probably will never be a time when Gene attends a sports show, dinner or any sports' appearance without someone in the audience asking to hear the story behind his attempt to fly away to Jerusalem, or where PumpsieGreen is now. Gene usually just laughs, the audience laughs and everyone leaves assuming it was just a prolonged "lost weekend".

The bizarre and mysterious happenings had started quite innocently enough but had turned into a three day media event. It caused a Mother and Father anguish with fear of their son's sanity, an owner's personal search, a media in a frenzy each hour of each of those three days, which included stake outs at our home, airports, train stations and bus depots. In some ways, the most deplorable of all, was the way in which some in the media crucified the manager, Mike Higgins, intimating that the team was in the early stages of anarchy against this mild mannered manager. With all this tumult exploding, the children and I were being quietly and contentedly, protected from "all hell breaking out". I was unaware of Gene's odyssey until it was reported to me over the emergency phone from the prodigal son himself, three days later.

During rush hour, the team bus was not making any headway through the Bronx on its way to Washington D. C. It had stalled on the outside lane encountering traffic left over from the previous light change. It was gridlock and nothing was advancing. It seemed that making a left hand turn would be an impossibility. All seemed so futile in this vintage pre-"facility" bus, filled with disgruntled players, manager and coaches who had enjoyed refreshingly cold beer in the clubhouse quite some time ago, and the poor "bussie" was absorbing a lot of abusive remarks to get on with it. The nearest rest stop would be some miles away. The Red Sox were down. Like their mood, the air conditioning was failing; the team parked and trapped forever it seemed, in the twilight zone.

All of a sudden, big Gene, always an independent thinker, got to his feet and proceeded down the aisle. As he passed Pumpsie Green, he tapped his shoulder and said, "I've got to go, want to come with me?" No one said a word. They must all have been a little bewildered about this sudden and abrupt departure with Pumpsie following Gene's exit from the bus into the corner bar to find some "facilities". Gene figured they could be out in a couple of minutes. Like I say, it

269

started innocently enough but when they returned to embark, there wasn't anything there to embark on.

Dusk was settling in but the humid, heavy air remained, and without their means of transportation, our fearless duo decided to go back into the bar for a little refreshment. "You know Pumps, since tomorrow is a day off, why don't we just do the town?" Every athlete in every sport knew, when you're in New York, you do "Toots Shore's". "Toots" was a big gregarious welcoming host and one of the greatest sports' fans in the country. He loved celebrities and made them feel wanted and comfortable. They had been dressed up for traveling so they went to some of New York's finest bistros before they wandered back to the Commodore Hotel where they had checked out that morning.

Before heading to D.C., a breakfast of "Bloody Marys" might do the trick and feeling a little wobbly and exhausted, they decided to go up to the room again and order room service; snacks and drinks. As Gene has admitted, "at that time, I was on the verge of becoming an alcoholic". Playing winter and summer now for five years had translated into 10 straight seasons of major league basketball and baseball and selling technical tape from Hawaii to New Jersey, his lifestyle was beginning to take its toll. The only bright side to this activity was that he was pitching his best ball without experiencing excruciating pain. Pain, sure, but not the kind that you can't handle.

Pumpsie was starting to worry. This wasn't the eighties with a strong Player's union to shield players who acted out their frustrations. Pumpsie was the first black player hired by the Red Sox, the last club to do so. Not playing regularly must have caused him a great deal of frustration. Pumpsie's display of independence had to be an anxious and fearful experience for him. This wasn't just a "missing a bus" incident, this was major disregard for the powers that be. It was thumbing noses at the "Lords of Baseball". This unorthodox disappearance would be unthinkable for a white player to attempt but think about the audacity of a black player to dare in those days? Surely his punishment would be most severe! I shouldn't wonder that he might not only be anxious about his situation but dreading the consequences. In 1962, discrimination was still a large part of the American fabric, even in sports.

"Gene, I'd better get gone. I'm going to get in trouble anyway. I need to get to Washington".

"You go right ahead Pumpsie. I'm in no hurry. They won't need me in Washington yet and during the All Star break, I'll just stay here in the room and get "tanked".

"Better still, I don't know what I want to do sittin' here in this room. I think I'll go buy me an airline ticket . You can go on to Washington. I'm headin'....I'm headin' for Jerusalem. You go to Washington and I'll go to Jerusalem."

"You, you ain't kiddin' me baby?"

"No, I'm not kiddin' you Pumps, I think I'll go to Jerusalem. You go to Washington".

"Well, I'm not going with you to Jerusalem".

"You don't have to, Pumpsie, but I'm goin'."

They checked out of the hotel to their separate futures. Gene stopped by the manager's office as he needed about two thousand dollars for the trip to Jerusalem. (This would be about seven percent of what he had signed to play) Gene didn't have a check with him and since this was the pre-credit card era, the manager called our bank in Foxboro to find out if they would have the money transferred to him at the Commodore Hotel.

So he went down to a travel agents' office and got himself a ticket to Jerusalem which I believe, was twelve hundred dollars. Since the plane didn't depart for a few hours, Gene had time for a few more drinks that afternoon.

Why Jerusalem? I think it is vital we examine what was going on in Gene's mind at that period of his life. Gene and I didn't have the opportunity to really examine and study the spiritual and religious questions he would sometimes inquire about. I have to admit, to me, baseball, basketball, the whole idea of competition, was not an issue that thrilled me. It provided our family's living and interesting places to see and things to do. It also afforded us the opportunity to visit the great museums in the country and meet celebrities we wouldn't have ordinarily met. We were able to purchase or receive complimentary tickets to the latest concerts and plays. It was a privileged life but we knew that it would soon be over and then what? I hadn't been a sports fan, but I adored the man who just happened to be an athlete, an athlete that performed well at the highest level of his professions. I admired him for that, but I knew the agony, the pain, and the loss that it all cost. The thing that concerned me most was his seemingly casual attitude towards spiritual matters, as I knew he was a very connected spiritual being.

We had a "God-centered" relationship but old habits die hard. No one is perfect. Salvation is a gift, it can never be earned. God's desire is to bestow blessings but somehow it just seemed presumptuous to ask for those blessings when we deliberately go contrary to His will. Our goal, our prayer was to live as God would want us to. The conscience always suffers when we don't and this drinking problem troubled not only me but Gene's realization of the potentially dangerous consequences if continued. Living on the edge was nerve wracking for both of us. To me, it became a problem as I wanted to warn, yet not wanting to interfere with his own religeous decisions, kept still. Upon reaching the highest point of a professional athlete's life in the "Majors" bears a tremendous responsibility, the pressures of winning is a constant. It not only involves the athlete but the media, the fans, the ownership, the league, the managerial staff, his fellow teammates, the opposition, the whole visible sports world. Every waking moment is devoted to this, everything else is secondary. His choice of playing all year long with its constant traveling, along with the additional responsibility of national account marketing, became impossible to do without the relief of a soothing "crutch". So, frustrated, he muddled through it all until he came to a point in his life where something dramatic stopped his forward motion into insanity.

His drinking started in high school. His buddy's Dad made wine in his cellar. He was from Germany and with each year's vintage, the boys became his master tasters. Since Gene wasn't a ladies' man, he and Bud would often park in a car and just talk about school, sports, their futures, etc. It was a rough government town, new and without youth facilities to keep the kids interested in a better way so most would just park and drink.

In college, living as a fraternity brother and owning a car, (thanks to an avid sports' alumnus) he was very popular with fellow frats, some of who were ex-world war II veterans who were in their late twenties and early thirties who had learned hard drinking in the military. It was the culture for young men then to have fun and party. He was so strong that alcohol didn't interfere with his sports endeavors at this time of his life. Even one of his professors would join him and the other frat boys in their fun loving ways. No one drank in the fraternity house, but after the games, it was the macho experience to get wasted.

His drinking stopped momentarily after he met me but it didn't prevent him from enjoying the bars, the camaraderie of the other players on the road as that was about the only activity available for those off hours, unless you were single or worse, a philanderer. Of course there always was the occasional egghead that enjoyed reading and museum hopping, but in this machismo world, they would be more or less shunned by fellow teammates or merely left alone. Most were able to handle just a few drinks but being six foot eight, two hundred and twenty five pounds, a "few" was hardly enough to lose those feelings of intimidation or social inadequacy. In baseball, his size made him feel like a giant among his average sized peers. His hunger for being accepted as just one of the guys alluded him without the comfort of alcohol, imagined or not.

Pumpsi went on to Washington and with an airline ticket to Jerusalem in his pocket, Gene began his quest for truth. But first, he decided to go to a bar. What else? He caught a cab and went to Al Schact's restaurant. He remembers sitting at the bar where he started telling the customers about his search for truth and his journey to where he perceived truth to be, in Jerusalem. They all knew who he was and as they listened in disbelief, came to the conclusion, he had cracked. He wasn't going to Jerusalem, surely(?). So to prove it, he showed them his ticket. He was very drunk by this time. They tried talking him out of it and of course, he took it as a challenge. So he left them, took a cab out to Idlewild to continue his pilgrimage. When he arrived, there were already a few reporters waiting for him. Someone there at Schact's must have called them. He greeted them with a handshake and a smile but he found that they too, didn't quite think it a good idea and tried desperately to talk him out of it. He wasn't to be humored and proceeded to the ticket counter to get his boarding pass. One thing prevented his determination ... no passport!

Now, he was embarrassed. He had already told the manager of the Commodore of his plan, people at the various bars and now the writers who would surely report seeing him at El Al Airlines, smashed and unable to board because of his lack of a passport. Now, the whole sports world, maybe those outside the sports' world would be told. His teammates, manager and coaches would have already been informed of his plans, as Pumpsi would have had to mention it to them in Washington. He said later, that if he had been suicidal, he would have killed himself.

"Well, I can't go back to the hotel as they'll think I'm an idiot" he reasoned. "Where am I going to stay? Well, I've got plenty of dough, why not the Waldorf Astoria?" So he checked into the Waldorf about 10:00 p.m. He was pretty exhausted by then and went right to sleep. The next morning, all that had happened came crashing down on him as he realized the whole of what had transpired the previous day. "What have I done? What have I---d-- o-- n-- e ?" He ordered breakfast and a paper where he read that "Gene Conley Had Disappeared" and no one knew where he was.

When Gene still remained absent, (AWOL) now for three days, reporters and columnists began inquiring the Red Sox office in Boston, the officials in Washington, our neighbors, etc. Mr. Yawkey even called Gene's parents to find out if he had gone home to Washington state. Eva and Les became extremely anxious about his frame of mind or wondered if something even more sinister had happened to him. Being well known, especially in New York, (all the cabby's knew him) and being six foot, eight inches tall, he would have been easy to spot but Gene's isolation at the Waldorf wasn't providing any clues.

In Boston, Saturday morning, the headlines read:

"CONLEY STILL MISSING; $1,000.00 FINE HITS GREEN "

Mystery Man Gene Last Seen Friday in Lobby of N.Y. Hotel, Hy Hurwitz

Washington--Baby faced Gene Conley has become a mystery man. The 6 ft. 8 in. right-handed pitcher of the Red Sox was still AWOL last night after his defecting team-mate Pumpsie Green was plastered with a stiff fine in the vicinity of $1,000.00 on rejoining the club here.

Late Thursday afternoon, Conley and Green left a traffic-jammed chartered Red Sox bus in upper Manhattan. Green returned to the club 27 hours later and after a dressing down from Manager Mike Higgins yesterday morning was handed a 'substantial fine.'

Conley has not been heard from officially since he told Manager Higgins that he was leaving the Red Sox bus near the George Washington Bridge. The bus was stalled in traffic. Big Gene faces one of the largest fines in the history of sports.

When last seen, Conley was in the lobby of the Hotel Commodore, New York, the Red Sox New York residence, at 3 p.m. Friday afternoon.

Manager George Howard of the Commodore told the Globe, Conley and Green returned to the hotel after they had left the Sox airport bound bus on Thursday.

Green took a jet plane to Washington the next afternoon and was so ill he couldn't go to the park for Friday's twinight double header.

Conley hadn't checked out of his room at that time. But when he hadn't returned on Saturday morning and as nobody had slept in the room, the hotel had him checked out.

... *'When I saw him Friday afternoon,' Howard told the Globe, 'Conley asked me to cancel the Monday reservations for his family. I've been looking for him since. Tom Dowd (Red Sox secretary) asked me to talk to him if I saw him and see if I could get Gene to fly to Washington and rejoin the Sox.*

I had my entire night crew on the alert watching for Gene. He didn't come back to the hotel Friday night. We had him checked out Saturday morning. I have not been able to talk to him and I have canceled the family reservations for Monday.' Conley's wife and their three children have been on a camping tour somewhere in New England ever since Gene left his trailer in Foxboro last Tuesday to go to New York with the club. The family was to be reunited Monday at the Commodore for a two-day holiday. (All Star break)

It was learned by the Globe that Green isn't the first player Higgins has fined. When the Sox skipper asked if he had fined anyone before he replied sharply. 'I fined Mel Parnell and Ellis Kinder in the past.'

It is possible that Conley may be plastered with the largest fine since Ted Williams was docked $5,000.00 by owner Tom Yawkey for spitting at Fenway Park fans six years ago.

After saying there was no excuse for Green to have taken off without permission, Higgins inferred there was even less for Conley.

'Nobody is happy about this,' said Higgins. 'I've talked with T. A. (owner Tom Yawkey) and he feels just as unhappy as I do.'

Higgins has apparently been told by Yawkey that he can make Conley's punishment as severe as he sees fit. Conley is one of the highest salaried players on the club. His pay is in the $30,000.00 class. He has been the best pitcher on *the team and would normally be entitled to a nice increase in his paycheck for 1963.*

At present, Conley's punishment will take a good chunk out of his `1962 paycheck and it may be that the Red Sox will trade or release him as soon as the opportunity arises."

In baseball at that time, it was tantamount to treason, to insult the game. His disrespect for "protocol" confused everyone. Gene just wasn't the type to disrespect anyone or anything.

In another article, *'Pumpsie told me he had every intention of returning to the bus,' said Higgins, 'but he said he got himself involved. He didn't say where he and Gene went or what they did, and I didn't ask him. He said he had no excuse for what he did and I accordingly handed him a substantial fine. I haven't heard anything from Conley'"...the mystery of Conley's whereabouts deepened as the Hose played the third game of the series with the Senators."*

There were articles of blame about Mike Higgins which was totally from left field as Gene's respect for Mike was never in question. Gene appreciated Higgins very much. Then the articles concerning his abortive Israeli sojourn began to circulate and still speculation as to why, what, and where he was now?

I was spared all this speculation and grief but Sunday morning, I was called to our emergency telephone. It was Gene. It was so good to hear his voice as we were planning on leaving for New York the next day.

"Katie, I've done something just awful". I braced myself for whatever this meant. I can't even begin to list all the possibilities that ran like lightening through my brain.

"Haven't you heard anything?"

"No, what do you mean honey?"

"I've been gone from the club since last Thursday". My first reaction was one of surprise but relief followed as this news was hardly as bad as the horrors I had imagined just moments before.

"I'm coming into Providence, RI as Logan may have reporters waiting and I'll join you at Camp Winnekeag. Can you pick me up in an hour and a half?

It was good to see him, especially since the experience had been so humiliating to Gene. He was so contrite, so shamed. He spoke of nothing less than quitting sports altogether. He had made up his mind to just get a job, change his life....maybe even get baptized. I was holding my breath, not wanting to change the mood, it seemed too good to be true. Maybe he was just trying to get my approval.(?) He said resigning would be the only honorable thing to do as he had embarrassed his club, his manager and the owner.

He was planning on looking for work the following day but first, he wanted to see the kids and spend the day relaxing by the lake.

All the little boys at camp, crowded around him upon our arrival. They had no idea what had transpired. All they wanted was an autograph and a chance to meet a major league baseball player. Our kids were crowded out, but they were used to that. They would fade into the background as they could wait.. They were just happy to be able to see DAD. At midnight, for the next twenty-five years, a small radio station in the greater Boston area would sign off broadcasting each night with, "Goodnight, Pumpsie Green, wherever you are". Thirteen years later, receiving the "Jack Barry Award" from the Boston Baseball Writers, Gene brought down the house when he ended his little speech with, "And I have but one more thing to say, ... Goodnight Pumpsie Green, wherever you are."

CHAPTER 27

CONSEQUENCES AND RESUMPTION

Turning off the highway into Foxboro, our plans were already taking shape. We were at peace and anxious to be home. The day before, Gene had sent a telegram to his manager, Mike Higgins, apologizing for his actions over the past four days, stating he might have other plans, but thanked him for all that he had done for him. At the time, Gene felt that explanation would suffice and the issue settled. That would be the end of it. We were stunned by what had been occurring since his disappearing act. There was a small crowd of both female and male reporters waiting for us in front of our trailer. Gene's telegram had just piqued their curiosity. Our neighbors later told us that reporters had been knocking at their doors for the last three days asking about our marital relationship, if they felt we were getting along, etc.

That morning had been a typical hot and humid July day. Gene had rolled up his pants and taken off his shoes to wade in the lake before taking off and had driven home that way. Myriad's of camping gear stacked high in the back of our station wagon was left unpacked as we all made a mad dash to our trailer door. Gene stood guard while the rest of us piled in. There were flash bulbs going off as he stood, amused, by the whole scene but there he was, barefoot, cheeks of tan,

Record American

LARGEST CIRCULATION IN NEW ENGLAND

8ᶜ CLOUDY, WARM
U S Report on Page 1

Vol 1 No 259 Boston Monday July 30, 1962 52 Pages

SUNRISE

RECORD AMERICAN FINDS GENE

Lost Conley Back Home, Ban By Sox

STORY ON PAGE TWO

STEALS HOME, FEET FIRST — Bare-footed Red Sox pitcher Gene Conley, missing since he left a team bus in New York Thursday, was located Sunday as he and his wife and three children returned to their trailer home in Foxboro. The strong-armed right-hander wore a big smile. (Story, Other Photo on Page 2)

pants rolled up, to be frozen in time at the door of our sixty foot trailer home. Even today, at odd times, someone will say, "you still living in a trailer?"

He said he'd talk to one reporter and picked out Joe Cashman of the Record American but asked if he could just have a minute first. To be honest, he didn't know what to say.

What could he say? He was caught with his hands in the cookie jar, he had embarrassed himself, the management, the owner and his team plus possibly alienating Red Sox fans. He asked me what he should say. I couldn't answer.

The next day when Gene went out to pick up the morning paper, there he was, on the front and back pages of the Boston's Record American, largest circulation in New England. Obviously, he hadn't made the American League's All Star team. Gene was mortified, the front office was angry and still deciding his punishment. His parents were relieved, but without too much in the way of explanation, they called to ask me as to his mental state. It was a great story for the newspaper game. Think of the many different hypothesis they could conjure up. Each one had their own ideas as to why such a bizarre and mysterious incidence had occurred. They were having a field day that lasted for what was left of the week. Along with the Record American's front and back spreads, the Boston Traveler had one and a half inch headlines on their front page. Outside of knowing his splendid and prolonged inebriated odyssey, the question of why Jerusalem (?) remained a mystery and has persisted so to this day. Speculations covered the gamut from problems at home, to the manager's problems with his players. He even made the church news page.

LOST CONLEY BACK HOME, BAN BY SOX, Story on page 2
NO EXCUSE, SAYS CONLEY

Joe Cashman, The Boston Herald American

"A contrite Gene Conley expects to meet an irate Mike Higgins Monday and hear his punishment for missing the entire three-day Red Sox series.... But it remains to be seen whether Higgins, who announced Sunday that Conley has been suspended indefinitely, will be willing to meet the big right-hander that soon.... Conley already has lost three days' salary, estimated at $175.00 a day and will receive no pay for the time he remains suspended. On top of that, a substantial fine probably will be imposed upon him for taking French leave of the Hose...

At no time during our conversation did Gene intimate he might not return to the Sox or that he had any idea of quitting baseball. He said he was anxious to talk things over with Higgins, and the sooner the better...

'I'm sorry for the way I've handled things, but I'm mostly tired and have other plans. Thank you for everything, Mike, the telegram read.

"We did not know about that wire while talking with Gene.....who was anxious to pay the penalty for his jumping act and get back on the Sox payroll."

'All I can say about what I did was that it just happened', he said. 'There was no excuse for it and I can't explain what prompted me to do it. It was simply one of those spur of the moment decisions. I've always been one to act on impulses, without stopping to think what the consequences may be'.

"There had been speculation that the failure of the Sox to get a run for Conley in his last two outings might have upset and discouraged him and had a lot to do with his decision to go into hiding for a few days."

'That had absolutely nothing to do with it.' Gene told us. 'Remember, I'm a pro. I've been pitching professional baseball for 12 years. Experienced players don't get unduly disturbed over a defeat or unduly elated over a victory. Sure, I love to win and hate to lose, but when a game's over, I forget it and look forward to my next game.'

"What about the report that he booked a plane passage to Israel before leaving New York?"

'We'll talk about that some other time' he answered with a shy grin. "Then it was suggested, there was some basis for the story."

'There was,' he confessed. But gee, I'm glad I'm here in Foxboro tonight now and not in Bethlehem. I understand it's very hot over there.' "It may be nearly as hot when Gene comes face to face with Higgins." "At the Logan Airport, Sox manager Mike Higgins, very serious, said: *'I'll be glad to talk to him, glad to meet with him.'*

"Other than that, Higgins had nothing to say of his flyaway pitcher, after the Sox had landed after their trip from Washington."

CONLEY: I'LL BE BACK! But His Future Up to Two Men
Boston Traveler, July 30, 1962 Tom Monahan

'If they want me back,' said the 6-8 righthander, 'I want to come back.' 'I went AWOL. Players have done that in the past and didn't quit. I'm not quitting. I have no intention now and never have had any intention of quitting.

'My record (9-10) may not show it, but this is the best season I have had in years.

'My arm feels great. I'm throwing the ball good. I want to continue in baseball. And I want to play out my baseball career right here in Boston, I also want to continue playing basketball ...

Now *I* was confused.

Time and again, reporters would and still ask the same question: *"Why Jerusalem?"* or *"What would you have done if you had a passport and found yourself in Israel?"*

It was always the same answer, *'I'd rather not talk about that but I'll admit I tried to get a flight out of New York.'*

Then came the speculations about how much Gene would be fined and how long he would be suspended. It would undoubtedly be over $2,000.00, largest since the William's fine but still the mystery remained. He was sorry for the embarrassment he had caused Mike Higgins. He even went so far as to say, 'I had no intention of missing the bus in New York. *I had no intention of missing the plane. I didn't know Pumpsie was behind me when I got off the bus.. Things just happened.'*

"Gene, Mr. Yawkey wants to see you in his office at 11:00 a.m. tomorrow." Beyond that, Higgins did not elaborate.

Gene hadn't been in Yawkey's office before. It was like a living room with a desk and shelves and a bathroom off it. Mr. Yawkey was busy shaving and directed Gene to sit down.

Before Tom had a chance to say anything, Gene made his apologies. Then he said, "Gene, you know, I've felt like that more times than I can count but Gene, you're a celebrity, you're in the limelight where everything you do is noticed and written about...you just can't do things like that anymore."

"You know I'm going to have to fine you, Gene, It's expected but if you keep your nose clean the rest of the season and put in a good year, you'll have that money back."

He was just about to end the conversation as he was just about through with his shave. "Gene help yourself to a beer."

"No thanks, Mr. Yawkey, I never touch the stuff."

Poor Tom, totally disarmed, bent over with laughter and told him he'd be watching him.

Mike was just as kind and generous in attitude and word. Gene would be starting in four days.

During Gene's days playing between college and the pros one summer, he had a semi-pro coach, Bob Dyer, who lived and breathed baseball. His uniform was neat, his shoes polished to a glossy black, everything about his appearance advertised, "Pro". Poor Gene, wearing baseball shoes that were at least two sizes smaller than his feet, his jersey too short to stay put often disturbed Bobby. Gene had cut the toes of his "cleats" open. Bobby often called them "alligator shoes" and threatened to take them away from Gene to drag the infield. Gene's general slovenly appearance was an affront to Bobbie's accepted view of what a baseball player should look like so he called him "Jeeter", the character from the book, "Tobacco Road". We received a telegram from him the same day of the Yawkey conference. It read, "Jeeter, Lay off that Mountain Dew or I'll come back and take your shoes away again, Bob Dyer."

After things settled down a bit, John Gillooly of the Boston Record American wrote, *"Well, I have known Gene all these years and I do declare that wherever he went, on a twister on a jet-flight to Bethlehem, his defection was justified. He should sue the Red Sox for non-support, and not be fined $2,000.00. This, technically, is his best pitching year, but what has he got to show for it? It would drive a man to a Manhattan. The Red Sox generally are blanked when he pitches. If not, they manage to lose by one meager, miserly pediculous run.*

Conley, you know, has been exposed to the Celtics, one of the great teams in the history of sports; a group of true major leaguers, each of whom does his job. How can he possibly be content to be associated with the Red Sox and their lallygagging? The Celtics are battlers; the Red Sox are badminton players, just tapping the bird about, old boy."

Gene wanted desperately to win. His first appearance after his fiasco was a 2-1 loss. His second time out, things were different. The Globe writer, Roger Birtwell:

"Maybe that $2,000.00 lost week-end helped Gene Conley."

"In a superb pitching performance before 13,489 last night at the Fenway, the tall right-hander of the Red Sox held the Cleveland Indians to four scattered hits and shut them out 6-0."

"At one stretch--from two out in the third through two out in the sixth--Conley struck out six of the 10 batters he faced."

Under the headlines about the Celtics, Auerbach, discussing his problem of not having a big man under the boards this coming season was quoted as saying, *'Don't think I wouldn't love to have Conley this year.'* *"Auerbach said, wistfully." 'We need a big man in the worst way. But Gene's not our property and furthermore, I don't even know if he'd be interested.'*

'Gene and I always had a rule that we wouldn't discuss basketball while he's playing baseball", Del Ninno.

His twelfth win of the season was a hot one! Literally, over 100 degrees in the shade in Kansas City.

"Gene stood out in the blazing sun at Municipal Stadium Thursday and pitched shut-out ball up to the ninth inning in leading the Red Sox to an 8-2 victory over the Athletics."

"Gene also got a double and single, scored a run, knocked in a run and was on base three times. Yet the big fellow looked almost as fresh and strong at the finish as he did at the start."

Gene was keeping his nose clean. "Gene was taken out of the Detroit game in the seventh inning, but was gone from the dressing room by the time the game ended."

"In the meantime the Celtics announced there would be a 'surprise signing at Walter Brown's office this morning.'

"It's been known that the Celtics were given permission to talk to Conley about playing this year. He had been claimed, via draft, by the Chicago club a year ago, but did not report."

It wasn't Gene but when the 1962 baseball season ended, Gene had 15 wins, his $1,500.00 back and a $5,000.00 raise.

In 1994, Gene was invited to Bryant Gumbels' charity golf tournament at Disney World to benefit the United Negro College Fund. At one of the banquets, Gene noticed Joe DiMaggio grazing around the many sumptuous food tables. Since Gene had missed playing against the famous slugger, he introduced himself. "Yeah, Gene I know who you are, you had to play two sports to make a living." He got that right. Playing the two sports the last two years, he only made $55,000.00

A couple of years after the golf tournament we were walking down Boylston St. in Boston trying to find Rochester's clothing store for tall men and some leather lunged guy yelled out from his car, in the middle of traffic and said, "Conley, ...Gene Conley, do you realize what you'd be making now, playing both sports?" "Yeah, I do", was Gene's reply. The guy then said, "You'd be making about ten million in each, how does that make you feel?" Gene yelled back, "I'm going home right now and slap my Mother around for having me so soon!"

Sal Maglie, who had been the pitching coach for the Red Sox the year before "the Jerusalem incident", had talked to Gene about his own decision to retire from baseball. Sal had been known as "the barber" because of his pin point control in just barely missing the batter's head to move him back from the plate. He was with Brooklyn in 1957 and when facing Gene, ("the batter"), walked him. He said that he called his wife that night and said, "honey, it's time I quit, as tonight, I walked a seven foot giant."

Getting back to the fall of 1962, Gene, did not want to go back into the ABL, which took him from NY to Hawaii to see every corporate purchasing agent while playing almost forty-five minutes per game, Gene, again, retired from basketball or at least this was the plan. We set ourselves on the road to normalcy. The children loved Foxboro and their schools so Gene began accepting charity appearances for town events. This led to purchasing a newly built Cape Cod home on Birch Tree Rd. in Foxboro. By October, he was baptized into the Seventh-day-Adventist church near Fenway Park.

Eddie Donovan, then coach for the NY Knickerbockers, called one day soon after that, before Gene had found employment, asking if they could have a conference with him as Ned Irish, the president of the Knicks had something in mind. They had just signed a 6'9", first round draft choice from Cincinnati University who had won the NCAA title that year. Paul Hogue, center, was also the Most Valuable Player in that tourney and was the third leading scorer in Cincinnati history, trailing pro aces Oscar Robertson and Jack Twyman. He had scored 62 points and grabbed 51 rebounds in three games at the Garden's 1961 Holiday Festival, but they needed a back up center with experience and since they had scouted Gene with the ABL, wanted him to fill that position. Donovan told him that he wouldn't be seeing too much playing time, and not to worry about taxing his energies. It was a pleasant meeting, although it seemed a generation away from the Celtics' homey "open door policy", Walter Brown and Company ran. The NY Knickerbockers were more "Big League". When asked what it would take for Gene to become a "Knick", Gene's hasty reply of $25,000.00, was quickly and easily accepted. One problem the Knicks weren't aware of, remained.

Gene's acceptance of *keeping all the ten commandments* would be the problem. One of the tenets of becoming a Seventh-day-Adventist is keeping the fourth commandment as written. These same commandments, entrusted to Moses on Mt. Sinai thousands of years ago, written on stone by the finger of God, was a major confession of faith in Christ at his baptism. These tenets, meant for the Israelites originally and then to "spiritual Israel" after Christ's ministry, were values Gene believed in. Gene felt that since he wasn't going to be a major factor with the Knicks, his absence from working Friday night and Saturday afternoon games, could be tolerated.

There was a major conference in the other room where Donovan and Red Holzman, the assistant coach at the time, had disappeared. After their reappearance, Eddie, very quietly asked Gene if he would please see his priest or pastor to find out if he would give Gene "absolution" from working on his Sabbath. This really threw Gene a curve. Red Holzman, such a great and wonderful man smiled, as if he knew this was nonsensical, but when in Rome..... It was also explained that it would be demoralizing for his other teammates to take this time off.

Gene said he would think about it. And think he did. He talked with me about it. Although the $25,000.00 was a temptation to both of us, I would rather he keep the Sabbath as written from sundown Friday night to sundown Saturday night when the day was established at creation. This was something Gene had to decide for himself, however. I would not pressure him either way.

It took him several days while the NY management waited. Then Gene told me his decision. It wasn't my set of values, nor the church's. It wasn't what the world would even know or care about but it was what Gene felt was right. When we married, I had told Gene that I had always tithed ten percent of my income, even gifts given to me as a child and if it would be all right, could I continue to do the same with what he made playing sports? Being a generous and loving person, this was no problem to him. His plan now, was not only to tithe his income, but to pay back to God via the church, the money he earned on Friday nights and Saturday afternoons playing for the NY Knicks. He didn't need to demoralize his teammates, nor disappoint Knicks' management. Most of all, he had a clear conscience about it. I did as Gene wanted me to do each paycheck. Since we lived so close to N.Y. and it was only a $13.00 one-way airline ticket away, Gene commuted to N.Y. on homestands so as not to disrupt family life which had become very important to him.

Between what the IRS took, along with what the states of Massachusetts and New York helped themselves to, giving up half his salary to charity, and the expenses of traveling, we probably only made a few thousand during the 1962/1963 Knickerbocker year. Not a very fruitful venture. Also, what was to be a back-up role behind Paul Hogue, turned out to be the complete opposite. Gene began starting as the Knick's center.

Bit of a Tussle — While Bill Russell looks on. Cliff Hagen and Gene battle for a loose ball while BobCousy struggles to get free. 1961

CHAPTER 28

THE BEGINNING OF THE END

CONLEY GROUNDED BY 'BOMB THREAT'

"New York— The FBI detained Gene Conley when Conley got himself into the word trap while he was getting ready to step on a plane from New York to Boston, near where he lives. He was on the way home to spend a night with the family.

'I travel so often,' said Conley, 'that I know all the guys at the airport, and we kid around a lot One of them said 'How're things going, Gene?'"

And that's when Conley made his mistake, His reply was, 'It looks good, we're going to BOMB the Celtics.'

The next thing Conley knew he was sitting in the plane, and a man came up and tapped him on the shoulder. It was the FBI, checking a bomb threat.

'He told me what it was about,' said Conley, 'and at first I felt pretty good about it, because I travel a lot and it's good to know they're on the ball.'

Four hours later, when the situation was finally cleared up, Conley didn't feel so good."

I was relieved when after five hours, Gene finally appeared. Knowing the Knicks were using him almost every night for longer than expected and knowing

295

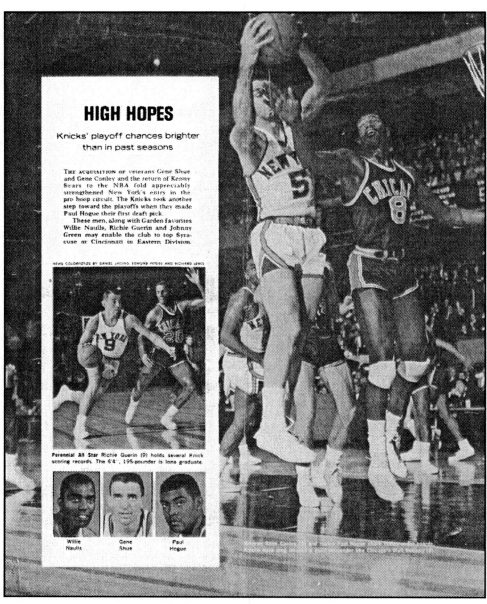

HIGH HOPES

Knicks' playoff chances brighter than in past seasons

THE ACQUISITION of veterans Gene Shue and Gene Conley and the return of Kenny Sears to the NBA fold appreciably strengthened New York's entry in the pro hoop circuit. The Knicks took another step toward the playoffs when they made Paul Hogue their first draft pick.

These men, along with Garden favorites Willie Naulls, Richie Guerin and Johnny Green may enable the club to top Syracuse or Cincinnati in Eastern Division.

NEWS COLORPHOTOS BY DANIEL JACONO, EDMUND PETERS AND RICHARD LEWIS

Perennial All Star Richie Guerin (9) holds several Knick scoring records. The 6'4", 195-pounder is Iona graduate.

Willie
Naulls

Gene
Shue

Paul
Hogue

**Gene and Walt Bellamy struggle at the boards
1963**

his exhaustion, had my mind actively going through the possibilities of his partying ways.

After a game with the Celtics, a NY paper (UPI) reported, *"The Hose's 15 game winner played the entire first half during which he scored 13 points. Then big Gino played all but five minutes of the second half. He finally ended up with 19 points.*

Knicks coach Eddie Donovan is getting plenty of mileage out of Conley -- something the Red Sox brass might not enjoy hearing -- and apparently there's no siesta in sight for Gino"

In New York, Heinsohn ate with Gene after the Knick/Celtic game and told him that at half-time "Red" was really dressing down the Celtics for letting Conley make a fool out of them to which Tommy replied, "but Red, he's playing more over here". All this activity was starting to take its toll. Starting for a last place club again after enjoying those Celtic Championships, was discouraging and physically draining. First it was just a little drink after games. Then, one time in Richland, Washington, where Gene had flown down from Seattle to see his parents, his father suggested that he, Gene's brother Sonny and Gene go down to see some of the guys he used to know at the VFW. Of course Sonny and Les left after a short time but Gene decided to stay and swap yarns. The next night he and the Knicks would be going against the San Francisco Warriors so the conversation naturally gravitated to how Gene would handle Wilt Chamberlain. After a number of drinks all around, courtesy of the big time ballplayer, Gene began to predict that he and Hogue could hold Wilt to under 20 points on Wilt's home turf. This seemed an impossibility when Wilt was scoring over 40 points per game so the bet was on. With little sleep, Gene deplaned for San Francisco and Wilt.

1964, March — Our Last Spring Training — Arizona

Upon arriving the next day, hours before the game, his first mission was to talk to his roomie, Paul Hogue. He told Paul about his bet and asked him to extend himself and between the both of them, they determined to hold Wilt to under 20 points. They both played their hearts out and at the end, Wilt had only 19. The Victory was an empty one, as it turned out, as he wasn't able to collect on the bet. His VFW buddies suddenly developed amnesia.

And so went the season. Almost predictably, another calamity stalked Gene's progress. His pitching finger, in a game against the Celtics, was broken in late winter. He was able to get a break but upon rejoining the Knicks, index finger resplendently dressed in tape, sustained his most serious injury, an ankle sprain that put him out of action for the last week of the season. The Knicks placed him on the voluntary retired list after he had met with president Ned Irish and other club brass. Asked by a reporter from the UPI news service if he would be retiring from basketball, Gene said, "I'd like to stay in both sports until somebody takes my uniform away from me." Being six weeks late for spring training wasn't anything new, but joining a Major League team for a full spring training for the first time in five years, was a pleasant experience, as was the Arizona sunshine and warm climate.

The Red Sox had a new manager and general manager that spring. Johnny Pesky who had been employed by them in some capacity since his playing days, was made manager when Mike Higgins was kicked up to the front office as general manager. It was obvious from Gene's limp and his taped finger, he was in no condition to pitch. He tried to run as best he could but his ankle would swell up to twice its size in the evening. He would attempt to pitch but his throwing was awkward, favoring his injured ankle but the bone chip in his index finger bothered him as well. It was a painful sight. Yet, with no complaining, took his turn. Then the team departed for exhibition games. In Denver, with the temperature around freezing, and snow falling lightly, Johnny started Gene.

The inevitable happened as everyone noticed his inability to pitch smoothly because of that ankle. Why athletes play hurt is a mystery to me. Times have changed since then but in Gene's era, I suppose it wasn't considered manly, not to. The most offensive insult a ballplayer could be accused of was to be labeled a "jake" so no matter what the injury, a player plays. Just as it was in Dizzy Dean's era when Diz pitched awkwardly caused from an injured ankle that ended his career, so it was with Gene's injury. No amount of cortisone each week, would heal his fragile shoulder now and after his third win, he was sidelined the rest of the season on the disabled list. Not knowing it then, Gene's Major League baseball career ended that fall of 1963. In basketball, the vintage Knickerbocker team of 1963/1964 was ending their year uneventfully so with Gene packing injuries and exhaustion, the Knicks allowed Gene to leave early for spring training. Everyone, including the Conley clan, were still hopeful that he'd have another baseball "comeback" and at times during that spring training, it seemed he would. When camp broke, pitching in Oklahoma City though, not able to pitch up to his standards, and upon leaving the ball park, he yelled at a youngster running for an autograph. "Hey, kid, you want a glove?" He saw no further use for it.

Mike Higgins called the house the day before the Sox left to go on their first road trip of the season. He told him of his "Notice to Player of Release or Transfer". It was a "waiver" of sorts, that within a specified time, if a Major League Player wasn't picked up from another MLB team, he would be unconditionally released. His remarks were personal and kind as he truly admired Gene and his admiration was returned in like manner. Mike thought it would be a good time for Gene to pick up his gear that day, while the team wasn't there.

Gene said, "Mike, thanks, for everything. You carried me all of last year and I appreciated it" and then it was over.

Driving in to Fenway that afternoon, we didn't speak much. Gene's reassuring hand rubbed my knee at times and his generous smile was a comfort. After thirteen whirlwind years, without ceremony all these attempts to redeem ones self, to fulfill the destiny that fate had handed him on a silver platter, was all coming suddenly to a screeching halt. No more chances. I hadn't expected the emptiness. My feelings didn't matter to me, but I knew what it meant to Gene, though he wouldn't admit it. He joked as he left me in the car to retrieve his belongings. By the time he threw the bats, shoes and remnants of uniforms into the back seat, tears were streaming down my checks. The clubhouse guy had given him some of Ted Williams things, his bat and a couple of Ted's old embroidered undershirts. Gene used those old shirts doing yardwork for years and gave away Ted's bat to one of his first customers, not even a very good customer at that. Strangely enough, it would be a sad and fond adieu from the Boston writers and columnists as they had enjoyed chronicling the Conley antics, it was fun and games to them. Their eulogies were numerous, heartfelt and interesting, two of which I'd like to add parts of:

CONLEY'S 'INTENTIONAL WALK'
PASSES INTO IMMORTALITY

"In a distant time, when baseball fans are rounding up memories over a few cool ones out in the kitchen, one achievement is certain to be recaptured and replayed.

It won't be Mickey Mantle's four successive homers or Stan Musial's four big blasts, or Bill Mombouquette's near perfect game, or Earl Wilson's no-hitter, or Sandy Koufax's 18 strikeouts, or Floyd Robinson's six for six.

301

The feat that will keep the 1962 season alive in memory was the historic stroll by Gene Conley, the wayward bus rider.

...Conley thus became the first pitcher in the history of the national pastime to issue himself an intentional walk. Behind this redwood of a man came his slender Boston Red Sox teammate, 6' Elijah (Pumpsie) Green. This modern-day Don Quixote and Sancho Panza march off together to tilt at the windmills of conformity.

Like the original Don Quixote, Conley ignored the timid voices that told him 'you can't do that here' or 'it will never work.'

...Conley became one with Rube Waddell, Rabbit Maranville, Charlie Grimm, Art Shires, Hack Wilson, and all the other delightfully mad geniuses who made baseball fun to watch and to read about.

Modern major leaguers don't leave the team bus but Conley did. Modern major leaguers don't fail to show up for games but Conley did. And then he added the most delirious touch of all to this wondrous adventure, the trip to Israel.

Instead of rewarding this inspired man by dedicating a statue (or at least a plaque) in his honor, the Red Sox management fined him $2,000.00. That's the same type of shabby treatment the unimaginative fired at the unbowed head of Don Quixote because he dared to be different.

Although his income from baseball and basketball is substantial, Conley surely will miss the two "thou". Long after the money no longer matters, however, Gene's intentional walk will assure him of immortality that he never could achieve through his pitching. Bill Gleason, The Boston Globe

"CONLEY HAD FEELING HE WAS ON WAY OUT

Larry Claflin, Boston Record American, April 24, 1964

Baltimore ... When word spread through the Red Sox the other night that Gene Conley had been fired, the story telling started. Just about everyone on the club has a favorite Conley story to tell, just as do the Celtics with whom he shared championships.

Some of the stories dealt with Conley's unpredictable behavior, such as the time he tried to take Pumpsie Green to Israel with him. Other stories were about Gene's incredible strength such as the time he is suppose to have ripped off a taxicab door with his bare hands. Yes, Conley left a memory of great strength, courage in the clutch and a body that seemed immune to wear and tear.

It wasn't always that way, though. Those of us who took the now legendary 'rookie rocket' trip to visit Braves rookies in the winter of 1952 remember Conley for different reasons. ... Among the players we visited were Eddie Mathews, Bill Bruton and Ernie Johnson. One of the last stops on the trip was Richland, Wash., where Conley lived.

Richland is an atomic energy center. Just about everything in the town was owned by the A.E.C. and everyone worked for Uncle Sam. Gene Conley's father was one of them.

The press had dinner with the Conley family in the Government Hotel on a Saturday night. Gene was only a kid at the time, but the Braves were very high on him. Especially Lou Perini. Gene had just won 20 at Hartford.

A few days after we left Richland to atomic fission, one of the Boston writers received a touching letter from Mr. Conley.

'His mother and I will worry about Gene while he is traveling and I ask you to keep an eye on him and write to us if Gene needs anything,' his father wrote.

Gene seemed like kind of a big boy for a 24 year old sports writer to be looking after, but the memory of that letter remained through the years while Conley achieved fame, wealth and championships in two major league sports. Maybe his father was right. In many ways, Gene remained a boy.

Last Monday, although it was not apparent at the time, the Red Sox career on Conley came to an end. He was sitting in the dugout talking to three groundskeepers while waiting to see if the bad weather would permit the Sox to play the Yankees.

'How's your arm?' Conley was asked.

'Not too good, but it will be okay once the weather gets warm. I'm always like this in the spring. One year I stayed in Bradenton until May before I joined the Braves so I could pitch in a warm climate. Then, Gene said something that--in retrospect-- proves he knew the handwriting was on the wall.

'But he said, 'when you get to be my age they don't wait for you that long.' Gene knew what was coming. So did most of his teammates. As Eddie Bressoud said when he heard the bad news about Conley: "We can't afford to lose a competitor like Gene, there aren't enough good competitors like him around.'

If this is adieu to Conley, then let it be with a smile and a story Gene delights in telling. A couple of weeks ago, while the Red Sox were in Oklahoma City, Gene met an uncle (by marriage) he hadn't seen for 13 years. When they met outside the ball park, Gene yelled out a greeting. The uncle said:'Gene, how did you recognize me?'

304

The uncle has only one arm."

A letter came by mail the next day from the Red Sox's traveling secretary, Tom Dowd.

"Dear Gene, As the old Irishman uncle of mine would say...' Tis with a sad heart to learn of our separation.' Knowing you was one of the pleasures of my baseball life. Never lose that fine sense of humor that is yours and things will forever have a bright side. If I can help you anyway at anytime, I'll be honored to do it. My best to Mom and the youngsters. God bless you'

True to his word, Tom couldn't believe his eyes when he saw Gene and his parents standing in a long line at the ticket booth to purchase tickets for a ballgame two months later at Fenway. He quickly took them into his office and produced the box seat tickets. Gene would never ask for favors, it would not be his 'nature' an old deacon used to say.

When we had returned from Fenway to retrieve Gene's junk, we soon received a call from the general manager of the Cleveland Indians. It was Gabe Paul, once the president of the National League. He said that Cleveland had picked up his waiver for $1.00 and if Gene would like to, work out with the Burlington, North Carolina team for $500.00 per month to see if his arm would come around. If it did, they would sign him to his Rcd Sox $30,000.00 per year salary.

Even though Gene's arm felt like there was "no tomorrow" there, he had to try. Like he once said, "I'll play until someone takes off my uniform". I would call after each game he pitched and it was always the same, "still no go". He had to play it out. While there he met up with the famed "King and His Court", a touring soft-ball group and their unbeatable pitcher, Eddie Feinger, who also hailed from Richland. When Gene informed him of his shoulder problems, he said he would fix him up. Satch Paige had given him this recipe a long time ago and it was a sure fire remedy for what was ailing him. As many pitchers are aware, there are all sorts of hot preparations that take hurt away from a great many muscle pains but Gene's was a torn rotator cuff from which no topically applied heat would alleviate. This injury could only be helped with surgery and in that era the medical community hadn't been that successful nor the owners that anxious to wait for a 33 year old pitcher to heal. There were hundreds of younger arms out there waiting in the wings. The druggist couldn't believe the list of ingredients Gene ordered that day and asked if he was sure he knew what he was doing. The results were deadened skin that peeled off like an onion.

He was slowly accepting his fate and while in a strange mood, went by a used automotive lot where he saw a large white school bus for sale, only $500.00. He thought about refurbishing it for camping trips, he knew the families' love for camping and sought a way to lessen our supposed disappointment and hurt. For the first time since his arrival at Burlington, his voice seemed so joyful.

"Katie, I bought this old school bus and we can rip out the seats, put down new carpeting, add cupboards, beds, a table....."

"Are you crazy, Gene? Where would we park it? You have trouble changing a light bulb, how could you refurbish it? The cost of having it refurbished would be prohibitive!" I'm afraid my diplomatic skills were sadly lacking. I wasn't aiding and abetting his grand plan meant to encourage. I just wanted him home.

When the old black pastor at the little white church on the outskirts of Burlington was given the keys to that large white school bus, he almost kissed Gene. Tears of joy were streaming down his face as he hugged Gene. "What a blessing, what a blessing", he kept saying.

Gene notified Gabe that it was no use, he was going to retire from baseball. It was Mother's Day Sunday and since his plane didn't leave until late afternoon, he decided to go over to the big Baptist Church for the morning service, to think about his future in quiet surroundings. He walked in and sat on the back row to try and figure this whole thing out. The pastor's sermon was on the virtues of Motherhood but Gene's mind was wandering, "now I *am* through, I can't pitch with anybody, my arm is killing me, I failed in the minors, I can't go back and play basketball. I didn't finish college and haven't got a degree, I haven't saved any money, what in the sam hill am I going to do?" The preacher kept preaching away as Gene continued his "mind talk", "It all seems so impossible, I can't think of a thing to do."

Tears welled up in his eyes and escaped down his cheeks.

"There was this old deacon standing back behind me in the back of the church and he walked over and poked me on the shoulder and said, 'what's the matter, son, did you lose your Muthur?'

"No sir ... I lost my fastball." The deacon slowly backed away. At Christmas, 2001, Robin Roberts sent his annual Christmas letter with these words, "Gene, while vacationing this summer, Mary and I went through Burlington, North Carolina and so we stopped in to visit the large Baptist church in the center of town. I asked to see the pastor. I asked him if he had found your fastball yet, but he replied in the negative. Merry Christmas, roomie."

CHAPTER 29

THE AGONY AND THE ECSTASY

The end of May, 1989, just before Joe Fitzgerald's feature was published on the back page of the Boston Herald tabloid, Gene accompanied me to the ENT's office. The usually rushed physician, Dr. Van Orman, seemed to be practicing a relaxed, off-handed manner as he casually lifted a clear plastic model of a disjointed human head.

After delivering his abhorrent news, Gene sat completely motionless as if hit by a colossal boulder. Swearing is a foreign tongue to me but this time, my reaction seemed the only logical thing to do and before I knew it, I had blurted out an expletive, which surprised even me. As he started peeling off each piece, I could feel the scalpel digging farther and farther into the middle recesses of my head. Then Gene started with his barrage of questions. Was the tumor operable? Was it a serious surgery? Can it be handled any other way? What if it were your wife or yourself, what would you do?

On and on it went until Dr. Van Orman said, "at this particular time, if it were me, there would be only three surgeons in the country that I would consider with such a technical procedure. One is in Tennessee, the second slips my mind right now but the third, is a Dr. Derald Brackman of the famous 'House Clinic' in L.A. He sometimes lectures at Massachusetts General Hospital. He was the one that President Reagan went to with his hearing difficulties."

**Our Fortieth
Christmas
Together**

The technical term for this type of tumor is "juglari glomus tumor" and this problem was not only location but all these invasive vascular tentacles had managed to attach themselves around the left ear drum, jugular, and left vocal chord. Not only that, they had continued to grow as it was able to draw in ever more blood on its voyage to the edge of my brain stem. Oh yuck!

After checking with our son who is a surgeon in California, we decided on having Dr. Van Orman contact Dr. Brackman in L.A. The scans were sent over-night and after viewing them, Brackman called me. His manner was kind but in a direct "matter of fact way", told me that after the surgery, I would not only be left with difficulty swallowing and breathing, but my speaking voice would be weak and somewhat inaudible. There also was the possibility that I could be paralyzed and that if I were a year older, he would not attempt the surgery. Ignoring these unthinkable possibilities, the only thing I could weakly ask was if I would ever be able to sing again which was answered in the negative. It wasn't as if I was this great soprano who's career would be shattered by this turn of events. It just seemed that at this time, it was the only thing I could focus on.

Not being a person to suffer in silence, I called and wrote everyone I had ever known or heard of to pray for me.

Ignoring this latest development, Gene and I continued that day to petition for the Oldtimers' pension by sending out letters to each NBA owner, player rep and NBA executive as well as our membership newsletters.

Up until this time, Gene had also been working with Early Wynn and Jim Bunning to improve the pensions of the older retired Major League Baseball player as the disparity of their pensions were grossly unfair. As a matter of fact, he was to meet with them in Washington D.C. the next week to discus their grievances at a meeting with Don Fehr, the MLB Player's Director. This was to be

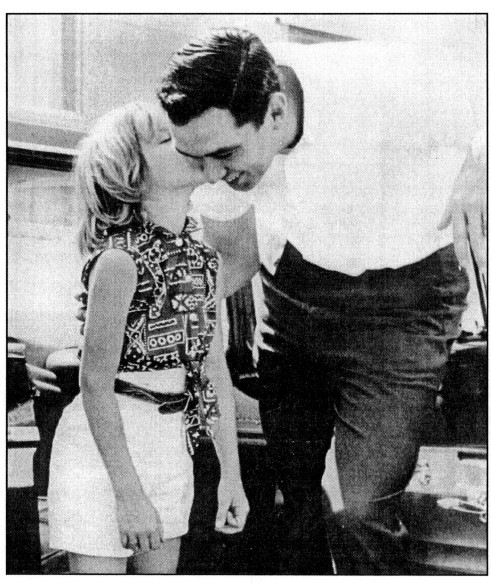

**Kitty Kissing Daddy Goodbye at Fenway Park for Another Road Trip
1963**

the same week of my scheduled surgery. With the recent news, Gene had to cancel his participation which was a disappointment to him. During the whirlwind of those last few months, working to gain a pension for the NBA Oldtimers, we had also heard from the pre-1946 Major League Baseball Players working towards pension inclusion. Former players in the National Hockey League and the National Football League had likewise called us during this time, just for advice and jokingly asked us to take over for them.

Coming home, arms loaded with boxes of copies to be sent out, I trudged up the stairs into our office. Gene rushed towards me with eyes glistening. I have seen that look before when he had a particularly good day at selling. He would play a little game of, "guess how much we made today?"

"Katie, WE GOT IT!"

"Wha....?????"

"I just received a call from Larry Fleischer". (the National Basketball Player's Association's Director at that time).

"He said, 'Well, Gene, you got the damned thing.'"

I don't know who started to cry first, but in unison, we fell to our knees. There we were in the middle of our office kneeling and crying, thanking God for this miracle!

Jesus spoke a parable that is recorded in Luke 18:1-8

"There was once a judge who cared nothing for God or man, and in the same town there was a widow who constantly came before him demanding justice against her opponent. For a long time he refused; but in the end he said to himself, 'True, I care nothing for God or man: but this widow is so great a nuisance that I

313

will see her righted before she wears me out with her persistence.' The Lord said, 'You hear what the unjust judge says; and will not God vindicate his chosen, who cry out to him day and night, while he listens patiently to them? I tell you, he will vindicate them soon enough. But when the Son of Man comes, will he find faith on earth?"

I could almost hear the Hallelujah chorus!

Gene prayed and agonized from the time we flew out of Logan until Dr. Brackman came in after sixteen hours and sixteen units of blood had been pumped into my system, to say that I had survived the surgery. However, three of the cranial nerves had to be sacrificed. The left vocal chord was paralyzed, the loss of the left ear drum as well as other smaller and sundry nerves which would interfere with facial, tongue and mouth function were gone. This meant a constant burning dry mouth and the inability to swallow water or ice chips without drowning. In other words, I was a real mess! Also, too weak to walk to a mirror, I was unaware that my face was temporarily on the paralyzed side.

In spite of that, Gene would come in each morning to say, "Katie, you're so pretty today". What a great fabricator! To say I was and will always be grateful to Gene is just way too insignificant as this sojourn lasted more than six weeks in the hospital. Not wanting to leave my side, necessitated a significant business loss.

Someone at the hospital had received Fitzgerald's article and had hung it up at the nurse's station which made me some sort of "floor celebrity", especially as the loads of flower arrangements started arriving from people all over the country. They would ask about the article and about the VIP's who sent the flowers and gifts. One of the attending physicians asked one day, "how many years did you play basketball Gene?" Then, "how much in pension does the NBA pay you now?" When Gene answered, "for seven years, I get a little over $400.00 per month Doc". He looked a little puzzled and said, "doesn't sound exactly right to me. Was all that work and effort to gain a basketball pension worth all those years of struggle?" Until that moment, we had been rather pleased with our accomplishment.

Almost immediately upon returning, two of our NBA Oldtimers sent us copies of the ***"post - 1965"*** NBA player's pension benefits which showed a glaring disparity with what we had been granted. The base pension and widows benefit was, for some, less than half what the ***"post-1965"*** player would receive.

Still, in all, we felt that recognition was a very important first step and we were grateful. If properly presented to the Player's Union and owners, we still felt something could be accommodated in the future.

Soon afterwards, the information of that disparity circulated among our ranks of a little over 150 Oldtimers, 22 of whom are inducted into Basketball's Hall of Fame, 5 of those, were voted the best players in the NBA's 50 year history. We were asked, once again to see what we could achieve in bringing pension equity to the Oldtimers. Exhausted from our shared ordeal, along with my voice and physical therapy sessions, at the same time trying to recoup our business losses, we were reluctant to continue. Still, we felt obligated to try.

So started another campaign. About this time, a new **Retired** Players Association formed, incorporating Gene as one of their board members of Dave DeBucherre, Dave Bing, Dave Cowans, Archie Clark, and Oscar Robertson.

We felt the new owners, who bought into the NBA needed to be aware of its rich heritage. Their gains have been tremendous, thanks to David Stern's progressive business acumen. The player's union has also benefited extensively under the leadership of Billy Hunter, their Executive Director. We still have the hope that these two entities will want to do the fair and honorable thing.

When honored for certain achievements in both baseball and basketball now, Gene feels unworthy because of the way he squandered his talents. I recall one such honor, when in the last days of the old Boston Gardens, just months away from its demise where so much of its history had gained its fabled championships, the Boston Celtics picked out thirty of their "legends" to represent their past glories. Chosen as one of those legends was Gene. He didn't feel honored, he felt humbled. Those other twenty-nine athletes had given their one hundred percent to their game. As Gene jokingly likes to say about himself, "I gave my full sixty percent", but with bowed head, he stood there with some of his former teammates. In street clothes, all thirty players which included players like; Larry Byrd, Bill Russell, Bob Cousy, Bill Walton, Tommy Heinsohn, Bill Sharman, Frank Ramsey, John Havelchik, Ed Macauley, Paul Silas, Jim Loscutoff, K.C. Jones, "Tiny" Archibald and Sam Jones among others, threw the ball around the floor finishing up with Larry Bird's dunk and Auerbach's hug. It was over, the last game in the Boston Gardens.

With tears in the eyes of the fans, they laughed, applauded and cheered their heroes one last and final time.

In MLB, Gene stopped appearing in Equitable's Baseball Legends' Games. His shoulder would not allow him to throw the full sixty-six feet, six inches. There have been many All Star anniversaries, MLB Championship Anniversaries as well as the Celtic World Championship celebrations.

In the seventies, he was awarded the first "Jack Barry Award" by the Boston Writer's Association for outstanding athlete of whatever era they were alluding to.

In 2002, April, he was asked to throw out the first pitch to open up the Milwaukee Brewers Baseball Season.

In 2003, the Retired NBA Players Association honored Gene at their All Star weekend Luncheon for his 10 years of service on their board and for his leadership with the NBA Old-timers.

In Sports Illustrated and a dozen or so books written about the era in which he played, include Gene's stories and comments. I really couldn't count the features in papers and magazines because of his two sport careers and his fine sense of humor.

He has made the Hall of Fame at Richland High School, Washington State University and Washington State's Hall of Fame. He is in Baseball's Hall of Fame in the Minor League Section as the only Minor League Player to win the "most Valuable Player" in their league *twice*. As a team member, he is photographically featured at both Baseball's Hall of Fame and Basketball's Hall of Fame. You could almost say he has been the most successful two-sport athlete, as he is the only two-sport professional athlete to win MLB's National League Championships twice, one MLB World's Championship and three NBA World's Championships. No other major league two-sport star has *"world's"* championships in two sports.

He has served on Foxboro's Industrial Board, Fuller Hospital's board, his church's board, the Retired NBA Players Association board and is still on the NBA Legends Foundation Board but nothing ever gave him more pleasure and pride than serving as director for the NBA Oldtimers' Association and complete what he and I had hoped to accomplish.

In the past 14 years, Gene has associated with some of the greatest basketball players of all time as all one-hundred-fifty plus Oldtimers truly honored and ennobled him. They were so grateful for being recognized by the NBA in a tangible way. The NBA's recognition of their efforts and sacrifices with a pension means more to them than any honors extended. The outcome has made life not only easier for them in their latter years but for some, a life saving dividend. We all look forward to next year's collective bargaining meetings as our hope is that the breach that exists between the NBA's pre and post-1965 player's pension will narrow.

This project continues and did continue while Gene and I managed our own company for thirty-four years. In the first few months when MSNBC first started broadcasting, they asked him if he would come on their television network to lobby on behalf of the **pre-1946** Major League **Baseball** players who were in the midst of their effort to gain a pension. Baseball left them out of a MLB pension in 1946 when the baseball pension was established. He was only too happy to add his small part to their effort.

Three years ago, in 2001, we celebrated our fiftieth wedding anniversary. It fell on Easter, the 15th day of April, tax deadline. At that time, two of our grandchildren, Kimberly and Buddy and their parents (Dr. Gene Conley and Annette) were busy serving at a mission in Nicaragua, three of our grandchildren, Katie, Patti and James were holding down the fort while their Mother (our daughter Kitty) was at a mission in Haiti while their father (Dr. and Colonel Greg Quick) was serving his country in Kosovo. Our other daughter, Kelly, was working at Bose as an occupational nurse in the Boston area while her daughter, Stacey, was attending her last year in a Virginia boarding academy and her son, Ryan, was doing battle with seventh grade math.

Nine years ago, right after Michael Jordan's first retirement from the NBA, in his attempt to have a baseball career, we were inundated with calls from print and electronic media from all over the country, asking Gene's opinion because of his own long career of doing both. They wanted to see what Gene thought about Jordan's chances of making it. NBC's "Inside the NBA" sent out a film crew for a day, chronicling not only Gene's career but to film three of our granddaughters who were then active in competitive ice skating, equestrian pursuits and gymnastics.

At that time, they asked our 10 year old granddaughter, how it felt to be the granddaughter of a famous person?

Her reply, "Well, just having a grandpa like that doesn't seem like any big thing but to other people, it's like, he's a great star, like Michael Jordan or somethin' like that".

Ramond Rachaud's response was, "While Conley was never known as "air Conley", even Michael has to admire the achievements of histories' most successful two-sport athlete."

Just before Christmas that year, 1993, Dan Shaunessey, celebrated author and columnist for the Boston Globe, wrote a very comprehensive piece on Gene. It won him second place in the nation for "best sports story of the year", a portion of which follows:

CONLEYS STRIKE IT RICH,
The Boston Globe, Friday, December 24, 1993
By Dan Shaughnessey

SHARON - In the space of a few short months in 1959 Gene Conley struck out Ted Williams and canned a hook shot over Wilt Chamberlain. No one else ever will make this claim.

Thirty years later, Conley faced a tougher challenge. He stayed by the side of his longtime wife, Katie, after she underwent a 13 hour operation that could have resulted in paralysis. For two terrifying months, Katie and Gene battled a foe tougher than Williams, Chamberlain, creditors, his drinking problem or the other fears and uncertainties that trailed them through four decades of baseball, basketball and family business.

Merry Christmas, 1993, It's a wonderful life."

The feature went on for two more pages of the Boston Globe but on the last page of the eighth column, what followed, pretty much summed up Gene's life. Actually, many media sports personalities have interviewed him over past decades and have always asked the same question that Dan pretty much covered in his last few paragraphs. The question most asked former athletes in their later years, "when all said and done, what would you like to be remembered for?" They may have thought he might reference his remarks about his many years playing both sports, perhaps the NBA pension struggle, the All Star games, the World Series Championship along with the NBA Championships. It remains a wonderment to them, and to me, still, as he humbly replies, (and he means it) "That I had so many great friends".

Winding up Dan's piece, referring, I'm sure to James Stewart's portrayal as George Bailey in "It's a Wonderful Life" under the sub Heading:

"SET STRAIGHT BY AN ANGEL"

"He couldn't pitch or hit the jumper anymore, but he could still drink. He kept pounding away until one night in Cambridge in the winter of 1966. He was drinking in a dive off Central Avenue when a young man came over and started talking to him.

'I don't know who he was,' says Conley. 'I still don't. He remembered me from the Red Sox days and he just kept saying, 'Gene, you shouldn't do this to yourself. I don't want to see you like this. You're too good.' He kept saying those things, telling how good I was. That was it. I haven't had a drink since.'

'I tell him it was his angel,' says Katie. 'Red Auerbach and a lot of people had tried to get Gene to stop for his own good, but there was something about that young man.'....

With Conley sober and free of professional sports, Gene and Katie went to work, Foxboro Paper. They buy, store, ship and invoice industrial packaging supplies. It's a proprietorship. They run the business out of their house. Just the two of them.

Who's the CEO?

Whoever's having a good day, 'Gene says, laughing.

They put their children through school. And now they enjoy the grandchildren. An NBC TV crew came to the house a couple of weeks ago. The network was taping a family spot to be used on "Inside Stuff" during All-Star weekend. One of the Conley's granddaughters, a 10 year old Patty Quick, was asked if she knew how good her grandpa was at basketball. She said, "He was as good as Michael Jordan." Conley loved that one. Another great story. Another laugh.

He knows he'll never have the fortunes of Michael, Bo or Deion, but he's got something they may never have. I was saying it again to Katie just the other day, 'no one will ever know it, but I'm the luckiest guy in the world. How many guys can have the life I've had - and here we are 63 years old and still enjoying life.' Merry Christmas to Gene Conley - the richest man in Sharon Woods."

EPILOGUE

Looking back on Gene's career, I began to realize just how fortuitous his life has been, as though some higher power was guiding him through all the confusions of life. His playing with the Tapers in the ABL led him to a job as an executive salesman with Tuck Tape. Mr. Cohen, owner and CEO of that company had given Gene his home phone number the year he had played for him. Many nights, after imbibing too much and too long, he would call Mr. Cohen, who patiently listened to Gene into the wee hours of the morning those last few baseball years. When Gene called Paul Cohen on his way up from Burlington, N.C. that Mother's Day Sunday when his thoughts had turned to tears which left that poor deacon bewildered, Paul encouraged Gene to come to work for him. Had he not played for Paul in 1962, he wouldn't have had that job that gave him the experience to start his own business as a technical tape supplier. If he had not defied Major League Baseball, and quit the NBA, he would not have organized the NBA Oldtimers in the mid eighties and we would not have gained a NBA pension which benefits us today.

His thirteen years of professional Baseball ended for Gene in the spring of 1964 but professional basketball didn't end at seven years. In 1966, the year we started our own business, the year Gene stopped using alcohol altogether, the Eastern League asked him if he would be interested in weekend basketball. Another windfall as a new business suffers from cash flow problems the first two or three years. Gene's physical endurance had improved remarkably; and having the games scheduled on Saturday nights and Sundays, our business wasn't

Sports Illustrated — April 2, 1979

disturbed nor was our observance of the seventh-day Sabbath. He was with the Hartford Capitols for two more years and coached/played for a short time with the New Haven Elms. He made the All Star squads each year.

One weekend night, Red Auerbach came down to scout the Hartford team as expansion had put a dent in that once large pool of All American college players to choose from. When he returned, Howie McHugh, the Boston Celtics' faithful publicity director later told Gene, "I asked Red if he saw anyone he liked?" To which Red replied, "hell, the best player I saw there was Conley and he's 36."

Towards the end of our second year in business, Bill Sharman, who was coaching for the San Francisco Warriors, called Gene to finish out the year with them. It was tough to turn down, but our business, which lasted thirty four more years, had just begun to turn a profit. It was a wise decision, as it put our three children through boarding school and college, plus a year of medical school for our son before the government took over his funding.

Gene won business awards in sales and marketing, served on his church's board, Fuller Memorial Hospital's Board, an Industrial Board in the town of Foxboro, Massachusetts, the NBA Legends Foundation Board, the Retired NBA Player's Board and led out in an effort to obtain a NBA pension for the pre-1965 NBA players. He still plays in charity golf tournaments. His life has been full and happy. Gene feels that his greatest accomplishment in sports was his success in being able to help gain a NBA pension for the NBA Old-timers. His humor remains intact but there are times he thinks of his days of wine and roses and his youthful inability to commit to sobriety, and has regrets about not quite fulfilling his destiny.

To my mind, with all its bittersweet memories, I am of the opinion, he did.

Happy Holidays

Gene and Katie Conley

GENE'S HIGH SCHOOL
AND
COLLEGE RECORD

JUNIOR AND SENIOR HIGH SCHOOL:

As a Jr. High School athlete (Oklahoma), Gene won over 40 first and second place ribbons against high school athletes in swimming.

Three letter athlete at Columbia High School in Richland, Washington (Baseball, Basketball and Track)

"All State" while in High School in the state of Washington in Basketball and Baseball.

Chosen to play in the National "Hearst All Star" game in NY (winning pitcher) from the state of Washington.

Came in second in the state in high jump.

Hall of Fame - Richland High School

COLLEGE: WASHINGTON STATE UNIVERSITY

As a sophomore, led the Northern Division in scoring in Basketball.

1955 - All Star Reunion - 1975
Henry Aaron,Ernie Banks, Gene Conley,..., Harvey Haddix,Ted Kluszewski,
Johnny Logan, Eddie Mathews, ..., Don Mueller, Frank Thomas

Made "All Conference" in Basketball and Baseball

His team came in second in the "Collegiate World Series" NCAA Baseball Tournament in Omaha, NE

Gene beat Alabama in that Collegiate World Series

The day before registering at WSU he was kidnaped by Idaho's basketball coach and three football players who took him over the state line into Idaho to the University at Moscow to entice him to register there instead. Idaho, along with four other Universities in the Northwest were fined heavily that year for their recruiting practices involving Gene.

HALL OF FAME STATUS

Gene is in the Hall of Fame at Washington State University

Gene is also in the Hall of Fame in the State of Washington

He is in Baseball's Hall of Fame in the Minor League Section of the "Hall" as the only Minor League Player to win the "Most Valuable Player" in the League twice.

As a team member, he is photographically featured at both Baseball's Hall of Fame and Basketball's Hall of Fame.

Garden tribute

For Red Auerbach and Gene Conley, it was a night to reminisce. GLOBE STAFF PHOTO / LANE TURNER

**Relaxed on the Big Island of Hawaii—October
(coutesy of son & family)**

**Our son's family: Buddy, Gene,
Kimberly & Annette**

**Grandma with 3 of her glamorous
granddaughters in N.Y. (courtesy of the NBA
Legends Foundations—All-Star weekend)
Stacey, Katie & Patti**

Grandpa with our other
glamorous granddaughter,
Kimberley

Our daughter, Kelly
a year ago she was
our only "breadwinner"–
now all our daughters work

Kelly's two children
Ryan & Stacey

Our daughter, Kitty & her family in Maui—Aug.
Patti, Greg, Katie & James

**Happy Holidays
Gene & Katie Conley
2004**

**Kimberly
Conley
Loma Linda
Medical U.
(granddaughter)**

**Annette
Conley
(daughter-
in-law)**

**Buddy
Conley
Junior at
Fresno St.
(grandson)**

**Lt. Commander
Gene Conley, Jr.
(Urologist
& son)**

**Col. Greg
Quick
E.R. doc.
(son-in-law)**

**James
Quick
H.S.
(grandson)**

**Kitty
Quick
another
nursing
degree**

**Katie
Quick
Graduate
U. Mass
Communications
(granddaughter)**

**Patty
Quick
(MVP) /
captain—tennis
Johnson St.
College
(granddaughter)**

**Kimberly—Pres. &
Dean's Medal Winner-
Summa Cum Laude
Fresno State U.
(granddaughter)**

**Daughter, Kelly & Gene
Nurse-Bose Co.**

**Kitty
Ghanda
(daughter)**

**Stacey Malcomson
(granddaughter)
Graduate at Southern
Adventist U. Cum Laude
Presently—
Loma Linda Dental H.**

**Kitty Quick
(daughter)
mission trips
Haiti & Ghana**

**Ryan Malcomson
Jr.—Foxboro H.S.
(grandson)**

Gene Conley is available for personal appearances and./or speaking engagements. For more information, email an inquiry to Gene at: GnKConley@aol.com

To order additional copies of this or other books, call ADVANTAGE BOOKS toll free: 1-888-383-3110 or visit our online bookstore at: www.advantagebookstore.com or visit: www.geneconley.com

Longwood, Florida, USA

"we bring dreams to life"™
www.advbooks.com

Printed in the United States
24052LVS00001B/1-12